Also by Dennis Wholey

The Courage to Change:
Personal Conversations About Alcoholism

Are You Happy?
Some Answers to the Most Important Questions in Your Life
(RELEASED IN PAPERBACK AS
Discovering Happiness:
How to Get the Most Out of Life)

Becoming Your Own Parent:
The Solution for Adult Children of Alcoholic and
Other Dysfunctional Families

When the Worst That Can Happen Already Has

Personal Conversations With:

Donald AuCoin

Marie Balter, M.Ed.

Gail & Richard Berendzen, Ph.D.

The Honorable Robert H. Bork

Jim Brady

Phil Buchanan, J.D., M.A.

Robert Buckman, M.D., Ph.D.

Tony Bunce

Marvin Bush

John Callahan

Margaret Chanin, D.D.S.

Charles W. Colson

Mihaly Csikszentmihalyi, Ph.D.

Dominick Dunne

Alex Ehrmann

Carol Fennelly

Betty Ford

Georgann Fuller, M.S.W.

Charles J. Givens

Socheat Hak

Phil Head

Bill T. Jones

I. King Jordan, Ph.D.

Reverend Edward Kelly, C.S.Sp.

Marguerite Kelly

Larry King

Lee Lawrence

Missy LeClaire

Lonnie MacDonald, M.D.

Josefina B. Magno, M.D.

Paul Marchand

Devin McCoy

Celane McWhorter

Richard Muldoon

June E. Osborn, M.D.

Pat Pomarici, M.A.

Reverend Edward B. Pritchard

Bill Russell

Peggy and David Say

Polly Schechter

Martin E. P. Seligman, Ph.D.

Secretary Louis W. Sullivan, M.D.

Rabbi Joseph Telushkin

Susan Warner

Paul Weiss, Ph.D.

Robert S. Weiss, Ph.D.

Jeanne White

Bob Williams

Patrisha Wright

Phyllis and David York

When the Worst That Can Happen Already Has

Conquering Life's Most Difficult Times

Dennis Wholey

New York

Library of Congress Cataloging-in-Publication Data

When the worst that can happen already has : conquering life's most
   difficult times / [interviewed by] Dennis Wholey.
      p. cm.
   ISBN 1-56282-985-8 : $19.95 ($24.95 Can.)
   1. Suffering—Case studies. 2. Adjustment (Case studies)—
Case studies. 3. Life change events—Psychological aspects—
Case studies. 4. Loss (Psychology)—Case studies. I. Wholey,
Dennis.
BF789.S8W46 1992
128—dc20
                                                    92-8338
                                                       CIP

Acknowledgments

The making of a book requires the efforts of many people. They deserve not only my personal thanks, but public recognition as well.

First of all, my appreciation goes to all of the participants who were willing to be interviewed in order to help others and who encouraged me with their hospitality, support, and generosity.

I am extremely grateful to Bill Brockschmidt, my research assistant, for his personal and professional dedication to the project. He did an outstanding job over many months—on the phone, in the library, checking transcripts, organizing credential materials, and at the computer doing anything that needed to be done. Bill's willingness and abilities have made a significant contribution to this effort.

Robin Thompson (our fourth book together) and Sandy Forsyth (our third)— my Michigan transcribers and typists—are the very best. Robin and Sandy handled the bulk of thousands of pages of material. The accuracy and excellence of their work is as fine as any in the country. When the crunch was on toward the end, we received top-notch assistance from Barbara Gibson of Takoma Park, Maryland; Carol Grant, Pat Cantrell, Joe Havley, and Pat Agnew of Pro-Typists, Inc., in Washington; and from Tom O'Neill and Bushra Finaish. I thank them all.

My gratitude also goes to my good friend John Knight for his initial enthusiasm for the project, assistance with the original proposal and correspondence, guidance in our computer systems conversions, and for his ongoing support over the months.

Others deserving of special mention are Rev. Ed Pritchard, Paul and Cindy Kasper, Gail and Richard Berendzen, Leslie and Sandy Dickerson, Donald AuCoin, Gene Schrecengost, John Coleman, Steve Lee, and Tarpley Richards Long. My gratitude also extends to the Friday Night Prayer Group at St. Patrick's in the City in Washington, D.C.

Some who helped out along the way opening doors, making suggestions, and being there for me and the project were: Wayne Smith,

Maggie Fogel, Sandy Birdsong, Ed Johnson, Steve Baron, David Dodd, Rev. John Mann, Jim Karayan, Fred Rotondaro, Tony Sheldon, Dottie McCarthy, Ann Wholey, Michael Sean Winters, Don Little, Nora and Peter Corrigan, Elsa and Tim Wholey, Joe Bentzel, J. Patrick Gannon, Ph.D., John Quinn, Ralph Wholey, Michael Graham, Megan Wholey, Lee Lawrence, Rabbi Charles Rosenzveig, Gail Cohen, Nonie Wholey, and Rob Hartman. I also thank Al Fisher, Marge and Jack Caldwell, Ed Alwood, Mary DeSimmone, Jane Wholey, Philip Movius, Betty and Ree Lasker, and the Murphy-Hutchins gang.

In the offices of the contributors my appreciation goes to Ann Cullen, Kimberly Kliene and Susan Gonzales, Judith Thomas, Sylvia Koski, Jodi Krizer, Mary Dickerson and Jenny Piekut, Muriel Strassler, Bonnie Robertson, Nelson Keener and Grace McCrane, Laura Hardy, Shelley Henson, Nita Rawlson and Marsha Barton.

At Hyperion I am indebted to Jenny Cox, my editor, for her belief in this book in proposal form and for keeping the book moving with her sharp editorial eyes—while at the same time delivering her first baby, Tony; her assistant, Paul Schnee—coordinator extraordinaire; Victor Weaver, Carin Goldberg, and Richard Oriolo for their art and design contributions; our managing editor, Lesley Krauss, meeting an impossible schedule; publicity director Lisa Kitei assisted by Simone Cooper and Annette Swanberg; the marketing and sales staffs of Hyperion and Little, Brown & Co., and publisher Bob Miller for his confidence in my work, his enthusiasm for this book, and making it all happen.

My very special thanks go to copy editor Mildred Maynard (with an assist from her husband, Mike) for the many hours she worked on the manuscript. A topnotch copy editor improves a manuscript substantially. Mildred is, and she did. I also thank Henry Price for his excellent line editing, and my sister Ann for her special photograph and my sister Nora for her final proofreading. I value the extra efforts of the folks at Musifex Video in Arlington, Va.; the staff and management at the Park Hyatt in San Francisco, especially manager Cheryl Phelps; Fernando Covarrubias and the gang at Federal Express; and Michael Haywood, Michael Smith, Gloria Frye, and Melvin and Patricia Smith at Spee Dee Que Printing in Washington, D.C.

My continued thanks go to Arthur and Richard Pine, my literary agents in New York City, their special assistants Lori Andiman and Sharon Mesmer. This book is the result of Richard's excitement and commitment to a concept, way back when. I am grateful to Richard for his ongoing friendship and support.

If, per chance, I've omitted someone who played a role along the way, I sincerely apologize and ask your forgiveness.

This book is dedicated to all the contributors,
those who have worked on it behind the scenes—and to
Gayle, Joe Lewis, and my dear Mother.

Contents

When the Worst That Can Happen Already Has

Life

All of man's celebrated accomplishments seem to pale in comparison with the magnificent ability of individual humans to transcend the very worst that can happen. What human beings achieve when they triumph over life's most difficult times is genuinely inspiring.

We seek emotional and financial security; all of us have responsibilities and obligations. However engaged we are—and we should be—in pursuing the rewards and joys of life, sooner or later we are faced with the challenge of the other side of human existence. The downside of life is suffering and it is a given.

Although we are surrounded by family and friends, co-workers and acquaintances, partners and helping professionals, we walk alone when we face our own "worst that can happen." During those difficult times, we confront our pain. Whether it is mental, emotional, or physical, major suffering provokes a crisis of the spirit. Within that experience and context we come to be more human and to appreciate that humanness as well. Our humanness is both our greatest asset and our greatest liability.

Catastrophe, misfortune, and hardship force us to endure incredible hurt, to struggle with hopelessness and despair, to accept shocking losses. However, when pushed hard against the wall of life, we discover deep within us remarkable resources of strength, courage, and coping abilities we never dreamed we possessed. Survival and victory give us new confidence and enhance our sense of self. After we have endured our suffering, we reach out to others with empathy and compassion. Our misfortune may force us to develop new skills, refocus our lives, and prompt us to use precious time in more productive and enjoyable ways.

Right now, in the lives of our families, friends, co-workers, and neighbors, there are people experiencing life's hardships: broken relationships, divorce, disease, accidents, job loss, physical handicap, financial difficulty, discrimination, mental illness, addiction, loneliness, the death of loved ones. Perhaps, at this time, you are experiencing a very difficult time yourself.

Being human requires dealing with day-to-day disappointments and problems. Some of us seem to handle frustrations better than others. Most of these problems are bothersome at best, energy-draining at worst. In the end, most of them are manageable. We muddle through them with some sense of relief when they are resolved. It may be said that if we don't have problems, we are not living. Adversity, however, stops us in our tracks. Time stands still. Our total focus is on life itself.

Perhaps it is the nature of man—certainly the nature of most Americans, because so many of us live the good life—to deny that misfortune will happen to us. However, regardless of comfortable circumstances and good fortune, all of us will encounter our share of suffering. Major defeats, serious illness, traumatic losses, and tragedy will make their way into our lives. It is part of the human experience.

Our pain and suffering help us to define who we are and to examine where we are on the path of life. The real journey of life is not upward; it is inward. Pain is life's greatest teacher, if we let it teach us. We are forced to accept, change, and grow; so we benefit from our pain.

My personal experience tells me that whatever sensitivity, generosity, humility, empathy, compassion, and forgiveness I have today has been learned through my pain. I have heard the phrase "grateful recovering alcoholic" thousands of times from men and women who apply that label willingly to themselves. I am one of them. Alcoholics are sometimes viewed by outsiders as a rather odd group of misfits who were at one time lying in the gutter or close to it. However, having paid the high admission price to sit in alcoholism recovery meetings myself, I can report firsthand the enthusiasm, joy, laughter, commitment, and love that occur within those meeting rooms. From my experience I can assure you that out of painful adversity can come freedom, growth, peace, happiness, and serenity.

This book is an extension of my own life. I knew where I went to get through the nightmare of my addiction to alcohol and pills, and I know where to go today for support when I suffer losses—personally or professionally. I know whom to seek out and what I must do to cope with my difficult times.

About a year ago, a two-part series by Brian C. Jones, in the Providence *Journal*, profiled a very special woman, Lee Green, whose son Jason got leukemia when he was three years old and died two years later. Mrs. Green, who now works as a parent consultant at the Rhode Island Hospital helping other parents facing similar circumstances, was quoted as using the phrase "the worst that could happen."

That phrase, which many of us use in daily conversation to describe personal tragedy and natural disasters, triggered some thoughts in my mind. I wondered where pain and suffering fit into the human equation and how other people navigated through difficult times. I knew what I did; I wanted to know what they did. I also thought if others who had conquered misfortune would share their experience, strength, and hope, perhaps many would be inspired to overcome their own hardship and learn the coping skills that would help them through.

Before beginning the interviews for this book, I asked a few friends and family members to write a list, as I had done, of what they thought were the very worst things that can happen to people. These lists became something of a guide as I sought out the people I wanted to interview. It is a humbling exercise. Why don't you try it, if not on paper, at least in your mind?

What Do You Think Are the Most Difficult Hardships a Person Can Endure?

_____

_____

_____

—————————————————

—————————————————

What you have come up with will, I guarantee, cause you to appreciate the positive circumstances of your life and will no doubt stir your feelings of compassion for those who may not be as fortunate as you. Interestingly, people—even though they may be currently experiencing adversity in their lives—tend not to put their own adversity on the list. As you read on, you will also note that many of the participants who have experienced extreme hardship themselves view others' problems as more tragic, and others' victories as more admirable than their own. Some of those who have coped with loss, disability, ill health, or circumstances beyond imagination see themselves as "fortunate." Some even believe they have led a "charmed life." Just as beauty is in the eye of the beholder, so someone else's misfortune is often perceived as greater than our own.

While the events of each individual's life may differ, the process of life is the same for us all. Each of us will endure hardship, tragedy, or misfortune, which will test us, strengthen us, and change us. We live, we grow, we die. The growth part is our concern here.

Gathered together in this effort is a group of truly inspiring people who have not only been challenged by life's most difficult times, but have been willing to talk with me about their very personal lives. Their voices are powerful; they need no intrusion from me. Therefore, I have edited out my questions, which would only get in the way.

Our role models of inspiration for overcoming adversity come from all walks of life. Some have been hurt by circumstances or events. Some have endured physical, mental, or emotional pain. Some have disabilities; some are victims of prejudice or war; some are facing death.

It may be that the reason we so often reject those who are struggling with adversity is that we want to avoid seeing the frailty of our own lives. "There but for the grace of God go I" may be invoked as a veil of self-protection rather than as an expression of gratitude.

A by-product of reading these powerful testimonies may be the realization that we are more the same, as humans, than we are different, and we can all be victorious in our own way. Perhaps in the future when we encounter someone who is in pain, rather than looking the other way out of fear or indifference, we will stop to help that fellow human being. The messages on these pages can have a profound effect on how you live your life today, whether you are experiencing adversity or not.

Shining throughout the personal stories of the contributors are wonderful examples of survival, coping, action, acceptance, and change. Hope and faith, meaning and purpose, humor and support—all are lessons offered in their stories. We can learn valuable information from the experts I interviewed as well. Their wisdom on our subject is priceless. In supporting others who are going through hard times today, I find myself caring for them in new ways as a result of these experts' professional knowledge. Their advice may help to make better partners, family members, and friends when those we love are hurting.

This is not a book about them—the people interviewed; it is about us. It is about the human experience of adversity and how we cope with it. "Strength" and "courage" seem lame words to describe the heroic virtues of brave men and women as they cling to life in suffering and then conquer their difficult times.

Adversity brings out nobility and greatness. So this is a book celebrating the very best of what human beings are all about: their ability to withstand suffering and pain, their capacity to grow from their experience, and their willingness to help others to heal. It is a book about a different kind of success—spiritual success—and the rewards that come from being human.

No one teaches us how to handle difficult times. Coping 101 is not offered in school. Acting efficiently is almost impossible when we deal with tragedy or hardship.

Lack of control and future uncertainty are common denominators of misfortune. To overcome painful circumstances is not a "follow the steps and arrive at a solution" proposition.

There are no rules for coping. However, when we are faced with adversity, we can benefit from the experiences of others and review what worked for us in the past. How we handle difficult times tells us a lot about who we are.

Robert Buckman, M.D., Ph.D., F.R.C.P.(C), is a medical oncologist and associate professor of medicine at the Toronto-Bayview Regional Cancer Center at the University of Toronto. Trained at Cambridge, he hosted the television series "Where There's Life," which ran for eight years in Britain and Canada; another series, "The Buckman Treatment," aired throughout Canada and in the United States on the Discovery Channel. Dr. Buckman is the author of *I Don't Know What to Say: How to Help and Support Someone Who Is Dying* and *How to Break Bad News: A Practical Guide for Health Care Professionals*. (The former is available through Vintage and the latter through Johns Hopkins University Press.) His new television series on alternative medicine, "Magic or Medicine," will be seen in the United States this year.

"Humankind Is Preset to Value Life"

Robert Buckman, M.D.

Adversity seems to reveal our individual differences. It's in the facing of adversity that you see the human being: the man and the woman. That is not all good. Sometimes it's magnificent because there are magnificent people; sometimes you see the absolute, horrible bastard that's there.

One thing society does not acknowledge at all is that if, for example, you have a guy rolling at the top as Donald Trump was three or four years ago, nobody ever says, "Gosh, Donald Trump, the richest, most powerful, most successful man in America—isn't it lucky he's able to do what he does because he didn't have leukemia when he was twenty and die of it?" Nothing has killed him. He was there because a whole load of disasters didn't happen to him. We like to think that Trump was a billionaire because he started off as a millionaire and worked hard.

There is never, in parentheses ("and also nothing awful happened to him").

Avoiding adversity altogether is, I think, impossible. Your coping strategies begin with a mild or marginal genetic component, which we don't fully understand, but I don't think we can shrug it off either. Your optimism or pessimism thermostat may be partly set by genetics; it does seem that depressive illnesses cluster in families, and that suicide clusters in families too. The optimism/pessimism thermostat mechanism also develops in your early environment, I assume. Say your family car runs out of petrol and you're a little kid sitting in the back, if your parents immediately have a row with each other and stomp off leaving you sitting in the car with the problem unsolved, you'll think, When a car breaks down, this is a major emergency. If, on the other hand, they say, "One of us has got to walk to a phone box and call the AAA," then you'll think, Okay, here's a car problem and here's the solution. The ease with which people grasp the solutions to problems probably sets some of their own coping strategies and their threshold for coping or non-coping.

My whole approach to helping people facing health adversities, challenges, reverses, or even death is to say, "Look, this is not the first big problem you've ever had. It's certainly the biggest or appears to be the biggest right now." Next, I go back through their life and look for the biggest disasters in their past. It might be the death of a parent or a divorce or a serious illness. Then I sit down with the person and ask, "Well, how did you cope with those particular problems in your life?" It often turns out that people have much better coping strategies than they realize, but they still think they cannot cope.

Not coping is really, in some respects, a frame of mind. You may get yourself through a day and at the end of it, in the midst of an adversity, you may say, "I didn't cope," but it may be that you really did. What most people mean by not coping is "I'm not in control of the situation." Nevertheless quite often they are, though they feel as if they're not.

Often people who are sick feel like cork in a storm with no control over their sickness; this is, almost by definition, true. The point at which they say their lack of control over the illness equals not coping is a very arbitrary one.

I was sick about eighteen months ago and lost the use of my right arm and leg; I had inflammation of the spinal cord. Since I was quite aware of exactly what it was, I didn't feel out of control except for a brief period about the second day when for five or six hours I felt adrift. Actually, it was very obvious why. Two days before, I was walking around perfectly normal and actually never in better shape, and then suddenly I couldn't do anything with my right arm and right leg. If you'd asked me during those few hours if I was "coping," I probably would have said no. Not coping is a subjective feeling of being directionless and literally powerless. At least I think that's what most people mean by not coping. They lie there and the waves push them this way and that, and they feel they have no engine, rudder, or sail.

Humankind is preset to value life and survival. That's why we're on Earth and we're quite plentiful. Our genetic makeup contains urges and drives and mechanisms to keep life going. We're probably programmed to fight our way out of misery and adversity and to think that by battling we can pull our way through it. The fact that we may be biologically programmed to fight our way out doesn't demean the more magnificent, admirable things that people do when confronted with adversity. Is there a preset purpose to misery and adversity? I don't believe so. Most serious illnesses are biological. The illness doesn't come with its own intrinsic meaning. The meaning of an illness is extrinsic to the illness itself. The real meaning comes from how one faces the problem.

I'm not in the slightest a great fan of suffering. In fact, I've spent most of my professional life trying to control symptoms for people. I was actually at a meeting on coping with cancer, a few years ago in London, and a chaplaincy student got up and said, "Since the magnificence of a human soul is shown by pain, shouldn't we forget about trying to relieve pain and just help people reveal their magnificence?" I very nearly strangled him. That is total nonsense. If you want to see humanity kicked out of a human being, visit a suffering person on the third day of a severe pain.

Illness is a real grind. Getting it all done in twenty-four hours would be just terrific. I had appendicitis and spent a week in the hospital. I felt terrible for a day before it began. I had the operation, woke up out of the anesthesia, had a couple of episodes of vomiting from the anesthetic, and the rest of it was just fine because every day I felt better and better. A week later, I was back to my normal self, and it was truly wonderful. If it had gone on for a year, my attitude would have been completely different. The grind is the fact that the illness isn't over in a week or two weeks or three weeks or a month. Most people don't realize how horribly awful and boring it becomes. You've learned your lessons. You may even have come to the conclusion that the experience has told you something about yourself. Now, thank you very much, you'd like it to be over.

I used to do a TV series with Miriam Stoppard called "Where

There's Life." One day she interviewed a man in his thirties who at the age of seventeen had dived into a shallow pool, broken his neck, and was paralyzed. He said, "This is the best thing that ever happened to me." And she said, "Oh, yeah, come on, that's ridiculous." And he said, "No. You don't understand what I was like. I was seventeen, I was a beery fog. I never thought about anything except drinking and fooling around with women, and I really didn't make use of anything above my neck." In fact, after the accident, he got married, had children, became the secretary of the British Association of the Disabled, and is a thoughtful, articulate man. What he was saying was that because his body worked so well previously, he never took any notice of the other bits. Having lost the use of his legs, he then realized that above his neck had to work. That is a process of self-realization. You can't inflict such a story on anybody. You can't stand next to a person who's broken his neck and say, "Now look at that bloke in England. Look at the man who became secretary of the Association of the Disabled. Now just pull yourself together and do that."

The journey is the important thing. People have to make that journey themselves. All you can do is recognize the steps they take that are leading them along the journey and applaud them, admire them, reinforce them.

The biggest wall mankind builds is in front of the gate labeled "randomness." We try to brick it up completely because we cannot stand the thought that adversity might be random, and that cancer of the esophagus or the bowel, or leukemia, or Lou Gehrig's disease, or bankruptcy, or divorce, or the death of a child or a spouse could happen to almost anybody at any time. We build this great, huge wall in front of that view to block it out, and we decorate it with all kinds of views about the way life works, about God, about divine plans and architects, and anything that disguises from us the possibility that terrible things can happen randomly. This is probably at the absolute center of my view of adversity. Yet if I dare to suggest that randomness actually makes up a lot of the world, I find it a very unpopular view right now. Even though I'm talking common sense, it's quite repugnant to a lot of people.

Uncertainty is probably the most horrible thing of all. The moment a doctor says, "I'm not sure, there's something on the X-ray, the bone scan doesn't look quite right," the patient thinks, What do I do? Is this the time to sell the furniture? Is this the time to call the relatives round and say farewell? Or is that scan normal and am I just going to carry on, driving up and down the highway without any worries? Those moments of uncertainty are probably more horrible than anything because you have no idea how to plan. You've got all your coping strategies organized, but you don't know whether to connect them or not. It's like having your engine revved up, but you haven't decided whether to go forward or in reverse.

There are definitely people who visibly cope better when they know that they have bad news to cope with than they did in the previous week when they didn't know whether the news was good or bad. Within the last year a married couple told me that the woman's breast cancer (she's completely disease-free at the moment) was the most important and exciting challenge to their life that they'd ever had. It really gave everything meaning to them.

In some respects, the way people respond to the good and the bad in the world is like the skeleton of their personality. Coping with adversity really tells you what kind of person you are. When you feel rotten, one of the things you could do is ask yourself, "What is this telling me about me?" If you suddenly lose a leg, that's not your fault. It's got nothing to do with you as a person; but the way you feel, the way you respond to that serious loss will tell you something about you.

That's what I do when things are really going badly. There's absolutely no question about it. Coping with the bad bits is what makes me; that's what I am. Anybody can do well when things are working nicely; anybody can be rich. It's when you're really grubbing around that you find out what kind of person you are. What I try to do even though I'm feeling rotten is to look at the best bits of coping I've done, try to acknowledge them, and in some respects reinforce them. You must pat yourself on the back for the bits that you're doing best, even if at that particular moment you're at the bottom of a slough of despond.

Death ends life but doesn't rob it of meaning. Death is merely the end of every life; that's all it is. If you really want to do something to stamp out somebody's meaning and existence, you're going to have to do a lot more than kill that person. What a lot of us fear is the total loss of meaning, the negation of the meaning of our life. If you're dying at three o'clock and your relatives are all looking at their watches wondering whether they can get to the cinema at four, it is apparent that you're not going to be missed very much. Ideally you should be as interesting as you possibly can right to the very end and leave a big hole when you go, a hole where people miss you. If you don't make any hole at all, if you're just one lobster in the pond, what was it all about?

In the James Stewart film *It's A Wonderful Life,* after the Stewart character, George Bailey, has become suicidal, the angel Clarence comes down and shows him what the town would have been like if he had never been born: his brother would have drowned, someone might have been poisoned by the pharmacist, and the housing project he dreamed of wouldn't have taken off. And there's the meaning of your life.

Death is an absolute fact of life—although we all like to think that an exception will be made in our case. We're all going to peg out eventually; we're all going to die. What we make of it is actually what we make of life in its total. My own major illness twelve years ago made me a little bit braver because I realized that I didn't fall to pieces under fire. Knowing that enabled me to risk more when it came to listening to other people, including patients. And though I came out of it equipped with a little more bravery for emotional investment in the people around me, it was five or six years after the illness that I really began to understand what it had shown me and the fact that my life had taken a change that was great and very useful indeed.

My friend Michigan psychologist Jack Gregory is fond of saying, "Life is good, bad, and so-so." The sequence of physical, mental, emotional, and spiritual experiences that make up the process of living is random and imperfect. Even though evidence tells us otherwise, we still believe that the worst that can happen—disability, chronic illness, the death of a partner, job loss, financial ruin—will never happen to us.

Yet the worst that can happen—something horrible, which is bigger than we are—does happen and we are forced to struggle with our own existence and life itself. In those dark days we summon up the very best of who and what we are in order to keep going. Our courage and instinct to survive help us triumph and conquer our own severe hardships.

John Callahan is a nationally syndicated cartoonist whose work appears in the Miami *Herald,* the Los Angeles *Times,* the San Francisco *Chronicle,* the Seattle *Times,* the San Diego *Union,* and many other newspapers throughout the country. He is also a contributer to *Omni, Penthouse, Harper's, The Utne Reader,* and *In Health* magazines. He is the author of the autobiography *Don't Worry, He Won't Get Far on Foot,* as well as the cartoon compilations *Do Not Disturb Any Further* and *Digesting the Child Within.*

"Anybody Can Be the One in the Wheelchair"

John Callahan

I was a twenty-one-year-old, out-of-control alcoholic, having just moved to L.A., looking to start a new life. I was artistically inclined, but I never could satisfy myself with any kind of creative endeavor. I really was a cartoonist waiting to happen. I was driving around in my newly purchased Volkswagen in the California sun. I had to drink every morning. I was barely able to make it back from the liquor store without the sky caving in on me. The inevitable catastrophe occurred on the last day I walked.

I got together with an acquaintance at a party and we drank excessively all day in the sun at a barbecue. In the early evening we took off to head down south to Long Beach for another party. We stopped at a bar and got drunker and drunker. It must have been midnight when we left the bar. I was too drunk to drive anymore so I let my friend drive. The next thing I remember was waking up in the hospital in Long Beach paralyzed from the chest down. The guy who was driving wasn't hurt very badly. We hit the entrance sign at Long Beach Community College. I don't know how many miles an hour we were going. I assume fast. My book suggested ninety miles an hour. We could have been going backward five miles an hour for all I know.

The extent of my injury is such that I am paralyzed from about the nipples down. My arms are partially empowered. I have biceps and some muscles in my hands and arms. My fingers are totally paralyzed. The hands are, too. All this leaves a patchy sensation up and down my arms, and it affects the diaphragm muscles to some extent, so it's difficult for me to cough very hard. It causes me to be dependent on a housekeeper in the morning to help transfer me out of bed onto the potty-chair. I need help showering. I have the illusion of looking pretty robust when I'm not, really.

In the evening somebody comes and does the reverse, which is much easier. Using straps that are above my bed, I'm able to support my own weight. The attendant grabs me under the knees and swings me like a sack of potatoes while I hang on to the straps with my arm. The attendant lifts my feet into bed after me. Because my arms are of normal or stronger strength, I'm able to be a big help to the attendant. I'm able to empty my urine bag during the day by myself. I'm able to use phones, buses, and public transportation. So there's nothing I really can't do, but I can get in a lot of trouble if I drop something. I'm not someone to stay home. The minute I'm done with my routine—it's about two and a half hours in the morning—I'm history. My basic habit is to roam the streets or ride in a taxicab to the tune of two grand a month.

I have some pain. Sometimes I've had anxiety attacks, feeling what I would call "phantom pains" in my feet. You really do a monstrous trauma to your body when you sever the brain from the spinal cord, but I stay busy and it helps. I'm able to feed myself, and manage in a restaurant completely independently because I've learned to use my fingers for a fork. I'm able to draw cartoons on my own. I kind of clutch the pen with one hand and kind of brace it with the other. My electric wheelchair weighs three hundred pounds. If the battery breaks down, I'm stopped dead, like a rock. Then I've got to call for service and repairs. My whole world drops in the pit of my stomach when my chair stops. It's happened to me twice recently. It'd be comparable to most people's legs stopping.

I draw cartoons in bed. My bed rolls up into a sitting position; it's much more comfortable, and I can think straighter. My cartoon stuff's shocking. What I go for is to please myself. I'm naturally interested in these edge topics. The one that got me kicked off the Carmel paper was the one with the dead dog on the street. The dog is lying flat on its back dead with a shard of glass through its stomach. A window has fallen and a piece is stuck in the dog. Somebody's walking by and is saying to the bereaved owner of the dog, "How much is that window in the doggy?" The one that caused more headaches is the title of my first book. It's a picture of a desert, and there's a broken-down, abandoned wheelchair half sunk in the sand. Coming up on the empty wheelchair are these horsemen in a posse, three or four of them. They've evidently been tracking this guy. One of them is saying reassuringly to the others, "Don't worry. He won't get far on foot." Whenever they run it in one of my new papers, somebody who doesn't know I'm disabled writes a long letter saying Mr. Callahan is extremely cruel to our brave handicapped friends. So the editor always gets a kick out of writing a retort saying, "This guy's indeed in a wheelchair; he's paralyzed himself."

Illegitimate child, adopted, alcoholic, quadriplegic—when I tracked my natural parents down, they both had died; it's a bad scenario. Who would ever buy a book like that? If somebody had written my life as fiction, you would say, "Sorry! Go back to the drawing board. It's a little too much." But it's true. It's been a tough life. I don't remember suffering that much, but I guess I have. I have carried a lot of emotional weight around that I didn't know I was carrying.

I came into the world with a chip on my shoulder. I was adopted by a family that was not compatible. I had completely different ways and looks and sensibilities from the rest of the family. My dad was pushy, repressed, neurotic, and abusive. I was a rebel, feeling unloved and acting out to get attention from him. It was a negative symbiotic, thing between us.

By the time I was twenty-one, I was at the end of my rope. I had no self-help tools whatsoever. All I had was cynicism, bitterness, and the feeling of being a victim. I had a lot of rage and anxiety attacks. What's that old quote? "Only his hate kept him alive." I didn't have a lot of support from my family. I felt on my own. I believe I really wasn't accepted. I had the self-image of plankton. After the car accident occurred, I drank six more years—twenty-one to twenty-seven. I drank like a madman. I was a complete fiasco and a total mess at that time, living in nursing homes and waking up in my own piss and vomit. It's something that no one would ever believe. The story of my life is complete hell until the time that I was able to get into a self-help program, and then I had a life. Not till the age of twenty-seven, when I began my alcoholism recovery, did I realize there was a way to look at things positively.

At the end I'd drink for two or three days and then I'd have withdrawals. I thought they were a reaction to drinking while being paralyzed, but it was just good old-fashioned withdrawals. After forty-eight hours, I'd feel that I'd ridden it out, and I'd say, "I can't go through that drinking again," but sure as hell, I'd get another drink and be off and running for another two or three days. It just got worse and worse.

I was in the chair one day half-buzzed and I dropped the bottle and couldn't reach it, couldn't get hold of it. I cracked. That was the straw that broke the camel's back. Able-bodied alcoholism is bad enough; quadriplegic alcoholism can't be described. I snapped. I rolled my chair back into the bedroom and I started screaming at God. It worked into a catharsis, a complete letting down of my defenses—racking sobs, the kind that go right through you and you are unable to breathe or stop crying. So here I was, having this big realization of what is wrong with my life: alcoholism. I was exhausted, and I felt a patting on my back, something comforting me. It sounds crazy. At the end of that, I rolled out to the phone and called an alcoholism support group. I knew there was something that changed in me; I was on a different footing. I've been sober now for thirteen and a half years.

The last therapist I went to asked, "Did you ever mourn the loss of your twenty-one-year-old body?" I had to say, "No, I didn't." You sort of have a hatred for your body because it's useless. It's as if it's somebody else's. It's so difficult for me to get in touch with feelings. I guess that's why therapists are around.

I was probably born with a good sense of humor. My birth mother was said to have been very funny and witty. I can laugh almost anything off. I remember being witty and very sardonic all my life. Maybe that humor's what helped me survive all the hell. It's a very big part of me. I consider myself a survivor. On the other hand, I would have committed suicide if I'd had more courage than I did. It seemed a very logical thing many times in my life, but I was so afraid of it.

What did I have to hang on to through those really rough years? That's the central question. I guess it's just the determination and the grit of a human being who's faced with no alternative but to survive. You cannot grow when you're involved with self-pity. If somebody doesn't understand what self-pity is and deal with it, it's very toxic. Self-pity will kill me. The minute you get into self-pity, you're a victim. Sitting there at the age of twenty-three with a beer bottle between my knees listening to the old people cry and staring out of a nursing home into a 7-Eleven window with the true feeling of having been screwed by life was a terrible feeling. Somewhere deep down did I really know

I had no justification for self-pity, and there was something in me that knew I was being dishonest and I was just being a rebel? I think there was a deeper me that knew I was not a victim and could survive.

We all have a tendency to sigh with relief when it's the other guy who's blind or got a divorce, or whose house burned down or who's in a wheelchair. It's a very hapless world we live in. Anybody can be the one in the wheelchair. Basically, you are the guy in that wheelchair "for whom the bell tolls." You may be the greatest, most intelligent, and richest person in the world, but if that banana peel's around that corner, and if you step on it, then you're a quad and you have no way to buy yourself out.

I think people sweat in their little gym shorts daily knowing that they could be the one that crane tips over on in the middle of Manhattan. Nobody has any power, really. It's an illusion. It's easy for people, able-bodied or not, to have the illusion of being autonomous. All somebody has to do is break a leg on the ski slope or have his girlfriend walk out or have the stock market go down, and suddenly he feels that powerlessness. When I think about these matters, it's often easiest for me to turn to cartoons. My favorite cartoons illustrate my feelings about these issues.

The fat guy's slipped and he's lying in a pile of worthless candy. His popcorn and candy bars have spilled, and he's obese. He's thinking to himself, "What kind of a God would allow a thing like this to happen?"

There's two cutoff heads on the street corner begging. One of them's got an eye patch. The other head notices that the other guy's got an eye patch. So the cutoff head with the healthy eyes says to the other cutoff head with the patch, in a patronizing tone, "You know, people like you are a real inspiration to me."

I've heard knotheads say that to me all my life. Really stupid people will come up and say, "You know, if I were you, I'd have killed myself." I feel, Geeze, thank you for the estimation of how much my life is worth. When people ask, "How did you break your neck?" I say, "I put one hand here and I put one hand here, and I just twisted it as hard as I could."

There's a kind of depth that I feel in terms of the richness of things in life. It's like people who've had a brush with cancer, or who are on their last legs with AIDS. When they look at a flower or a bumblebee, it means something different. Well, I escaped something, and I feel I have that capacity too.

Survival

The concept of the word "survival" has been weakened over time. It does not convey today the sense of continuing to exist after a horrific period of time filled with intense fear, dread, and terror. Survival should imply a personal victory of heroic proportions. A hero is a person who is endowed with great strength and ability, who demonstrates true courage, and who is admired for resource and achievement.

Some individuals have survived the worst physical, mental, and emotional abuse that life can offer. Survival gets to the very essence of what we appreciate about the human instinct to cope with and triumph over tragedy. Those survivors, those heroes, can inspire us to scale our own personal mountains. In doing so, we become heroes ourselves.

Alex Ehrmann is Executive Vice-President of Alaron, Inc., in Troy, Michigan, a company that imports home entertainment electronics.

"Somehow It Will Work Out"

Alex Ehrmann

My trials and tribulations began in 1938, when I was twelve years old. I was born and raised in southeast Czechoslovakia, an area that's predominantly Hungarian and that was annexed to Hungary as part of the deal that Hitler made with Chamberlain in 1938. We were Jewish. The Hungarians had already at that point two anti-Jewish laws on their books. When we became Hungarians, we had to go to Hungarian schools and the faculty were anti-Semitic. The teachers in class would refer to Jews as "damn Jews" and "stinkin' Jews," so we soon felt a very sharp contrast to what we had been used to.

We were a family of six children: three boys and three girls. I was the middle son. My oldest sister got married in 1939, and she received a very nice wedding present from the Hungarian authorities. In the middle of the merry making, the gendarme patrol came into the hall and ordered all males to line up outside. They accused the guests of singing Slovak nationalistic songs, which wasn't true. They marched everybody off, including the bridegroom, and beat them up.

My father had a beer-bottling franchise, a wholesale liquor business, and a small hotel with six rooms, a restaurant, a dance hall, and a little game room. In Hungary the Jews were said to make a lot more money than anybody else and that was a good reason for them to pay more taxes. So they taxed us more than we were able to pay. They came and said, "We will auction off your house." We moved into a house that used to belong to my uncle who had died. We also lost the business and my father started angora-rabbit farming. My middle sister and I were working for farmers.

We were struggling that way until March 1944, when the Germans marched into Hungary and Budapest and started talking about resettling the Jews. We had read early accounts of what was going on in Germany. We knew about Dachau. We saw pictures in the newspapers, and we had accounts from people who were deported to Poland, had witnessed massacres, and managed to escape. But we said to ourselves, "Well, yes, it's true. It happened there but it's not going to happen here, not with us. It's being done in Germany but it won't be done with the Hungarian Jews. The Hungarians are more civilized. The Jews have contributed to Hungarian welfare too much. Hungarians are not going to let that happen to their Jews." To the last minute, we were fooling ourselves with these kinds of excuses.

The last day of Passover, word got out that the next morning they were going to gather up all the Jews from town and the resettling was going to start. Prior to this, my older brother had been called off to the military service. There was a lot of commotion in the Jewish community. Families were getting together: "What shall we do? Should we run away? Should we stay? What are we going to do with our valu ables?"

That night in our house, we started digging down in the basement and burying silver candelabras and jewelry. We lifted the floorboards and put suitcases of linen under the floor. About four-thirty or five o'clock in the morning, we heard heavy boots marching down the street. We looked out and saw the gendarme soldiers going by our house. About twenty minutes later, they were leading Jewish families who lived farther from the center of town to the synagogue. A few minutes later, they knocked on our door and said, "Jews, get ready. Take the bare necessities with you. You'll do a lot of walking. We'll take good care of you." They took us to the synagogue and by about two or three o'clock in the afternoon they had gathered up all the Jews in the area, about two thousand people, and ordered us to march down to the railroad station.

We were marching down the middle of the street just like cattle coming home from a pasture. Our neighbors were standing out in the gateways. Some of them were openly weeping. Others were standing around dispassionately and some yelled out insults and spat on us. At the railroad station, there was a boxcar train waiting for us. They told us we were going to a town about thirty kilometers away where we would have to find our own lodging with other Jewish families until they prepared one part of town designated for a ghetto. They were going to concentrate us in that area and then transport us to our destinations, wherever we were going to be relocated. That's exactly what happened. When we arrived, my father looked up his cousin. Later they moved us into a different quarter of the city, which was encircled with barbed wire.

They jammed us into houses, buildings, and warehouses, wherever they could. By now our spirits were broken. We were exposed to all kinds of abuses in the ghetto; hunger and very, very poor sanitary conditions were just two of them. Our family was given a small hallway about twelve by ten feet, and that's where we had to sleep and live. The sentries would often come and beat us.

We were told that they were going to liquidate the ghetto and there would be four transports in which they would take us to other towns, put us in factories or on farms, but keep families together. Our family was told that we would be in the third transport. Each transport was leaving about a week apart, and by the time the second transport was leaving, we had postcards from people on the first transport saying they were working on a farm or in a factory and "work is hard but we have it relatively good." The postcards were postmarked Hungary. Later on we found out that those cards were written by people who had arrived at Auschwitz. They were forced to write the postcards.

The morning of the third transport, around eight-thirty, we were ordered to line up. They marched us down to the railroad station. There was the train, the cattle cars, and German soldiers with the dogs waiting for us. The Hungarian military turned us over to them; they loaded us on the cars, closed the doors, sealed them, and the train started moving. We were told we were going to go to inland Hungary, which was south, but we headed north. So we said to ourselves, "They're taking us in a roundabout way because they don't want to use the main lines. Those lines are important for military purposes." Even when we crossed into Poland, we still didn't want to face reality.

On the third morning, around two o'clock, the train stopped. We looked out of the little windows and saw in the distance tall chimneys, flames on top of the chimneys—something like what we see now in the oil refineries. There was excess gas burning off and a terrible stench. We couldn't make out what it was. It was not oil. Outside, we heard all kinds of yelling in German. The doors were flung open and we saw little figures in striped uniforms yelling at us in Yiddish, "Get out! Make it fast! Don't ask any questions, just get out! Leave everything on the train. You don't need it. Get out and start moving forward!"

There was not much time, really, to talk and to speculate. We had to move. They lined us up, five abreast. My parents and my older sister with her baby were in the row ahead of us. My two other sisters and my kid brother were with me in the next line.

At the head of the column, there is this good-looking German officer waving his hand, right or left, right or left, and people follow him. They go to the right or to the left. My mother is told to go to his right. My sister carrying the baby is told to go to his right as well. He asks my father, "What is your occupation?" My father says, "Farmer." So he tells him, "Go to the left." Then he stops us and yells to my father, "Come back, old man. What did you tell me your occupation is?" And my father tells him again, "Farmer." He says, "Show me your hands." And he looks at his hands and he smacks him across the face, "Go to the other side." Then he tells us to go to his left. There are SS with dogs telling us, "Move, move, fast, move." And there go my parents, my sister, and her baby, and it's the last we saw of them.

We are walking down a barbed-wire alley and to the right are piles of tree branches and empty suitcases burning, smoldering. The stench is there but we still can't make out what is going on. I hear in the distance babies crying. As we approach one of these piles, I look in the flames and I see a baby moving. That's when it finally sank in and I realized that this is it, this is Auschwitz. There is such a thing as Auschwitz, and we are there.

We were told to come to the barracks where they would give us a bath and change our clothes. I started wondering, Is this going to be a bath or is it going to be gas? They told us to shed our clothes and line up. They shaved us, cut our hair, and disinfected us with a liquid. I was lucky; it turned out to be a real shower. We came out, dried off, and were given starched clothes and shoes. We were marched into another barrack. There they took our data—names and occupations—and told us to go into another barrack. After that barrack was filled, we were ordered to get out. They counted us. Again they lined us up, took data, asked us all kinds of questions, and gave us a number. Then they told us, "Forget your name. It's not important. Remember your number. This is your identity from now on. Your name doesn't mean anything anymore." This is how it was all day, about four or five times: lining up, asking questions, writing, grouping us according to occupations or education, then back into the barrack, beating us in the process.

Beyond the ditch in the back of our barrack were other barracks where we saw women moving. We couldn't recognize them because their hair was shaved off. We yelled out to them in the little German that we knew. They asked, "Where are you from?" I said, "Hungary," and so we started talking Hungarian to them and they recognized us. They were girls from our town. They said, "You're the Ehrmanns. Your sisters are here—wait, we'll call them." And, sure enough, my two sisters came out. I jumped the ditch, gave them a half a loaf of bread, and started talking with them. In the distance I saw an SS approaching. My brother yelled, "Hurry up! The sentry is coming!" I said goodbye to my sisters and jumped back just in time and got lost in the crowd.

We were in Auschwitz for about seven or eight days. One day they put us on a train that took us to Warsaw. We arrived and we were taken into the Warsaw ghetto. That was exactly a year after the uprising was squelched. There were two concentration camps inside the ghetto, between three and four thousand people in each camp.

There were several incursions into our camp by members of the underground who were trying to liberate us. Every time after such an attempt by these partisans, the next morning truckloads of young people stripped to the waist were brought to the ghetto blindfolded. As we marched out to work, we met these trucks. We heard they just blocked off streets and searched. Wherever they found young men, they took them away, no questions asked, and brought them into the ghetto. An hour later, we heard machine-gun fire, and in another hour we smelled flesh burning.

In August, the Russians approached Warsaw. At night we saw rockets flying. The whole area was lit up. We were hoping we would be taken by them, but that did not happen. Instead we were ordered out of the ghetto, and we marched for about six days. During that march, we lost about half of the people to exhaustion. We were not given any food or water. Those people who couldn't keep up were shot by the SS.

When they finally put us on a train, there were only half of us left. They gave us bread twice, and once they gave us salted meat in cans, but no water. People drank their urine; it was terrible. We were wet from rain. We had to sit in each other's laps. To the left, to the right, people were dying. They took us to Dachau, and by the time we got there, another fifty percent of the ones who were loaded on the train were gone as well. When I got off the train five days later, my seat was raw and bloody from wet clothes.

At Dachau they gave us food to restore those of us who were in good condition, which luckily included my brother and me. Four days later, we were taken out on a transport from there to Upper Bavaria to build an underground aircraft factory.

By now, we had developed an attitude of getting to one more day, surviving to tomorrow, not beyond. We didn't think beyond tomorrow. Just one more day. And the next day again, one more day. We didn't think. The only thought that remained with me was that someday I was going to meet my older brother.

By now we knew that our parents were gone. We knew our sister and her child were gone. My faculties were so stiffened that I didn't really deal with it. I just stored it away as a fact. This was common among the survivors. Those who were bemoaning lost loved ones didn't make it. One man constantly cried over the loss of his wife and child. He died. People drove themselves to suicide or just gave up and died because they did not separate themselves from their emotions.

We didn't know what had happened to our two other sisters. In Warsaw, we didn't see any more women prisoners, but we were hoping that our sisters would eventually come back, that there would be an end. "It cannot last for long," we said. Would we survive? We didn't know. But in order to get there, we kept hoping for one more day, one more day. Our principal aim was to get food, clothes, shoes, shield ourselves from the cold weather, get away from hard work as much as we could, and survive one more day.

In Germany, we arrived in a forest area that was surrounded with barbed wire. We had tents to sleep in. But on the next day, my brother and I were told we were going to another camp a few kilometers away. We were kept in that camp for a few days before they took us into an area in the forest where we had to mix cement in giant cement mixers. We had to carry eighty-pound bags of cement up about twenty-five feet to the top of a cement mixer and pour it in. There was no gas chamber, no crematorium, but they didn't need it. The cement took care of it.

As we were mixing the cement, the dust settled in our lungs. On the average, people lasted there maybe three weeks, four weeks at the most, and they expired. Their noses started running, their lungs clogged up. I recognized this danger and said to my brother, "We've got to get away from this."

My brother got a job in the kitchen peeling potatoes, because the Germans had an affinity for children and gave them easier jobs. He was able to give me some raw potatoes, and finally he got me into the same commando. The man in charge of this commando was a German criminal, a sadist, but he liked the kids. I was older, so he threw me out and I got into another kitchen and was finally put into a clean-up unit. We were ordered to clean up the bomb damages.

In April 1945 I was coming in from the railroad station where we were working and I felt ill. I developed a temperature and I got worse. We were infected with lice, and the lice carried typhus. That's what I had. I was able to stay in the barrack for a few days before they took me into the quarantine part of the camp. My brother was bringing me coffee and aspirin. Even today, I don't know where he got the aspirin, and when I ask him, he says, "I got it somewhere."

One evening I was shaken awake by one of the quarantine inmates, a friend of mine, who said, "They're calling your number. The officer who is in charge of human inventory is looking for you." I went in a shirt. That's all I had on me. The man asked me, "What's your number?" I gave him my number. He said, "Okay, sit here." Then he got another prisoner, and he took us out of the quarantine and into the hospital barrack and said, "They'll take care of you here." What happened was my brother and another kid had cornered this officer and pleaded with him, "Save our brothers. Get our brothers out of there." The following morning, that whole quarantine portion of the camp was liquidated. Next to my brother, I actually owe my life to an SS officer.

My brother saved my life once more. One day I came in from work and there was a selection going on in camp. Mengele visited us. At one end of the camp there was a big crowd, and my brother yelled to me, "Don't go there! There's a selection going on!" He managed to steal me away from there. The fact that my brother was with me and vice versa was for us a strengthening factor. I witnessed several instances where brothers were together or father and son were together, and when one of them died, the other died right afterward.

Two weeks later they evacuated the camp and put us on another train. One day the Allied bombers swooped down with five machine guns firing on us. They thought it was a military train. We climbed out of the train and spread our starched clothes on top of the cars. They came back for a second pass, but when they saw those clothes, they didn't shoot anymore. We buried our dead and got back on the train.

On the 30th of April, while we were stopped at a station, the stationmaster brought out a radio and we heard the German military's orders to lay down arms. There was jubilation, and fellows started running away. I didn't have a choice. I was so weak I could hardly walk. My brother wouldn't leave me, so we stayed. About an hour later we heard Göring on the radio ordering the Air Force back into arms. The guards rounded up those who had left, brought them back, and the train started moving again.

Next morning, a beautiful sunny day, we were stopped in Bavaria on a tall embankment. We looked out; it was quiet. We didn't hear the sentry walking up and down. We dared to look out the door. We saw rifles leaning against the wheels. Not a soul was around. We dared to get out. There was no sentry in the caboose either. All of a sudden there was a tremendous noise. We saw huge tanks rolling down the road with a white star on them. We knew the Russian star, which was red. This star was white. We didn't know what it was. We knew the tanks were not German, so we started running down the road. The lid opened up and out popped this beautiful black face, smiling, white teeth. We knew right away they were Americans.

The Germans had fled. The American Army asked us whether we wanted to stay there and wait until they could emigrate us or go back home. My brother and I chose to go back home. We found out that our two sisters were home already. Nobody knew about our brother.

We made our way home in a roundabout way. An uncle of ours in the next town offered to take us under his wing. So we moved in with him. One day a fellow came to the house and told us that he had been with my older brother. My brother had skipped the work force and got himself papers as a master sergeant of the Hungarian Gestapo, the Arrow Cross troop. He was rescuing Jewish people and putting them into protected houses. If he saw other Arrow Cross members leading Jews to concentration points, he would tell them, "Brother, let me take care of these bloody Jews. You go two blocks over—there are fights going on. Go help our brethren there." Then he took our people and hid them in the protected houses. One day he went into a theater and this man telling the story was in the same theater. It was dark, and all of a sudden a shot rang out and the lights went on. There was a commotion and they were carrying my brother away. He had accidentally shot himself in his groin. They took him to the hospital. On the operating table they recognized my brother as Jewish because he was circumcised. They took him out to the Danube, and a firing squad executed him. The man who was telling us the story followed him all the way and witnessed it.

My younger brother went to school and became a dentist. I learned the jewelry trade. In 1948, the Communists took over. My uncle fled to France, and finally to Canada. Another uncle bought us fake Paraguayan visas so that we were able to get transit visas to France. We wound up in France for a year. My sister married and had two children; she, her husband, and children traveled with us to France, Canada, and, finally, the United States. My brother-in-law and my other sister were already in Montreal with my uncle, and it took us a year to get visas to emigrate to Canada.

My experience in that period of fifteen months has had a profound effect on my entire life. Luck? Obviously there was a lot of luck involved. My distinct luck was that I was with my brother and that both of us made it and neither of us succumbed; we were able to fuel each other. We pondered trying to escape many times, but we saw the fate of those who tried and never made it. Several fellows were shot. Others were caught, brought back, and tortured in public. There were many instances of suicide. One morning we came out to the marshaling area at work by the railroad track. A young man threw himself at an oncoming train. He was physically healthy but couldn't take it mentally. Several people hanged themselves. They gave up because it was hopeless for them. They saw no sense in continuing. If there is no light at the end of the tunnel, why continue?

One factor that kept me going was hoping for my older brother to make it home. Somehow there was a strong drive to continue the family. Our parents were gone but we would be together again. Another factor was my religious upbringing: unmistakably faith. I prayed a lot and I kept going, hoping that God would not leave me. This was the toughest period of my life, the period of least hope. There really wasn't any logical hope. We were totally closed off from the world and did not know what was going on. Since we couldn't follow developments, we couldn't draw conclusions as to the time when salvation would come. I had to find something that would carry me, and that something was blind faith.

My religion tells me, "Throw your faith on God and He will nourish you." I know that faith was fuel for me. That it empowered me. It was self-generated, evidenced by the fact that I would pray. So, afterward, during my lifetime when I didn't have immediate solutions to my problems, I would borrow from my experience and say, "Just go ahead, continue. Don't worry. Somehow it will work out."

Others who were not necessarily believers had other goals they believed in, such as getting back to a wife or family again. One fellow kept telling me he didn't believe in God but, as a strong Zionist, he was going to make it to Palestine. There's no question about it in my mind: faith, as such, was a strong factor. In my case, it happened to be religious faith. Once when I talked to a fellow prisoner, he said, "If God allows this to happen to us, there's no God." I was able to tell myself, "Well, the man is off his rocker. He's not right. Who am I to question God?" I kept on believing, I kept praying, and I kept the faith within myself.

During incarceration, I had no real choices: Either I give up, I thought, or I continue fighting; and I chose to fight. But after the war, when I found myself thrust into the world, I experienced fear because of all the uncertainty. During the war, I managed to insulate myself from that fear. I built a wall of protection. I did not expose myself directly to that fear. It was too dangerous for me. Fear would have consumed me if I'd been conscious of it. I let myself be governed by instinct. "Go this way, don't go that way. Get away from the cement commando. It's not good." If I was very hungry: "Eat the raw potato peel. It's rotten. It doesn't matter. Eat it." There was a lot of action by instinct.

I live my life according to what I learned in those fifteen months more than in any other period in my life. During those months, I was experiencing things on my own. It was no longer theory. That was the proving ground. In addition to seeing people who hanged themselves or threw themselves under a train, I also witnessed cannibalism. A fellow inmate was so hungry that he took a knife and cut out a piece of the dead person next to him. Another fellow, who saw that, beat him to death. So I saw human behavior sinking to a low level, and I also saw discipline, an unwritten law being practiced, and I accepted it. I explained it to myself as cannibalism being a level to which a human cannot sink. If he does, something is hideously wrong.

Society has to be governed by laws. Survival is not necessarily the paramount authority. There is a certain respect that one has to give another person as a fellow human. From this cannibalism incident I drew the conclusion that my ego is not paramount. Society is superior to my ego. I am subjected to society.

A situation doesn't have to be as grave as that incident. When I'm chivalrous, I do it out of respect, not out of self-interest. When I do something for you, I do it not only because I like to do it, but also because I chose to do something I accept as right.

That experience has played a major role in the moral code I have today. It's there guiding me in what I accept as right or wrong. I act out something that I accept and profess to be right. Because I feel good about it, I will do it. The learning process was witnessing the act: the cannibal was wrong, and the enforcer was right. I accepted that, stored it away, and I live my life accordingly. That incident taught me that human values are more important than self-interest.

The events that took place in that period were the worst things in history that I know of. For me, the depth into which humanity sank at that time surpassed all the previous destructive happenings in history. I'm talking about all that was going on, not only what was happening with the Jews. One man generated the whole machinery and was able to draw out all the elements of evil in human behavior. I would not like to relive those experiences, but I have no regrets about what I learned.

Over the past few years, we have become aware of the shocking extent of physical and sexual abuse that exists in our country. However, in order to avoid its heartbreaking implications, we tend to deny its reality except when we are confronted with the flagrant cases that make their way into the media.

The labels "victims of incest" and "victims of sexual abuse" still seem to convict the abused instead of the abuser. The abuse of a child by an adult is an assault on the very being of the individual. This maltreatment, which cries out for understanding and healing, becomes for the abused child or adult a personal nightmare of shame and guilt, the pain of which is hidden with whatever that individual discovers to anesthetize it.

Saying of those abused as children, when they recover from their trauma, "He's a survivor" or "She's a survivor" is to bestow on them, in the true sense of the word, the accolade of respect they deserve.

Richard Berendzen, Ph.D., was President of American University from 1980 to 1990, when he resigned. A few weeks later in the Fairfax, Virginia, court he pleaded guilty to two misdemeanor counts of having placed "indecent" telephone calls. The subject matter of the phone discussions—according to the prosecutor in Virginia and staff members at Johns Hopkins Hospital, who had listened to the tapes—centered almost exclusively on the issue of childhood sexual abuse. According to the report released by the Johns Hopkins University School of Medicine, Dr. Berendzen "was sexually and emotionally abused severely as a child. . . . The phone calls appear to have been a troubled attempt to make sense out of his own childhood victimization."

According to Dr. Paul McHugh, who headed up the psychiatric team at Johns Hopkins—as quoted in the *Washington Post Magazine*—it was "as severe a sexual abuse as you can suffer for a limited amount of time—a couple of years of his life—as bad as you can get."

The calls, which were made to someone who had a day-care position, were not placed for "prurient interests"; they were placed, the prosecutor said, in a rather sad and pathetic way to seek information, quite inappropriately. As quoted in the *Washington Post*, he said, "I would not dignify the calls by calling them cerebral, but in a way they were cerebral." The hospital, the court, and the Fairfax County Police Department called them "indecent" phone calls, a term that the Johns Hopkins staff stated was more accurate than "obscene."

The court ruling was thirty days' suspended sentence with a proviso that Dr. Berendzen continue with therapy, which he did for a year.

Richard Berendzen returned to American University as a professor of physics in January 1992. During 1991, while on leave from the university, he served as a consultant to NASA and actively participated in numerous public service organizations.

Gail Berendzen is active in numerous community service organizations and is the founder and president of Women of Washington, Inc., a nonprofit organization that provides a forum for women to come together to hear speakers on national social issues, to exchange ideas, and to network with each other in support of their professional goals.

"Hope Is Always There"

Gail and Richard Berendzen

Richard

It hit like a thunderbolt. Our lives changed dramatically in a very short time. I gave up the presidency of the university I love dearly and a position I enjoyed. We moved out of the president's home, where we'd lived for ten years. We disposed of roughly a third of our belongings. We put a lot of things in storage, and we moved. There was the crescendo of the experience of the hospital, the public press attention, the shame, the humiliation, the pain. But then there was the other part: the healing and understanding, the lifting of a weight like a boulder off my shoulders, and, in a curious way, a sense of peace and freedom, which I had not known before. It was freedom from my attempts to suppress memories of childhood sexual abuse and being my own one-man self-control system. I had made being a workaholic a trivial term. To me, eighty hours a week was hedonistic and slovenly. A hundred was better. A hundred and twenty, if one could do it, was better yet. In twenty-some years of marriage, we had taken only a week of vacation.

Today there is freedom from that kind of frenzy, pressure, and drive and greater sensitivity about myself, my wife, my family, and everyone around me. So, with enormous, almost indescribable pain, there has come a personal peace and a greater concern and compassion for other people and their suffering than I could have imagined a year and a half ago.

As we drove to Johns Hopkins Hospital that first time, I kept saying, "I'm so sorry, I'm so sorry. I'm sorry for intruding in anyone's life, sorry for humiliating my institution, my wife, my family, and my city." I love Washington, D.C., and I was on various committees, boards, and commissions. I felt I'd let them all down. I said to the doctors, "I'll do anything. Please help me." They helped. They're scientists, but they went beyond being scientists with their ability to reach issues I didn't know people could reach. I didn't know the talents and skills that could be marshaled. I'm not talking about one doctor, or even three or four; it was as if they had a veritable army of psychologists, psychiatrists, therapists, and clinical social workers. It seemed that every few hours there was somebody else. They just kept coming. It was this test and that test; four polygraph tests (all of which I "passed"), a sodium amytal interview, and group sessions. If there was anything to find, they were going to find it.

For three and a half weeks, I stayed in Johns Hopkins—possibly the nation's foremost hospital. There I found myself in a psychiatric ward, self-admitted, with the unrelenting barrage of therapists pounding and drilling from early morning until late at night. They were kind, they were sensitive, but they were unrelenting. Seven days a week, every hour, males, females, young, old—unstopping. That was part of the pain—the pain of reliving experiences from some forty years earlier—which they forced me to relive, and relive, and relive.

Before the hospital experience, I had decided I would never tell anyone about that part of my childhood. I would die an old man, carrying those secrets to my grave. At Johns Hopkins they forced me to discuss it all in detail with one therapist, then two, then five, and one day with a group of about two dozen for two hours. Every time I'd say "I have nothing more to say," they'd say, "Yes, you do. Now, let's get back and tell us about your feelings at the time." Then they forced me to tell Gail, in full detail, about all of it.

Gail

I didn't know why I was going into the room to talk. I remember sitting down. It was a small room. I remember thinking it looked like a dorm room at the university. As I sat down, I noticed that Richard didn't look the way he usually looks. He seemed very nervous. He talked for three or four hours. I lost track of time. I sat there thinking, God, what am I listening to? I couldn't believe this was coming out of my husband, that this had happened to him. They told him to describe everything in great detail, and that they were going to talk with me later. He had no way out. He couldn't just say, "Yes, I told her everything." He knew they would test what he said. He talked and talked, and cried and talked.

When he had talked himself out and there wasn't anything more to say, I said, "I have three reactions to what you've said. One is that I love you even more now than I did before. To think you've held this in you for the twenty-six years we've known each other. You are such a good man and you did such good things, and you had all of that underneath. Second, if the person who did this to you as a boy were in the room, I think I could murder her." I had never felt that way before, and I don't feel that way now, but it was a very strong feeling knowing someone I loved had been hurt so badly. The third thing I said was "You were a victim once, and now you are a victim again because of the first time. It's just overwhelmingly unfair."

I remember looking at him, and it seemed that pounds had been taken off of his shoulders. I once saw a statue that was inscribed: *"The truth shall set you free."* Not feeling guilty or having to hide one's problems anymore is freedom. The truth has opened doors for Richard. When he was through talking, he just looked different; it was as if somebody had lifted him up.

Richard

I had thoughts of suicide, but not seriously, because of Gail and my daughters and the realization I had so much to live for. Suicide would be the ultimate shame for them. Generally, I believe very strongly that if something is difficult, you face it. I've felt that since I was quite young. There were a few days at Johns Hopkins, and some weeks later, when I was as down as a human could be. But Gail was there, the doctors were there, and I dug deep within myself to find courage and reasons to go on. Everybody has that ability. I also began to realize how I was magnifying my trauma. I would find strength by looking around me and realizing the nobility of people who had encountered incredible challenges, and yet somehow had survived. Surely if they could, I could. And so I did.

Clearly, before the crisis, I had not handled the situation properly. I was obviously very troubled at the time. I should not have made any such calls under any circumstance. I should have sought professional counsel, but I did not for a number of reasons. I didn't trust therapists. I didn't understand the linkage to my past. What I had done was wrong. Since the time of those calls, I have not made any more of that kind of call. Absolutely not. There's no need, there's no interest. It's now a resolved issue. It's done.

Mark Twain said, "We're all ignorant on different things." I understood a quasar, I understood the birth of the cosmos—insofar as we understand those things—but I didn't understand the young Richard Berendzen. I surely didn't understand how the professional, presidential Richard Berendzen was but an extension of, and still a hostage to, the boy Richard Berendzen. He was the boy who had determined to work hard to avoid reflecting on things he didn't want to reflect on, and who had learned self-control mechanisms and survival techniques. I discovered at Johns Hopkins that the ones I invented for myself were commonplace. It's a human response. They had served me—as far as I could tell—quite efficiently for a long time, until they finally failed.

Gail

Richard was a workaholic from the day I met him. On our first date, we were supposed to go dancing; instead we went to finish a paper he had been working on. It was always work. We had to keep busy. We would take walks on the campus. That was my way of forcing him to exercise. But he'd have a 3 x 5 card in his pocket and a pencil. We might not go more than ten feet before he'd stop and write, "Light's broken; bushes need trimming; door is unlocked." A student would stop him and talk; then he'd write, "Student needs help. Contact so-and-so." That began to be a joke: "Let's go for our work walk." Toward the end it got really "off-scale" busy. Some of the time I'd get mad at him: "Richard, you've got to slow down!" That's when I bought him a treadmill so he'd exercise.

Richard

It was as if the clock struck on January 1, 1990, as the beginning of an unusual year. Gail was determined I was going to exercise. Before using my treadmill I had a stress test. It appeared that I had an abnormality in my electrocardiogram. I thought back to my father dying of a heart attack a few years earlier. Then Gail underwent a serious operation a month or so later. By March, I didn't feel well at all. Physically, psychologically, and emotionally I felt awful. I knew it and Gail knew it. I didn't understand the problem but my pressure cooker was at full boil.

Gail

Life always seemed very upbeat to me. I'm a cheerful person and I was happy. When this whole thing first started and Richard called me, it was as if I had walked through a door. When I look back on it now, I am on the other side of that door, in another room of my life.

My faith has always been very strong and very much a part of me. So throughout all this, when I made the long drive to the hospital in Baltimore, I never drove alone. I always talked to God. Most of the time I asked for strength and knowledge and insight. "Help me to do the right things."

Richard

Losing the presidency of the university was bad, but what was far worse was my childhood loss of innocence. A loss of childhood itself. That was a warping of what nature and God had intended. It was illegal. Most important, it was profoundly wrong.

I had asthma and rheumatic fever when I was a kid. We had to leave Oregon and move to a drier climate. I spent three years in bed. I had no brothers or sisters, so I had nothing with which to compare. The downside was feeling I was behind and had to catch up.

I have very mixed feelings as I think back to those days. The abuse part was wrong. It scarred me. It's a scar like any other scar. Scars don't go away. Time covers them over, but the tissue is still there, sometimes more tender than at other times.

As a child when the abuse was occurring, I felt profound confusion: "What is this? Why? I don't understand." To a child, the simplest thing can be confusing. At the time, I would get intensely angry, as angry as I knew how as a child. At the same time, there were lots of positive, developmental, creative aspects to my life. Even then, I was aware of the paradox. My childhood certainly was not negative the way some people's are. My parents were not alcoholic. We lived in a stable neighborhood, with no drugs or violence. I went to a respectable school. My father was diligent in his job, honest and loyal and hardworking. My mother and father wanted the very best for me.

Nevertheless, there can be little doubt that what happened for a period of some time was "wrong" and "evil." Those are insufficient words. Certain issues are cataclysmic. They are anti-nature. They're against the flow of what ought to be for human beings. The abuse of a child surely has to rank at the top of a list of such issues. You're dealing with the most vulnerable, sensitive, unprotected part of life. A child has an entire lifetime ahead. When you encounter trauma face-on, like a sledgehammer to your forehead—not only as a child but also as an adult—it has a profound, deep, jolting effect on you. It certainly has increased my sensitivity, awareness, and concern for other people.

I've received a few thousand letters. The people I've heard from are not just adult survivors of child abuse. I've heard from recovering alcoholics, from women who have been beaten by their husbands, from people who have undergone unexpected bankruptcies. I've heard from people with cancer and from people with loved ones who have developed mental illness. I feel their pain. People have called us or stopped us on the street, wanting to reach out—sometimes to give us a helping hand, sometimes to share their troubles with us. The commonality is grief and pain. It's the human connection.

Gail

Richard is strong now. He knows who he is. He has a purity that he didn't have before. There's a tremendous strength in that. So while things may happen we don't like, and some people may have made judgments based on lack of information or erroneous interpretations, I certainly don't see him as a victim anymore.

I feel a lot stronger now and I'm still very optimistic; yet I never go anywhere these days—supermarket, movie theater, restaurant, or even stalled in traffic—that I don't think some percentage of the people around me are in pain. People approach us now and you can almost see it in their eyes; you can sense that they are dealing with something. And they feel that we'll understand.

Richard

This last year's been a period of healing and rebuilding and rebirth. The year 1990, the full calendar year, was hell; 1990 entered with pain and ended with the pain subsiding. But 1991 has been quite different. We're getting on with life. I'm doing consulting with NASA. I enjoy it enormously and admire the people there. Gail and I are involved in a group of volunteer programs that we really enjoy. Some of them we sought out and others came to us.

In the scope of space and time, how important is all of this? To me, mortal, fifty-two-year-old husband, father, professional, Richard Berendzen, it is extraordinarily important. But I'm a tick in time. I'm a speck in space. I am but one of several billions of people, including many tens of millions in this nation, who have faced challenges equal to or more severe than mine.

Out of bad can come good; out of pain renewal. I fervently hope that out of my mistakes and my crash and hurt there can be an object lesson for others. If that is so, then I find some solace in it all. I hope that others out there who have not yet obtained the help and support they need will be motivated to do so.

In many ways I'm quite lucky. I'm lucky to have my wife, my daughters, my friends, my faith, and my education. I know that life goes on, and I hope someday, somewhere, I can serve in a proper role again. I'm also fortunate that I was forced to deal with issues I should have dealt with long ago and that I got expert assistance in doing so. Putting all the pieces of this labyrinth together, I have to say—ironic or not—I feel better now than I've ever felt before: bruised, pained, and scarred, but better. And I'm confident of the future.

Three things carried me through the last year. My faith, my family, and my friends. In the darkest hours, even when I was alone, I dug down deeper within myself than I ever thought I could reach and found more there to hold on to: hope, resolve, and determination. I'm glad I found them because I know they are there and won't leave me. Education has been my life. But during the twenty-five days at Johns Hopkins, the weeks following that, and in the subsequent year, I learned more than in all my formal education combined. It was an education I would never want to replicate; but it was real, strong, and indelible.

There are two powerful messages that people should learn. None of us know the future. The most we can do is attempt to influence it and possibly surmise what it might be. If you allow yourself, you can imagine the worst possible scenario for the future. When you are down, when you're hurting, such pessimism comes naturally: "It's been this bad, and it will probably get worse. And then it's going to get worse still." But you don't know that. You also don't know that it may become miraculously better. Rather than assume the worst, let nature reveal itself. You may find that the worst case of all is not in the real world; it's in your mind. If you can free yourself from that, you can unburden much of your own problem.

The second message is also an important lesson. Not all problems are soluble. Some are not, and some require such strength that I can scarcely imagine what it must be like to face them. People who have AIDS or cancer, and other such tragedies, face life with dignity. Somehow they find hope and strength. I admire those people enormously. The vital word is "hope." Hope is always there. You must never give up.

America is filled with millions of men, women, and children who, with strength and courage, grace and humor, resolve and hard work, rise above their pain to live in the face of continued suffering. In our own lives, we may know some of these special people.

Occasionally, someone comes along who uses his or her personal experience to inspire others in a more public way. Such a unique person becomes a modern-day hero for everyone.

Jim Brady is Vice-Chairman of the National Organization on Disability, in Washington, D.C. He served as White House Press Secretary under President Ronald Reagan. He and his wife, Sarah, are active in lobbying for passage of the Brady Handgun Violence Prevention Act, which would require a waiting period before the purchase of a handgun. The "Brady Bill," as it is called, has been passed by the U.S. House of Representatives and the U.S. Senate, and is awaiting the President's signature.

"Quitting Has Not Entered My Mind"

———

Jim Brady

The survival rate for the type of brain injury I had is one in ten. My doctor says he told my wife, "He's fighting it like hell." And I was. I said, "If I'm a statistic, it's going to be on the other side of those odds, maybe make that two in ten or something like that." I certainly found out I wasn't ready for the alternative. Some have said it's Irish stubbornness. I think it goes deeper than that.

Day in and day out I'd have small victories. One day I'd be able to sit up, another day I'd walk, another day I could hold something in my left hand. I said, "I see a trend emerging here. If I keep fighting this, I can keep doing more of these things." Then I got this quirky wheelchair, and I said, "Gosh, I can move this thing along with my feet." Now I can get around with this damn cane. People have said my grip has gotten a lot stronger.

When I was shot, in March of 1981, I was in the hospital for six months at least. I got to know all the nurses on a first-name basis and I got to know more doctors than I cared to know. I had a motorized wheelchair at Mount Vernon Hospital, but it was quickly taken away from me because I took out my frustrations with it on the staff. I'd drive into the gymnasium, where they made us do all these terrible exercises. They said, "You're too damn dangerous to drive that thing. We're going to give it to someone else who's a little more advanced in their rehabilitation."

Setting small goals along the way served me well. I'd go from ten feet to twelve feet in my wheelchair one day, and from twelve feet to twenty-four feet the next, running over the terrorists' feet. I refer to the PT people as "physical terrorists." I said that on "Donahue," and these people totally went off. I've been admonished by the American Physical Therapy Association. They said, "Don't you understand these are professional people just trying to make you better? How insensitive are you?" I said, "Right now, I'm fairly sensitive. Every part of me hurts from these people." I had a woman physical terrorist that I called the She-Wolf of Auschwitz. I said, "Had the Germans or the Japanese had these people, the war would have been over ten years earlier." They said, "Now, you know because of them you talk better and you walk better today." I said, "I limp better today because of these people." It's against the rules in that profession to have a sense of humor. How can they keep on doing what they're doing if they look down at some guy and see the tears streaming down his face? How can they stay the course and keep on doing what they're doing? Their hearts have to be made of granite.

The physical terrorists know exactly how I feel about them. Their textbook was written by the Marquis de Sade. Only the Marquis would know the subtleties of pain and how to twist a joint past a point where it will not twist anymore. It takes someone who majored in pain to really know what they are doing. I've traveled in all fifty states, and I've probably been to every rehab hospital in the nation. When I go down the receiving line, I know which ones are terrorists. When I'm shaking hands, all of a sudden I get someone who has a catcher's mitt for a hand. You know he's just had it around somebody's neck. But their mission is to make us walk and make us better, and we do and we are.

I remember the day I walked. They'd been bugging me so much I finally got the head terrorist over, and I said, "If I walk, will you leave me alone for ten minutes?" He said, "Yes." I said, "Where are the parallel bars?!" Bump, bump, bump, I went right down the parallel bars. Then they all started coming back for me to do more. I said, "Wait, we made a deal. Back off, back off." They backed off. That was about five months out of the brain trauma.

Before that I would lie there and make a noise the speech terrorists called whaling, a kind of moaning. Then I'd go into spasm; I'd start shaking. That's hell if you're having lunch with somebody. Next thing you know, you've thrown the table all the way across the restaurant. I may reach under the table and my guest asks, "Is there something the matter?" I say "Yes" while I'm making a noise like Thumper the rabbit. Those muscle spasms still come back every night. The circumstance is called "bed." I once thought, Gee, maybe I can get some small sandbags, and when I get in bed I'll put the sandbag on my leg, because I'm knocking the covers off myself and it gets very cold. My metatarsal bones are such that you could almost shuffle them like cards and put them back together.

I love horseback riding; large horse, larger victory. I hope my horse Birney doesn't read this because if she sees I've called her "large," I'm in deep trouble. (Never stand on the right side of Birney; she'll kick you through the goalposts of life.) Riding is a sense of freedom, and if you haven't been able to control anything else and you can control a seventeen-hundred-pound animal, then that is a victory. I told my riding instructor, "Anything I say and anything the horse does is purely coincidental." He said, "That's not true—you're a good rider." I said, "Right." I was quite the Middle Western boy. I'd slip out into the pasture and get on a stump, put the bridle over the horse, and then ride in the wind. The horse and I were one. I wanted to relive a little of that, because I could get around in those days.

It's always darkest before the dawn. I found that to be true with what I'm going through. You don't know the day you're going to be able to hold something in your left hand, or the day you can push your wheelchair backward with your feet. You don't know the day that you're going to walk. You never know when it's going to happen; it happens. It happens when He wants it to happen.

Another thing is to keep your sense of humor. If I look back on trying to do some of the things that the PTs told me to do, I know that without humor I wouldn't have made it. Geri Jewell has cerebral palsy, and she says that it's not the CP that gives her trouble; it's how people regard her that causes problems. Because of the way she walks, she says, people think she's drunk or on drugs. She said one day she was walking up to a bank machine to get some cash and a fella came up behind her and said, "Next time, young lady, just say no."

They say when one sense is taken away from you, another sense becomes keener or you're compensated for it in other ways. In other words, if you're deaf, perhaps your eyes get better; or if your eyes are bad, you might develop better hearing. I think I got smarter. That's the way I rationalize it; I grew more brain cells. I was smart enough to hire the right physicians. The neurosurgeon who saved my life is a genius, Dr. Art Kobrine. I owe my life to him. If I'm lying on the floor and the legs are just kicking up and down and I'm really having a bad time, Sarah can call him, and in fifteen minutes he'll be over. The world's not filled with people like that. You don't have a whole city full of physicians who will drive that far to take care of one of his patients. He does, and he will. He doesn't take any diddly-squat from me, though. "You will do this, and you will do it now. You will do it this way, and you will feel better for doing it this way."

Don't pay the price I did to join this club; sometimes I wonder if I'd do it again. Being the real article is a bitch. I can remember the doctor telling me at one time, "You're not going to like what I'm going to tell you, but it's true." He said, "You probably wish there was some kind of pill I could give you that would make the incident not have happened. There is no such pill in all the world. If there was, I'd give it to you." But he said, "You'll find that you'll get much better with the passage of time." He said, "I know no one wants to hear that. Just live a little longer and you're going to get better."

I'm still fighting. I'm not back as far as I want to come back yet, and I know it. I'm going to keep fighting till I come back farther. Quitting has not entered my mind. A good bear is a hard thing to get down. I am a bear.

I didn't ask "Why me, God?" Nor did I go through protracted denial, as if nothing happened to me; something did. "Have you always been in a wheelchair?" "No." "Then something happened to you." "Did you always walk with a cane?" "No." "Then something happened to you." "Do you have muscle spasms at night?" "Yes." "Then something happened to you." I know it happened; God knows I know it happened. It hurt and it hurts to this day, but I'm not going to give up. Whether that's just quintessential stubborn Irish or what, I don't know, but I am not going to give up. I'm not ready for them to dig a hole with a backhoe and throw dirt on me. It would be a shame to give up after having done hard time, done pain. To quit now? I'm not going to do that.

God has a major role in all of this. You're talking to a lad who has more hospital chaplains praying for him around the country than you can imagine. Remember the nuns? If you got hurt, they'd say, "Offer it up for the poor people in purgatory." So I've offered this up for the people in purgatory. If pain is any measure, then I know that thousands of them are coming out.

There isn't any way that I can take this experience off and put it on you and let you feel some of the frustration. What is a bump for other people is a cliff for me. This, too, someday shall pass. I'm a testament to the fact that it does. It gets better and it's amazing.

When I want something, I have big brown eyes, and I get right up in somebody's face and give them puppy-dog eyes. They say, "No, no, anything but the puppy-dog eyes. We give in." I'm not reluctant to use them either. I thought perhaps it was a cheap trick. Then when I found out it worked, I used it.

God could have killed me dead, boom. But Our Lord up there was looking down on me saying, "Make him miss, make him miss." When I go over to the Handgun Control Office and I see the TEC-9s and the MAC-11s, I think, My God, if Hinkley had bought one of those in Dallas instead of the cheap-ass little handgun, there would have been a whole bunch of us down there on the street in bad shape. Praise the Lord, he didn't.

The worst thing would have been if he'd have killed me dead. Then I would have had to figure out how to resurrect or have someone resurrect me, which is a lot harder to do than going through PT. Probably I would have found someone who could have instructed somebody on how to do it.

I'm going to continue as long as the Lord gives me the will to continue, and I think I have the will to continue, because He's given it to me.

Loss

Adversity is about loss. Some of the most traumatic pain we suffer is when we lose those with whom we have developed a special bond of self-revelation, trust, and intimacy. With the exception of chronic physical pain, almost nothing hurts more than the loss of a person who has played a significant role in our life.

Mutual interests, shared pleasure, affection, common goals, similar values and life-styles, and deep love are characteristics that create the bond of intimacy. When that bond is severed, shock, loss, grief, despair, and depression come together to form indescribable pain.

Therapists and clergy agree that the loss of a significant person through death, divorce, or breakdown of a meaningful relationship has equal impact. The loss may take years to overcome. However, time and the grief process help heal the hurt, and people who have loved and lost move forward to love deeply again.

Robert S. Weiss, Ph.D., is a Research Professor at the University of Massachusetts (Boston), where he is the Director of the Work and Family Research Unit. He is also a lecturer in Sociology in the Department of Psychiatry at the Massachusetts Mental Health Center of the Harvard Medical School, where he was previously Director of the Group for Research in Community Psychiatry. Dr. Weiss is the author of eight books, including *Staying the Course: The Emotional and Social Lives of Men Who Do Well at Work; Marital Separation: Managing After a Marriage Ends,* and *Loneliness: The Experience of Emotional and Social Isolation.*

"People Have a Need to Come Together . . ."

Robert S. Weiss

People need to come together in some kind of special, intimate relationship, and there's a need for people to come together in some sense of community. There's a readiness to experience the attachment need, and it looks as if there is a fair amount of chance involved with whom you get attached. People have a very wide range of potential attachment figures; under pressures of loneliness, the range gets wider.

The critical issue in relation to establishing a bond of attachment is whether the image of the other person has been incorporated into the attachment system: the way the person looks, sounds, and feels. You see a lot of eye-gazing when two people are in the process of forming an attachment. A particular constellation of features is going to be what one will call up when in need of this other figure. Also when one sees this person, there's going to be that sense of "great . . . wonderful . . . terrific." It's like being at home with this image of the person. It isn't as simple as seeing the person and thinking, That's my wife. It happens before there's even a chance to react. It lasts. That's what is so eerie and unsettling for people whose husbands or wives have died: the image persists. They anticipate seeing their partner even after the person is dead and buried. They think they see that person walking down the street. They look at a picture and it has an emotional impact. All of these are consequences of the incorporation of the image into the emotional system.

The attachment system seems to be linked to feelings of security, well-being, and completion. The incorporation of the physical image into that system is probably only one of the ways in which the other person becomes a way of triggering it. People feel reassured when they talk to an attachment figure over the telephone. Even a letter from an attachment figure is reassuring.

What most people have in mind when they talk about loneliness is probably emotional isolation. The experience of emotional isolation is like being at a wedding alone. It shows up at times when you feel inadequate by yourself. It's a feeling of being edgy, as if everybody at the wedding is in color and you're in black-and-white. They seem to be in another world. They don't touch you. You don't touch them. You're separate from them. They all seemingly have their lives together. They have it made and you don't have a thing. Your feeling is: I don't want to do this. I don't want to be here. I don't know what this is keeping me from, but I can't stand being here. You feel enormous restlessness and inability to connect with people. If, on the other hand, somebody comes by who looks like a person you could connect with, you go through a chemical change. You're now engaged, focused, and energized because you're organized to establish a linkage, and whatever interferes with the possibility of establishing that linkage feels hostile to you. Just the possibility of attachment interrupts the feelings of loneliness. The absence of an attachment figure gets triggered when you feel as if you need somebody because you aren't adequate yourself. That's the loneliness of emotional isolation, and stress brings it on.

Social isolation is different. You have to have a place where you have a right to be when you show up. Maybe all the people don't like you, but that's not the issue: you have a right to be there. Work is the very best community, because your job establishes your right to be there. When you get paid, that absolutely demonstrates it. That certifies your membership. No matter how it's put to you, it is very hard to feel that the loss of a job isn't a declaration by the people at work that they don't want you among them. People often take job loss personally, with a lot of resentment, and with the feeling of not having measured up.

What's left in its place is a sense of being an outsider.

We're doing a study of retirement, and we're finding there is great gratification in not having to get up and fight the commute and worry about what's going on at work and be subject to all the accompanying stresses. There's freedom and relief in being retired. But the other side of freedom is "I don't count." There's a feeling of being outside the action; there's often the feeling "If I were to show up at work, they wouldn't be happy to see me. And as time goes on the retired person may even think, What the hell am I living for?"

Family is a community and the world of friends is a community. Family community goes on lifelong. It's awfully hard to understand why it works and the way it works, but it's pretty clear that it works. In most instances, it doesn't matter how long you are separated from the other people you feel are your family. There is almost always a sense of mutual obligation and loyalty, the feeling that we're going through life together and we ought to look out for each other even if we don't.

Loneliness is pervasive as hell. Everybody's experienced it. The groups that are most susceptible to emotional isolation are those in late adolescence, those who aren't married, and those who are shy and introverted and don't make connections easily. People who experience social isolation are those who move around often, including business-men, because they're separated from their families. Students have problems too. The first year at any new school is a time when they experience social isolation. They know nobody, and that's scary. What they lack are allies who will make them feel they're not all by them-selves.

If one attempts to think of the bad things that can happen to a person, my own sense is that number one on the list is the death of a child, even an adult child. Number two on the list is the death of a spouse. And number three, way up there, is divorce or separation.

The loss of a significant person may be the most severe psychological trauma most people will encounter in a lifetime, and it's tremendously complex. I've been working for a while with people who've been told that they are HIV positive, and that, of course, is *very* traumatic. Once a person hears that news, it's always in the back of his or her mind. One never gets away from it. But as near as I can tell, it doesn't obliterate functioning as severely as does the death/divorce situation. In the divorce situation the person seems to be assailed by pain, experiences extraordinary mood swings, and is overwhelmed by anger. Some people feel themselves so out of control that they are worried they're "losing it" and that they need psychiatric intervention; many people do benefit from it. I don't see that in the HIV-positive situation.

A person is told he or she has a stigmatizing condition that is life-threatening in the short run, and probably fatal in the longer run. It's a way of dying that is going to be terribly tough to tolerate. And yet when people get over the shock, they start thinking about what to do. Sometimes they do have suicidal thoughts, but it isn't as though their capabilities for self-control have become deranged. Yet that is what seems to happen with bereavement and divorce. With divorce, it's more visible because there are mood swings and anger. There's an expression outward, reaching out to the former spouse by calling on the telephone or getting the help of lawyers. With bereavement, the loss of control isn't that obvious because people are more inclined to turn inward. There aren't such physical expressions of pain, although people are terribly restless. It's impossible for them to think, impossible for them to develop coherent plans. They can't sit still. It really is more damaging to emotional functioning than learning that you have a fatal illness, even though it doesn't seem to make any sense that that would be so.

I don't want to suggest that the person who goes through divorce is in some existential sense worse off than the person who's about to die; that's not true. Four years from now, the person who's about to die is going to be dead. Four years from now, the person who is now going through a divorce may have a functioning life. From an existential standpoint, it's not worse; but from the standpoint of what's happening to the person's emotional organization, the divorce has more impact.

The sameness of death and divorce is that they're loss; they're loss of an attachment figure. They both trigger the built-in emotional reaction to a threatened or real loss of that attachment figure.

There's a major difference, though, in divorce and bereavement. In bereavement, the cause of your distress is cancer or a doctor, a drunk driver, or some other outside agency. In divorce, you're distressed because of the absence of the other person. It's the other person who did it. You want to kill the other person. You are in the peculiar situation of wanting to kill the person that you need. That can make you crazy. In bereavement, sometimes there's anger at the person who died. "Why did he take those risks?" "Why didn't she quit smoking?" There's sometimes anger at the self, but it's much more muted compared to the anger in marital separation and divorce, which is like nothing you've ever seen. The only example I can think of that comes close to it is business partners who've discovered that one of them is trying to embezzle from the other. Even then it isn't the wild rage that you find in marital separation.

The initial reaction to trauma generally is "I've got to do something about this." For most people, it's a time of mobilization. When a woman hears that her husband has died, her first reaction is "I've got to do something." "What's going on?" "Where can I see him?" Enormous energy is released. It's later on, when a person has given up hope and has fully internalized "No matter what I do, it's not going to work out," that one gets depression.

There are really just two steps in the bereavement process itself: mobilization and depression. An early reaction to trauma is an inability to grasp: "It doesn't make any sense." "It's not real, it's a dream." "I'm going to wake up from this shock." You don't have any feelings. You are taking it in cognitively, but it doesn't mean anything to you, really, in terms of your feelings. We don't find that with forewarned separation where you've had a lot of trouble along the way. We do, however, find it pretty regularly in bereavement. It's a fairly reliable immediate reaction, but it doesn't last very long. The next reaction the distinguished psychoanalyst, the late John Bowlby, calls "protest." "How am I going to deal with this?" "How am I going to manage it?" "How am I going to undo it?" Some of what happens is trying to undo it. People go through the "if only's." "If only I hadn't" is a way of undoing it magically. During this phase, people are vigilant toward anything that will resolve the loss or the hurt.

In marital separation, many people associate the partner's car with the person, and they discover they are suddenly aware of every blue Plymouth on the road. There's a vigilance toward the return of the other figure. People feel impelled, according to Bowlby, to regain proximity, to get close to the other figure. I had a divorced man once tell me that he established a routine. He'd come home from work, think about fixing dinner, be unable to do it, get in the car, drive down the street where his ex-wife and kids still lived, feel better about things, go back home and start dinner.

In the bereavement situation, people are alert to all kinds of indications that the other person's spirit is still there. They hear footsteps. They think they see the other person still sitting in the living room. They hear a noise and it's the house settling, but they wonder, Maybe it's him. Maybe he's letting me know he's still here. It's as though the rejoining has so overwhelmed other concerns that everything gets interpreted in terms of it. Then people give up. There's always a certain amount of giving up early on, and there's always a certain amount of protest later, but what predominates is "the only important person in life isn't here. It doesn't matter what I do, there is no way of making it happen. Nothing I do matters." No point even in getting up, no point in getting out.

Experts talk about a phase of adaptation or recovery in which people re-establish a workable life. It takes a while. The attachment system is marvelously tenacious in relation to images once incorporated. It doesn't give them up easily. If you think about it, you can see why that would have to be so. That's what makes a pair relationship reliable. It doesn't matter if you have a fight, you stay attached. It's a retentive system, it doesn't listen to reason even after the other person has died. It takes a long time before you have free attachment energy and it's possible for you to become attached to a new figure. It may take the best part of a year before people have an afternoon when they don't remember with pain they're now alone. That's how pervasive that kind of linkage is.

Men are able to form new relationships early in bereavement—two months or three months. That does not mean they are no longer grieving. One of the premises of the new relationship, with absolute reliability, is that the new woman will join him in grieving and will understand that he's bereaved. In bereavement or in divorce or relationship termination, we're talking about the period of adjustment being two to four years. It's probably somewhat longer for bereavement than for marital separation, possibly because people feel less comfortable moving toward recovery. It seems to take about a year before people have established a new way of functioning that gets them through the day accepting, without being depressed, that the other person isn't there. But they're still pretty raw. The first anniversary is very tough, and people are still vulnerable to anniversary reactions for a long time after the death.

It isn't that you recover a hundred percent. You don't really get over it; you get used to it. It becomes one of the givens of life. Certainly by three years—with people for whom the recovery process is going well—it's in the past. They can call up the image of the other person if they want to, in a way re-establish the sense of presence if they want to. If they don't want to, it won't happen. For the most part, it's put away. Obviously, the emotional health of the person plays a large role in the recovery.

An unforewarned loss, one that comes out of the blue with absolutely no warning, is very difficult to accept. It's also difficult to deal with a relationship where there are strong negatives as well as strong positives.

If a relationship is all negative, then the hell with it. But marriages very seldom are. In a divorce, people will say afterward, "Well, it wasn't the best marriage in the world, but there were often very positive elements as well." In situations in which people have hurt each other, and the resentments were never resolved, that's a tough situation too.

Dependency is another thing that makes divorce or bereavement harder. You're a little agoraphobic and you don't like to go shopping; or the other person was responsible for your social life; those kinds of losses set you back, and it's often very tough to recover.

One woman with whom I talked divorced her husband, and then he died. In the period during which he was alive but an ex-husband, she was perfectly happy being furious with him. It all made sense. He was a lousy father, slow on support, a lowlife. When he died, she was flooded with feelings of loss and nothing made sense.

What is the cause of pain? What causes the hurt? What causes the suffering? Some of it is terror of abandonment in a mysterious and dangerous world. There's a helplessness that feeds anger; there's a feeling of betrayal. There may also be something that is primitive around "This shouldn't have happened." "This isn't the way it should be. This is wrong. It's wrong, wrong, wrong." Somehow it all seems to come back to there being something insufficient about you. There's something fundamentally flawed or missing, so that part of your rage is toward yourself. Part of your rage is toward the figure that isn't there.

The rage toward yourself is part of the pain. The pain is terror, self-directed anger, enormous dismay and distress. The only thing that's important in the world isn't there. For the one who has been left, there's a tremendous sense of rejection, of inadequacy.

People deal with their rage in many different ways. This includes people who are afraid that if they were to express the rage, the other person would really never come back. Only by pretending the rage is not there do they have a chance that the other person will reappear. So they blank themselves out emotionally. Dealing with all that energy can be a problem because you don't know what to name it. All you feel is jumpy, restless; you can't settle down, you can't concentrate, you can't make sense of anything.

Loneliness is one of those things that don't go away gradually. It goes away all of a sudden. That was one of my first observations. When I saw that and thought about its implications, it was really stunning. You're never half-lonely. You are or you aren't. It's on or off.

Lonely people aren't lonely all the time. It's in the evening when they come back to an empty apartment, and weekends. Work time tends to be a less lonely time. Even so, the loneliness is always there. It's always pushing you, it's always an irritant, and you try different things. Most of the time, you're sensible. One evening, you just can't take it any longer, so you're going to be not sensible and you do something dumb. You go out to a bar. If you're a woman, you let yourself get picked up. Guys get on the telephone. People get telephoneitis. A couple of drinks will help that come along. You answer ads in the personal columns; you know that makes no sense, but what's the difference? "I'm so miserable anyway."

The most sensible thing to do is to establish a place in a community of friends. It's something that you can reasonably expect to work out. If you get into a group of people who have interests similar to yours and who are more or less like you, and you keep hanging out with them, you will be accepted. After a while you'll have a place. Communities do look after their members. There are resource pools of every sort, including resource pools for making connections. Somebody will have a party, and there will be somebody you'll meet.

If you expect to be able to deal with emotional isolation by next week, you're in trouble. If you can give yourself a one-year time perspective, that's reasonable. Put yourself into opportunities to meet other people and to form a new attachment. The best bet is to have a place in a community of people who are more or less committed to one another. This isn't what the community's going to be about. It's going to be about something else: work, politics, a hobby. But things will happen.

Two people come together to form a special partnership. They are committed to each other's growth, security, and happiness. The goal is to help each other become the best person he or she can be while simultaneously sharing hopes, dreams, joys, hardships, successes, and failures.

The two share a special commitment to each other as well as the happiness of being together. What greater satisfaction are humans capable of experiencing? Yet, as happens in life, partners die through illness or tragic circumstances. Since the pain of that loss cuts deeply, life loses meaning for a long while. It is not only the loss of that special person that hurts so much, but the ruin of hopes, dreams, and security as well.

Georgann Fuller, M.S.W., is a therapist and certified social worker specializing in addictions and substance abuse. She holds a Master of Social Work degree from the University of Michigan and is currently working toward a post-Master's degree at the Center for Humanistic Studies in Detroit, Michigan. She is a frequent public speaker on coping with sudden traumatic death.

"I Prayed, 'Please Give Me Peace' "

Georgann Fuller

Jim was coming back on Wednesday from Frankfurt. It was to be a very short trip because our son was celebrating his eighteenth birthday on Thursday. Jim chose his flight because it was the only one out of Europe where he could leave there during the day and arrive here in Detroit by midnight. Then he would sleep, get up, and we would spend the day with our son.

Even though the Pan Am flight originated in Frankfurt, he got on another carrier, flew to London, and boarded Pan Am 103 at Heathrow Airport. About thirty-five minutes into the flight the bomb exploded over Lockerbie, Scotland. It was 7:03 in the evening there; it was 2:03 in the afternoon here.

That morning I'd gone to the airport to pick up my son, who had been visiting his girlfriend in Ohio. We had meandered along, and we stopped at a Taco Bell to have lunch. I think that was where I was when Jim died. When I pass that place today, I can still taste the tacos in my stomach.

As we came into the house, the phone was ringing. The daughter of my closest friend here, my college roommate, was on the phone. She asked, "Is Jim coming home today from London?" And I said, "Yes."

She asked, "Is he on a Pan Am flight?" And I said, "Yes." Then she asked, "Is he going from London to New York?" And I thought, Why is she asking me this? I said, "Yes, why?" "Well, there was a Pan Am flight that just crashed," she said. "It was 103."

As she said it, I was shuffling through some papers in front of me and Jim's itinerary was there. My eyes went to "Pan Am 103," and I said, "Kellie, I have to go now." I sat down in a chair and I thought "Jim is dead. Jim is dead."

I remember that night my house being filled with people; they were in and out all evening long. I handled myself very well because I'm a crisis person, but I was in shock. I hauntingly remember that the television set was on all the time. I recall walking past it and seeing the burning over and over again—the fire at Lockerbie—and not having any feeling at all.

Jim was vice-president of Volkswagen and the head of Volkswagen Division of Volkswagen of America. We had a really good marriage. We'd take walks and hold hands. We always held hands in the movies and often in the car. We were really best friends.

The bomb only weighed a pound and a half, so it blew out a very small section of the plane. The plane broke up primarily because of its weight, and it dropped in various sections around Lockerbie. Jim was in first class. There were seventeen bodies found in there. That section fell on a farmer's field five miles outside of Lockerbie, about a hundred yards in front of a beautiful little Scottish church and graveyard. It was very comforting for me, first of all because there was a body; second, because he was protected in the first-class section; and last, his falling in front of the church. It was symbolic to me, and I held on to that. Those things have helped me in my healing.

Two hundred and fifty-nine people in the plane and eleven residents of Lockerbie on the ground died. After the tragedy I really needed to read everything. I was not treated well by Pan Am or the State Department. Getting the body back was an absolute fiasco. They'd call one day and say, "His body's going to be released tomorrow." Then they'd call back and say, "No, we can't send it." It went back and forth, back and forth. Finally, Jim's body arrived, on January 1, eleven days later.

Also at that time we were beginning to find out that it was a bomb, that it wasn't a plane crash, that there had been warnings, and that some State Department people had been pulled off the flight. (A couple of weeks before, there had been a posting of the bomb threat at the U.S. Embassy in Moscow.) I started to get phone calls from some of the relatives, and I went to a meeting in March in Connecticut. We were outraged at how we had been treated by Pan Am, how Pan Am had not done what they were supposed to do in checking unreconciled baggage, and how they had not taken heed that there was a bomb threat. We were angry at the FAA and the State Department about our treatment and that some people were notified about the threat and some not. There was a lot of anger. That's typical. Where are you going to put your anger? You direct it toward those different agencies. I was in shock often; there's a lot I do not remember for about six months. Actually I was probably in some shock until I went to Lockerbie a year and a half later.

In many ways I functioned as though the loss wasn't there. Then I would have jabs of my loss. I made some decisions about how I was going to handle it. Some of the decisions came from the fact that I was having so much pain. I decided I was going to go through this and come out of it a better person. It might take more work and cause more pain. If I succumbed to the pain and to my "poor me" and my "awfulizing," I wouldn't make it.

I'm a nice person. I go to church. I've never been arrested for anything. How could this happen to me and my children? My husband murdered? Somebody murdered that I love? There was a tremendous sense of vulnerability and lack of control that was extremely difficult to handle. In some ways I still have that vulnerability. It will take a long time to heal. But, I thought, I'm going to grab where I feel I have some power and I'm going to use it.

I was lucky because I had training as a therapist, not only a therapist of people who had problems but of people with addictions. One thing I learned is always to ask myself what I can change and what I can't change. I lived my life with that in my mind daily. I know what I have power over and what I don't. I also learned, "one day at a time," "one hour at a time," "ten minutes at a time." Those things really helped me a lot in the first few months, the first year and a half, and sometimes even now. I also decided that I would allow myself to cry whenever I felt like it. I was going to let the feelings come out. I was not going to keep them in, because I knew they would manifest themselves physically and I didn't want to be sick. I really have been very healthy throughout all this. I also made a decision to exercise, and to watch caffeine; caffeine really set me off and made me very sad.

Another thing that I think was really helpful was I don't have any guilt. A lot of people have guilt, particularly in a sudden death, because they have unfinished business. I don't have any unfinished business with Jim. I would have loved to have been there and held him as he died. I feel some sadness but I don't feel guilt about it. I know he knows how I felt about him and I know how he felt about me. Not all relationships in my life are like that. I've tried to do it but I haven't always succeeded. I certainly try more now. I tell a lot more people that I love them. I really do. I hug people who are important to me a lot more, and I don't give my hugs away to just everybody. One of the reasons I haven't gone back to work full time is that I still need people. I want to feel that I've done certain things for people and said things I need to say.

My daughter and son are doing pretty well, considering their age. I've gathered from a lot of people I know who have lost a parent sometime around my children's age that they often don't deal with it until they're thirty or more. After Jim died, my daughter went out to Colorado and struggled. When she wanted to come back, I suggested therapy and she agreed. She's really getting her life on track; I think she's done very well. My son is still quite angry, but he's beginning to get things together. He goes out once in a while with several friends whose fathers have died and I think that's a good sign.

I struggled recently because I got Jim's autopsy report. I was really devastated; almost every bone in his body had been broken. There was a lot of mutilation. I kept having a recurring picture of this horrific situation. I found myself wondering, How am I ever going to be able to erase this picture? Is this going to be something I'll have to carry to my grave? It's baggage I just didn't want. So I thought, I need to look at this differently. I decided that I had to look at Jim's death not from my point of view but from his. The survivors can only see the aftermath of the destruction, so that gets imprinted. Sometimes when you think of the person, that's the picture that clicks into your head. I decided I had to think about it from Jim's point of view, because if he knew, it was only for a second. He went very quickly and that destruction was his body, not him. It was a better death than wasting away in a bed, in severe pain, watching yourself dying. It's been helpful to me to look at it that way rather than from my view as a survivor.

My father died of cancer about eleven years ago and I did not grieve after he died. I had done all the grieving beforehand. I was ready for him to go because I could not stand what I saw and what it was doing to my mother. So I've had the experience of that kind of death versus this very sudden death. The shock of a traumatic or sudden death lasts longer because there isn't any preparation. The shock comes WHACK! For me it was as if a big capsule of Lucite or ice came down over me and enveloped me. It gradually got chipped away by reality. If I tried to handle all the reality of what had happened immediately, I'd have gone crazy. Jim was fifty and to a certain extent that's untimely. There's that part, too, that makes it more difficult. The average age on that plane was twenty-seven.

About four or five months ago, I was dating a fellow and just decided to stop because I'm still not feeling ready. I don't want to get old feelings mixed up with new ones. I'm becoming a new person, I'm changing. I'm looking at life differently. I'm smelling the roses a lot more. I'm choosing to do things that I enjoy doing. I'm not doing them because I feel as though I have to. People who know me certainly see the difference. I'm becoming a really neat person. Unless I'm a neat person I'm not going to attract neat people. I want to be the best possible person I can be. As the grief leaves and I become more of my own person, then I lighten up more, and I can attract those kinds of people in my life. I don't mean just men; I mean women too.

The day of Jim's memorial service I asked myself, "How am I going to get through this without falling apart?" That night I prayed, "Please give me peace." At that moment a tremendous feeling of peace came over me. The only drink I've ever had that I feel out at the end of my fingers is a margarita. It was as if I'd had about three gulps of margaritas. The peace was just there. It was as though God said, "I'm here with you," and I just took off from there.

I have taken sudden death to be like Good Friday. The period that you go through is really Holy Saturday; then you come to Easter Sunday, resurrection. The Bible promises new life if we accept it. It doesn't say "Stay stuck." That's helped me a lot. I really had to think about my belief in everlasting life; that was important. I think Jim's there on the other side. They're all over there on some other side.

I feel that I can go on with my life. I feel as though Jim's there and that he's going to be okay. He'll go on and I'll go on. I also don't want him with me all the time, because I can't be with him and he can't be with me. So let's just go. We always gave each other freedom, and we give each other freedom now.

Pain and suffering are there in an imperfect world, but we have free will. We can choose to think, feel, act, as we want to. Sometimes we create our own pain. We have the power to do what we want with pain, but we don't have power over whether it's there or not.

At some point, many of us have experienced the hurt of a broken relationship. In the United States, almost half of all marriages end in divorce. So many good people come together with great hopes and expectations. While their relationships may have been successful for a while—for many, a long while—those intimate partnerships, because of conflict, could not continue.

When any very close relationship ends badly, the profound sense of loss is accompanied by feelings of fear, rejection, abandonment, and defeat. For those who grieve that special kind of loss, time can heal, lessons can be learned, regrets and resentments can be put into perspective, and new opportunities can be discovered to love and commit once again.

Polly Schechter is Assistant to the Secretary of the Catholic University of America in Washington, D.C. She serves as a protocol and special events coordinator for the president of the university.

"I'm Going to Be Who I Am"

Polly Schechter

My ex-husband and I met in high school when we were seventeen years old. That was back in the early 1950s, when men and women looked at things a little differently from the way we do today.

My focus at that time centered around getting married, establishing a home, and having children. We were married when we were both about twenty-one years old, extremely young, immature, and inexperienced. We had a daughter, and three and a half years later we had another daughter. My goal was having everything appropriate for our children—the station wagon, Mom, apple-pie kind of thing, and his was directed toward getting an education and furthering his career.

As I look back on it now, I can see that from very early in our marriage our lives really took different directions. There were parts of my personality I never allowed to develop; he was a strong personality and not always the easiest person to live with. I swallowed some of my desires, as he probably did his.

For a long time I felt I really wanted to pursue a career, and I did not do so because I didn't get the encouragement I needed. I also didn't know how to go about it. I had a Bible-school education, which didn't suit me for any particular kind of career other than one that was church-oriented. I am very much of a people-oriented kind of person, but instead of being out in the workplace over the years, I did a lot of volunteering.

Our lives never did seem to be headed down the same road together. My idea of love and marriage was very much a fantasy idea. It resembled a fairy tale—Cinderella and the Prince. In reality, my ex-husband and I had some distinct differences from the beginning, and those differences did not change. As our marriage went on, they increased.

My ex-husband was very much the kind of person who needed to be alone. He did not care to be out with groups of people in a social setting, whereas I was more extroverted and my energy came from being around people.

As our children became teenagers, some of the ways we approached discipline began to show. Instead of bringing us together, our methods, which were quite different, separated us further.

My ex-husband and I also had extreme differences in our backgrounds—economically, socially, and psychologically. I think what made us click was that he had a strong need to be liked and loved, and I had a need to fill that. The mothering side of me hooked in to it. As he continued to grow and mature, he was able to get away from that, and so I felt very unwanted. He was getting what he needed from inside himself; conversely, what I had been contributing wasn't necessary and I felt empty.

Many times over the years I had thought, I really don't want to be in this marriage, but because of the fantasy, I was doing everything I could to make it work. Nothing in our marriage was ever dealt with completely. All the things that were never dealt with were put in the closet, and after a long time it was so full it burst.

One day I needed to talk to him about something we were doing in the house that involved money. It had to do with some drapes we were putting in the living room. I had one understanding of what the agreement was, and he apparently had another. For days before I sat down to talk with him about this, I planned what I was going to say.

I look back on it now and realize I spent a lot of time in those twenty-seven years of marriage being afraid to deal with many issues because I was afraid of his verbal reaction to me. So I said what I planned to say and he blew up at me. His words to me were "I want to live alone." The next day, he took me to lunch and told me this again, and I realized he was serious about it.

Our older daughter had gone to California to school and our younger daughter had already graduated from high school and was living in her own apartment. So we were not faced with the children being at home. I realize now that he had gone through a whole planning process to get to the place where he could say to me, "I want to live alone." He had not planned to say it that way that day, but he did because he was ready. I wasn't.

Our younger daughter was to be married in September. This was in May. So we agreed that he would stay in the house, that we would not live together as man and wife, and that we would not tell either of our children that we were planning to separate in the fall.

I spent that entire summer trying to get us back together again. I went through some individual counseling. I remember once stopping on the way home to buy a rose to give to him. I was just pushed aside when I offered it to him. It took me a few months to realize he really meant what he said.

He had spent a lot of time searching his soul. Along the way I could see he was making some significant changes in his own behavior, and he had hoped that I would grow as well. But I didn't come along. I was afraid of the changes.

However, I remember that summer as one of the healthiest I have ever had in my life. I spent a lot of time alone reading, thinking, searching, and reaching out to myself to make some discoveries about me. I also began to think about how I wanted to approach a separation from a social point of view. I talked to friends. I have a group of women friends—there are four of us—and we're all about the same age. At that time two of them were separated and divorced. One was in a marriage. Many times we sat around the kitchen table, crying and talking together. I worked through most of the issues in my separation and divorce with this group of women.

It occurred to me I could join these other two "unattached" women, and the three of us could socialize in the singles world. So we started going out. This went on for a period of a year or so.

During that time, I met someone who told me about an organization that I became very deeply involved in, called New Beginnings, an organization for separated and divorced people. It's a place where people can go to talk in a safe environment about loss. It was an opportunity for me to share and to listen to what people were going through. It offered me hope and it provided me with the knowledge "I'm not alone out here," and that I would be able to make it on my own as a divorced person. I also read a lot of psychology books. I still have a whole shelf of books that I read during that period. Slowly my life began to take directions that were important for me.

We stayed together in the house until after our daughter was married. He physically moved out of the house the first week in November. The day he moved out was as hard for him as it was for me. When he left, I had to fill those spaces in the closet and in areas left vacant by the furniture we had agreed he would take. I had to fill those spaces so I didn't have to see them as voids. Consequently, I could see my life moving into those spaces over time.

My growth process involved discovering I could do things for myself that I didn't think I could do. I could take care of my own business affairs. I realized that I could not only live alone, but be alone and be happy. That was something new for me.

During that summer, I was making other discoveries about peace with myself, contentment, and happiness. I think of one day in particular, being at home alone. It was raining and I was looking outside at the trees in the backyard and feeling peaceful about the scene and that I was a part of it.

On the other hand, I can remember another situation very close to that time. My ex-husband was living in the basement of our house. I recall getting up in the middle of the night and going down there crying, "What am I going to do? I'm so scared—don't leave me." I was growing internally and gaining some knowledge of myself but, at the same time, I was scared to death. I experienced a great sense of abandonment, too. He was walking away from what it had taken us twenty-seven years to build. I saw a picture in my mind of the old house left to rot.

What I felt internally when my ex-husband said "I want to live alone" was what I felt when my parents died. You feel as if you can't get a deep breath or that your heart is in your feet. The emotional response to loss is overwhelming.

That summer of introspection—socializing differently from anything I'd ever done as a single person, being involved in a group setting, and talking with people who were sharing loss together—was an energizing process for me. I began to live my life in other directions, I to branch out of suburbia. I came downtown to George Washington University and took a Continuing Education Program in Fund Raising Administration. I also began to explore a little of downtown, which was really fun for me. The first evening I went to a night class, I was scared to death—not of driving into town, but of the whole process, this new direction my life was taking. Yet I remember driving home that night and being so excited with what was happening, what was going on.

About a year after my separation, I met a man with whom I got involved. It developed much more quickly than I had anticipated. Ultimately I married him. I was in the final counseling process with my ex-husband when I started the relationship with my present husband.

We have been married now for three years. When I first met him, my life began to take a whole different direction. I was fortunate to meet someone who has provided me with a completely new focus.

The experience of the divorce has turned out to be positive. I feel better about myself. I do feel it changed me positively. I think I am a different person now.

Most of the time my life is better in this present relationship because I feel free to express myself as a person. I do the things I really want to do. Part of that is because the man I am married to enjoys many of the same things that I do. Socially he is very good about coming along and I feel very comfortable with that kind of outlet. When there are things that I feel strongly about, I feel free to express myself. I guess I'm sort of coming out as a human being. If something's troubling me, I say it. In my previous relationship I couldn't do that because I was afraid. I've decided I'm going to be who I am.

My ex-husband and I are friendly. In the separation process we went through a closure counseling. At the time we said, "Look, we're hurt and angry today but ultimately we want to work through that. We want to be friends." We chose that as a goal. We were able to agree that in separation we wanted to be friendly because in fact we shared a history and we had two children. We wanted to be able to continue to talk with one another. There was so much hurt for our children. Even though they weren't living at home, they were blaming themselves. We didn't want that to go on. So we kept working at it.

I'm not sure how we finally overcame the hurt and anger, except to say that it was through time. Because we kept in touch with each another, time helped to resolve a lot of the hurtful things and we are able to look at the historical past. We touch base every week or ten days. We say, "Hi. How are you? Just calling to see how everything is going." In those conversations we exchange stories about the children or the grandchildren that we now share. We keep our conversations about our personal lives very general. He is always involved in family get-togethers. We always invite him and he always comes. Time has healed a lot.

My ex-husband gave me a poem some time ago. It's on the side of my bookcase in my study, over my desk.

> From time to time
> Two paths will cross
> Then merge together
> To appear to be one

And as such will travel
Many miles

But so often
The fortunes of the world
Make it necessary
For them to separate
In order to reach
Their own destinations

Javin

I like "to reach their own destinies." That's the way we both have looked at it.

I don't see him as the man I was married to for twenty-seven years; I see him more as a person who is important in my life and with whom I have a certain kind of relationship. I would be very hurt if that were to end, and he feels the same way. People we know say that they are really amazed and impressed that we have been able to have this different kind of relationship.

I'm pretty happy today. Many of the things I wanted to accomplish in my life, and many of the needs I have are being met in this marriage. It is more fulfilling and more joyful today.

Suffering

In the earlier stages of life, it is normal to focus on self. Not until we get older, and encounter setbacks in our own lives, do we develop empathy and compassion for others. Because of our experience with pain, we connect with others in a deeper and more fulfilling way.

According to Father Edward Pritchard, "It takes a long time to make a human being." Suffering forces people to recognize their own vulnerabilities and to appreciate the humanness of others as well.

While there are some who give up, most people benefit from their pain; they appreciate their own life, themselves, and others more, as a direct result of their suffering. Our adversities and hardships transform us from takers to givers. Suffering softens us and, in the process, allows us to experience the good in life more fully.

Reverend Edward B. Pritchard is an Associate Pastor of St. Patrick's in the City Roman Catholic Church in Washington, D.C., and is one of three priests in the Washington Archdiocese active in the healing ministry.

"What Am I Learning from This Suffering?"

Edward B. Pritchard

We bring our children up to think that everything is going to be wonderful because we want it to be wonderful. That's a disservice to them. We send them to the best schools and we try to provide the idyllic life for them by giving them so much materially. It's not reality. Suffering and pain are part of what it is to be a human being. Without them you can't be human. Suffering teaches us that there are "no"s in life. Sometimes it's physical; sometimes it's emotional. It's learning that we have limitations.

There's a very thin line between pain and suffering. We say suffering is a result of pain; one follows from the other. Pain is the initial negative situation. Suffering is the enduring of that situation. I could make an equation: "Adversity plus pain equals suffering." Discomfort is a sort of Geiger counter; it's the beginning of realization that pain's coming on.

In counseling I can see quickly if a person will not accept something the way it is. They don't want to face the reality. There are other options that may be just as good for them, but they're not giving themselves the chance to see them. I've had people come in for counseling because their mate wants a divorce. A marriage is supposed to last forever yet sometimes it doesn't. Still, they want the marriage to be the way they want it. The partner may not be capable of relating in the marriage and have the desire to do it, nor even want to do it. Often what causes the divorce in the first place is they want the mate to be the person they want him to be, rather than accepting the person as he is. They've probably never accepted that person.

People who are handicapped physically and do not respond to rehabilitation are people who are totally involved in the loss rather than being able to accept reality. I knew a man who was crippled in a car accident. Even though he was a very athletic person, he was able to move on and say, "Okay, I'm not going to be able to do some of the things I used to do, and I certainly feel the loss of my limbs below the waist, but this hasn't killed my mind and my heart. There are still other things I can do."

The purpose of suffering is growth. We're people who run around frenetically. That's our society and we get caught up in it. Suffering helps us stop and ask, "Is it all necessary? Is this all there is?" I'm not saying God comes along and strikes us down to help us grow. But you could ask, "What am I learning from this suffering?" It's a real stretching of your emotional, spiritual, and psychological muscles to find meaning in suffering. All suffering experiences can be growth experiences. Suffering often forces us to let go of situations, jobs, or people. It also opens the door to receiving a lot more as well. Adversity builds character. Crisis gives human beings a proof of their abilities that they probably wouldn't even try to use unless they were forced to. People are healed because of their attitude and spirit.

Suffering changes our perspective on life. It often strips away the luxury of time. People are basically good, so they want to do good things; they want to do something positive with their life. Suffering puts important things in focus. People who are dying of cancer or people who are dying of AIDS want to accomplish things. I don't know if it's a need to immortalize themselves or just a need finally to do what they've always wanted to do. People often want to write about their experiences to help other people. When you're faced with accepting some type of permanent change that you can't avoid—even death— you start paying attention to the things that really are important in life. Some of them may be your own needs, which have never been expressed. I don't mean in a self-centered way. I mean in a very healthy, self-giving way.

People who are suffering become much more sensitive, much more caring, and much more aware. Maybe it's the depth of pain that makes a person much more sensitive to others. When you are suffering, you empathize with everybody's suffering in the world. You become much more attentive to the least suffering of other people.

I receive much more from people who are suffering than I can possibly give to them in consolation. They're more willing to share with me their personhood—who they really are. It may be their fear, it may be their anxiety, it may be their hopes, it may be their dreams, it may be their joy. That's really quite a beautiful gift to be able to give another human being. It's really an honor.

Basically we're taught to be superficial in the way we socialize and conduct relationships. For those who are suffering, their need for intimacy is much greater. Human beings need intimacy, and when we feel we don't have much time, we want to develop that intimacy as quickly as possible. Some people seem to be able to achieve it more quickly because of their openness. They're willing to share who they are inside. Maybe that's part of greatness, too. Isn't it sad we wait so long to express those intimate feelings to one another? The sense of losing something makes us realize the value of it.

People are afraid to be with people who die. One of the graces I get for being in my vocation is that I am there. We tend to regard somebody who is dying as already dead. They're still very much alive, probably more alive than they've ever been, because they're reaching that apex that all humanity reaches in transition from life to eternal life. The privilege of being involved in that process continually shows me the incredible courage of human beings.

Suffering is something you have to do yourself. However, because of pride some of us suffer alone; there's a big difference. We confuse pride and dignity: Dignity is your awareness of your self-worth. It doesn't make any difference what other people think, so you are able to share your suffering with somebody else. People are not going to think less of you because you share your suffering. Pride has to do with being insecure in who you are. Pride causes us to put up a façade. Along with that come anger, distance, and isolation. Because of pride you don't allow others into your suffering.

To see what people go through, what they pull through, and what they accomplish is very edifying. It's more admirable than amazing. Human beings are incredible entities in themselves. To see what I believe about people put in action convinces me how terrific human beings really are.

It is difficult to imagine the extent of pain and suffering endured by those who experience traumatic physical disability. Mobility—once taken for granted—is gone forever. Every facet of life is altered in a split second by a fall, an accident, a stroke, a gunshot, a dive into shallow water. Hopes and happiness turn into depression and despair.

Those who live that experience dig deep within themselves to adjust and accept a new life in new circumstances. Those who are closest to them—partners, parents, children—must make corresponding changes too.

Slowly, the pieces of shattered lives are put back together. From this crushing blow, a deeper and closer bond may develop and a new appreciation for the gift of life itself emerges.

Phyllis and David York are the co-founders of Toughlove International, Inc., a self-help program for families and communities struggling with unacceptable adolescent behavior. They are the co-authors of *Getting Strong in All the Hurting Places*, *Toughlove*, and *Toughlove Solutions*. The Yorks are also the co-founders of Toughlove Ventures Ltd.

"You Can Survive Almost Anything"

Phyllis and David York

David

Our marriage was excellent; it was wonderful. We were having all kinds of good feelings and doing exciting things together.

Phyllis

We had been busy traveling and came home for two or three nights. We were tired, too. We were scheduled to go to California to do a workshop for Tough Love International and to promote our book *Tough Love Solutions.* I got up in the middle of the night to go to the bathroom, and I think I fell asleep. We were redoing the house. Instead of going through the bathroom door next to the stairs, which had recently been moved, I fell down the steps and broke my neck. I became instantly paralyzed from under my arms down. I knew it immediately. I later learned that the sixth, seventh, and eighth cervical vertebrae were compressed, and had crushed my spinal cord. When they took me to the hospital, they compressed the fracture to get the weight off the spinal cord. They thought there might be some physical changes by doing that, and there may have been, because I got back more hand and arm function than they expected. I was in a general hospital on a floor for spinal cord injuries with acute medical care for a month; then I was in rehabilitation for five months. It felt like five hundred years. I had one operation to stabilize the vertebrae, and then they put me into a halo.

David

A halo is like a metal cast that goes around your head. It's actually screwed into your head.

Phyllis

I have the two scars to prove it. It has hinges on the side that attach to a vest that go down to your legs. On a man it would only go to his waist, but since I'm female, it practically went down to my knees. In the halo you're not moving your neck or your head. The halo has very sharp points at both ends. You sleep on a special pillow. You could kill somebody very easily.

I went through a tremendous amount of physical rehabilitation. At the beginning I had only minimal hand function, but I finally learned to type. I did a lot of finger and arm exercises. I went to feeding class, too. The halo put my head at the angle where I was always looking at the ceiling, and I had no peripheral vision. If you feed yourself like that, especially when you don't have hand function, the food often ends up going over your head or in your eye. It's also very hard to swallow in that position, so I was constantly choking.

Since I had the accident, I can't remember that people "bend" their legs. To me, someone takes me and folds me. I don't even remember how to walk. I can't think of how you do that. I've lost what it feels like to walk, so then "I don't know how to do it" is in my head. I did a lot of upper-body exercises, too—at least two hours a day. I was also sick a lot in rehab, with bladder infections and falling blood pressure. The injury affects your lung capacity and your ability to breathe.

David

My first response was to be the person who was going to do physical things for Phyllis to help deal with this problem. I would go to the hospital and learn how to lift her, how to move her, how to change her, how to do whatever had to be done. That activity and physical stuff was a protection for me. It was a way not to feel so overwhelmed by what had happened. In those early days, when I got a chance to go away to do a workshop, I would be relieved to go and then felt awfully guilty about being relieved.

Phyllis

As soon as I had the accident, when I was at the bottom of the steps and Dave came down, I said, "I ruined our life." I didn't ask, Why did this happen to me? I already knew.

Way before the accident, when I lived in California, someone called from a dance studio and said, "We want to offer you these free lessons at Fred Astaire." And I said, in my smart-ass way, "Oh, I would love to take them but I don't have any legs." Well, I found out that Fred Astaire is God and he punished me for telling that lie. I expect to be blind because I once told an Encyclopaedia Britannica man on the phone I couldn't see, so "forget it." So in my old age I'll get blind, and it's not from you know what.

The thing that I wanted immediately was to die. I felt at some level that I had died. I had to grieve for every single part of me that had died: ability to have an orgasm, my ability to walk, my ability, at that time, to hold my grandchildren, to put my arms around my husband, and to go to the bathroom. That grieving process still goes on. When my kids got married, I couldn't walk down the aisle. That was part of the grieving, too.

I did not want that halo off because I knew it meant my condition was forever. Everybody kept saying, "Oh, you'll feel so wonderful when it's off you." I wanted to kill them. But the minute it came off I put on makeup. I wanted to see if I had enough hand function to be able to get made up, and I did, and that was pleasing. However, as I was putting on this makeup, I was talking about killing myself.

David

Phyllis asked me to help kill her lots of times. Whenever she'd have low blood pressure when she could barely move and had no energy, she'd say, "Kill me." In the beginning, I used to treat it with rational response. I'd say, "Well, I understand how you're feeling about that." I'd get into the counseling bullshit. I'd say, "We don't know what's going to happen. We don't know what our life will be like. You have to wait and give yourself time." Inside I'd feel terrible. It's someone you care about and you love and you value. And yet I wouldn't want to live either.

It's a feeling like "I understand that you want to die, but I don't want you to die," but then that means that I become responsible for her living. I wouldn't want to live and feel I was a burden. But on the other hand, being the uninjured person, I thought, Well, I'll do the caring. I'll make it happen.

Phyllis

He used to drive me crazy. He'd say, "We'll make it good. It'll be a great life. You won't have to worry." It was impossible for him to make it different from what it was. Stop telling me this bullshit, is what I felt. I was seeing a reality, maybe not "the" reality.

David

I think denial's a very protective thing. It's a way not to have to look at the reality, whatever it is.

Phyllis

This accident was different in that I was alone with it. No matter what anybody could say or do, it had happened to me. There was nobody who could enter my body and understand from my viewpoint. When people would say to me "I understand your wanting to kill yourself," to me it meant "Do it," because if they did understand what I was saying, it meant "I wouldn't want to live with it either." To me it meant "Go ahead." It was not good for me to hear that. I thought of a lot of ways to kill myself. I thought about glass, but I'm such a coward I didn't want to cut myself.

David

Phyllis's thing about suicide was another thing. I eventually said to her, "Shut up. I don't want to hear that anymore. I don't care how you feel. Don't ask me to kill you, because it's not something I can do. Suicide's not an option—we're going to live."

Phyllis

There isn't a person who has this injury who doesn't have to redo their house, redo their job, redo their life, redo their relationship, redo every single thing in life. You eventually get a normality, but it's redoing. It's still going on in our life. Our kids were wonderful. They were great. They took care of me, they took care of the house, and they took care of David too.

Friends came through tremendously. I had too many friends. I had so many visitors I was going nuts. Once, I had eighteen people all at one time. People came from California. I got five thousand get-well cards. They brought them in by loads. I was still getting them five months later. Somebody remembered that when I was sick as a child, my mother read me comic books, so they sent a man up with comic books for me to read. I got more Serenity Prayers than there are drunks. They were hanging all over the hospital room. Helen Steiner Rice. People sent me books of hers. I'd say, "Who the hell is this broad?"

I had so many visitors the guards asked people to leave the hospital. I had people who came regularly and brought food and learned how to take care of me. They learned how to catheterize me, to help me with bowels, they learned bladder stuff, they learned how to move me, they learned how to take me out in a car, they learned everything they needed to learn, and they came all the time. I had such good friends they would come at times when I didn't want them there. When I went home, they were so helpful they put me to work immediately and almost killed me.

We had three dear friends who worked for one year without pay for the organization. They really worked for me. They got me out on the road by coercion in July to show me that I could do it. Then they forgot to let me stay home. By the following February, I could not keep up the pace. I could not function. It might have been good to show me what I could do, but it was killing me.

David

At some point, I realized how nuts it was trying to drive her, force her, and make her be normal. I was beginning to accept the reality of it all. When Phyllis first got hurt, I denied that she was as hurt as she was. When she got to the hospital and the guy who took the X-ray said "I can't see anything broken," I thought, Well, thank God there's nothing seriously wrong. It's just a little thing.

Then, as you hit each medical wall and they say something like "The neck is broken and she may not have hand function," you accept more of the increasing reality even though you don't have the slightest idea of what the hell it means. So each time you confront that denial.

Traveling, going on workshops and watching Phyllis relating to people with that dynamism she has, and getting positive feedback from other folks was all very powerful. Wanting to keep that up, I was not seeing the physical effect it had on her.

We'd come back from a weekend workshop, and she'd have to stay in bed for two weeks. She couldn't get out of bed. She was just too tired. I was not willing to accept that because the excitement of the workshops was something I got pleasure from. Getting into this house, I felt, We'll be able to manage it. Then I finally had to face the reality that this injury stops us from being able to be as productive as we were or able to do the things we used to do. There's never a time when you're not dealing with the injury. It's always there.

Phyllis

We met a young person in the gym of a hotel. He asked if he could help us. I asked, "Do you know the meaning of life?"—being very funny. And he said no, he didn't. Then I asked, "Well, what's the meaning of adversity in life?" And he said, "So I can reach for higher goals and appreciate them."

David

When I was young, I went into a home-school orphanage. There was a kid who used to beat me up. I was six at the time. I remember lying on the ground with this guy on top of me. This other bully friend of his would cheer him on. He was pounding on me, and I was thinking, I have no idea why I'm lying here with this guy hitting me. The next time he does it, I'm going to roll over and beat him up. And that's what I did. That was dealing with adversity and seeing I could do it in the physical way. Later on in life, I became a phys-ed teacher and a jock. It's always been important for me to be able to manage adversity with my physicalness.

With this accident, I never think what I do as helping Phyllis. I think of it as helping us to be able to do things.

Phyllis

I love David more. I see him as so patient and giving. If the accident had happened to David, I don't think I could be as good.

David

I think we have a very loving relationship and that's remained. If anything, that's gotten even better—the sense of commitment to each other. The dependency gets to be a real pain in the ass sometimes, but I can laugh at that mostly.

Phyllis

I can live with this and I will live with this. I can end it if I choose; that's always an option. Maybe that's exactly why I can live with it. The other reason I want to live is that I'm so curious. I want to know what's going to happen next. Even if it's bad, I want to know. I want to know what's going to happen to me, to other people, to the world. I have my creativity also. A concept. An idea. Something grabs me. What might come into my mind? I haven't yet written the fiction I want to write. Intellectual curiosity and being a *yenta* are part of what keeps me going.

Humor is important. That keeps me going too. There's always something funny. We do funny stuff back and forth with each other all the time.

David

Phyllis will say, "Is there a banana over there?" So I walk into the kitchen and say, "Sure, there's a banana over there." And then I walk away.

Phyllis

We play a lot. I think that's increased at some level because we're together so much. You should see Dave's Marlene Dietrich impersonation.

David

I tend to do more of the day-to-day stuff and not worry too much about what's going to happen on down the line. Even this injury. Well, it happened. We'll do what we can do. We've got to make the best of it and we'll go on from here.

Phyllis

I guess the thing you learn is that you can survive almost anything. I wouldn't be here now if I didn't think that I would survive and I would live. I'm still me.

It is human nature to feel we have played a role by omission or commission when bad things happen to those we love. "If only we had acted differently" haunts us: it also gives us a sense of power in situations where we have been rendered powerless. These painful and confusing feelings occur to us all. Not only are we presented with our loss, but with our guilt feelings as well. Such feelings can remain a long time.

Our feelings and actions are about us when others whom we love suffer. Our feelings are different from their feelings. Their lives are their journey; our job is to heal ourselves.

Carol Fennelly is a leading advocate for the homeless with the Community for Creative Non-Violence, in Washington, D.C. For more than thirteen years she was the companion of the late homeless activist Mitch Snyder.

"I Forgive Him"

Carol Fennelly

Mitch Snyder was magnificent, mad, brilliant, terrible, wounded, angry, and obsessed. Our relationship over thirteen and a half years was all of those things as well. Our working combination was genius between us. Our creativity became such a meld that it was hard to tell whose idea was whose because we built them on each other. I fell in love with him from a picture on a brochure, and I knew I had to know who he was. Then I met him at a demonstration and that was it.

The Community for Creative Non-Violence began in 1970. We were an anti-war organization of primarily Catholic leftist types who came out of George Washington University. We spent our first few years opposing the war and finally made the connection between war and poverty. In 1972, we opened up a soup kitchen and have evolved from there. We are all volunteers. All of the CCNV lives in a 180,000-square-foot building, which is the largest shelter in the United States. We house fourteen hundred men and women, and a few children.

There are probably three million homeless people in America. However, when you talk in numbers, it's all a guess. Nobody can count the homeless.

One of the things that homelessness does is steal from people their ability to dream and hope. When your consuming endeavor in life is where you are going to get dinner and where you'll sleep, the ability to dream and hope is devastated. We deal with primarily African-American men, who are a devastated part of our population anyway. Add to that homelessness. For many people who come to the shelter, the only things they own are their names and their bodies.

Social change is addicting, particularly when you're succeeding, and we had Camelot for ten years. We put homelessness on the national agenda. We passed the first and only ever voter-mandated right to shelter in the history of the United States, for the District of Columbia. We were involved with the passage of the Stewart B. McKinney legislation, which put about a half a billion dollars a year into homeless programs. We caused the Reagan Administration to bend on giving us a building for a shelter. There were lots of those kinds of victories in moving the agenda forward. The shelter stands as a monument to that progress.

In the last months of his life, Mitch became very obsessed with me. I became his final campaign. He fasted for forty days to try and get me to come back to him. I don't think I'll ever really understand what happened. But during the nine months before the "Housing Now" rally, Mitch was traveling a lot. He went on four road trips where he drove to two or three cities a day, speaking and trying to organize coalitions to get people involved in the march. He was absolutely exhausted. At the same time, there was a lot of anger and resentment growing toward him in the movement. It became accepted to be mad at Mitch and blame him for everything that went wrong. That hurt him a lot. Being really burned out, I think, got him to a point that made the rest possible.

I had been living at another staff house with my kids. After the march I moved to the shelter. I had waited for years to be able to be together again—we had lived together before. For three weeks he wouldn't even come downstairs to visit me, let alone spend a night with me. To this day I don't know why. So after three weeks of that I said, "Enough already. I've waited a long time for this, and you're still not here. I'm going to take a break." I'd left him before because our relationship was very volatile and very difficult.

I met someone praying one morning who was exactly the opposite of Mitch. We started praying together, and it became the center of our relationship. That began to make Mitch nuts. He just got preoccupied with me and went on his forty-day fast, which further deteriorated his health. Fasting made him more tired on top of the fatigue from the year before the march, and the deep wounding he felt at the movement having turned against him. The march was October 7. During November, we were in the process of ending our relationship.

At the end of December one of our key CCNV members, a man Mitch had great affection for, got very ill and went to the hospital. His death a few weeks later was another blow. When this man died something very dark happened at the shelter. Another "friend" proceeded to run around trying to turn people against us. It all finally came to a showdown. This guy had organized a coup to throw Mitch and me out of the Community. Mitch found out about it the night before and quickly rallied his forces. The guy finally backed off, but Mitch felt the Community had turned on him. It further destroyed him. He was in incredible pain, yet he kept trying to win me back. I wanted to come back but he was having a nervous breakdown, and I didn't know it. I knew he was in a lot of pain but I didn't understand the depth of it.

In April, I went to Russia for three weeks. It was a trip for homeless activists and service providers. However, we found out when we got there, the organization that invited us had ceased to exist. We were stuck over there for eighteen days with nothing to do but sightseeing. While there, I decided that Mitch and I, in spite of how difficult things were, had the best thing, the best vision. We shared that, and if nothing else worked between us, that worked. So I called him, and I agreed to marry him.

I came back with very high hopes. When I got off the plane, Mitch was waiting for me, but it wasn't Mitch; it was an old man, small and shriveled and worn out. Because our relationship had been so painful and because there had been massive rejections from him of me, to go back was very difficult for me. He was a stranger. I didn't know him anymore.

I was utterly and absolutely consumed with love for him for over thirteen years. I was obsessed by him, and he owned me. He abused me, he treated me like trash, but it didn't matter because I loved him so much. However, somehow I couldn't settle for that anymore. I'd found a level of dignity I had to have in a relationship. I couldn't be owned anymore. I was still utterly consumed with love for him, but I had also started liking myself a little bit better. So I was different, and he read that as me not loving him. He read that as me still being in love with this other man. There wasn't anybody else; it was just that I didn't want to be owned. Every week—at least once a week—there was a massive blowup.

I was closing down the old house up on Emerson Street; my son and daughter were moving out to live on their own. I'd spent the whole week up there cleaning and packing. It was an enormous job. The last day of June 1990, I ended up working there till eleven o'clock at night. I got home and Mitch wasn't in our bed and the blankets and pillows were gone. I thought, This is weird. So I found another blanket and just fell into bed. About midnight he came stomping down the hall demanding to know where I'd been. I said, "Well, I was cleaning the house. You know where I was. I told you I was going to be late because I didn't want you to worry." He started screaming at me. He went off and slept somewhere else. He came back again in the middle of the night and screamed at me again.

I got up about six in the morning. I just couldn't deal with it anymore. I just couldn't be yelled at anymore. So I went over to this guy's house, taking my laundry and the bookkeeping, to spend the day. I needed to get some peace, and nobody would know where I was. As it got later and later, every time I'd call home I'd say, "I'll be home in a couple of hours." It'd get even later and I'd call again, "I'll be home in an hour." I just couldn't face going back. So I went to sleep on the couch.

The next morning, I went back to the shelter. When I pulled into the parking lot, I was so afraid that I threw up before I got out of the car. I came upstairs and said to Mitch, "I just can't do this anymore. This is nuts. We're killing each other, and I'm sorry." He started yelling at me again. Every muscle in his face was shaking. I was numb, brain dead, emotionally dead—everything dead. As I walked out, he chased me down the hall shouting at me, calling me names, telling me he hated me and never wanted to see me again. That was the last thing he ever said to me; he killed himself the next day and wrote a note blaming it on me.

The thing that I live with today is knowing I could have saved him. That was the nature of our relationship; I always put him back together. I took care of Mitch. And this time I didn't take care of him. I know that if I had put him back together we would have ended up in the same place again, but I wished I'd done it.

He hanged himself at the center. The note that he left said: "I loved you an awful lot. All I ever wanted was for you to love me more than anybody else in the world. Sorry for all the pain I caused you in the last thirteen years."

He'd been playing with suicide for months. There's a part of me that thinks it was just a game, that he wanted me to come in, find the cord hanging from the ceiling, and freak out. There's one line more. It's the guilt line and I blocked it out completely. It was "All I ever wanted was for you to love me more than anyone else in the world. Too bad you couldn't."

Everyone tells me I'm supposed to have anger in the grief process, but I haven't reached it yet. I don't know when I ever will. I get real depressed and sometimes it's hard to work. There certainly hasn't been an overwhelming amount of joy, but I love my work and I'm grateful that's a thing we shared.

I miss him every day. I go between remembering only the bad stuff and remembering only the good stuff. I can't remember reality anymore. There are days when I'm liberated by the bad stuff. There are days when the good stuff just haunts me. I thought I was the only one who was addicted. But I guess in the end he was too.

I understood the only thing that would heal me was to continue to be faithful to what God had called me to do. So I just stayed extremely busy and did the work that's important to me. By doing so I did take care of myself in the end. When I have a hard day, I go to bed and I tell people, "I'm having a bad day." I put a "Do Not Disturb" sign on the door and turn off the phone. I disappear. I do that from time to time.

I spend time listening to tapes of Mitch in the car when I drive. It's nice to hear his voice again. It inspires me and challenges me. No matter how mad I got at Mitch, all I had to do was listen to him give a speech and I was as in love with him as on the first day I met him. A particular speech of his in *Promises to Keep,* a documentary about the shelter, erases everything. His brilliance is all that is there. It just takes my breath away. He was so incredible.

The message isn't in Mitch's death, it's in his life. That's the only message there is. Mitch would have said, "Bury the dead and fight like hell for the living." The way he died had nothing to do with the way he lived.

Mitch never understood this, but I always told him I would have loved him if he'd been a plumber. We were "soulmates." Lots of people told me I should leave him, over the years.

I've ended up a semi-famous person because my lover hanged himself, supposedly over me. I don't like that. Mitch and I had such a volatile relationship that I began to believe I was a volatile person, which I'm not. I'm discovering that about myself. I'm a much calmer, more peaceful person now. I take my relationships more seriously today. I'm a much more outgoing person now. I never had any friends. Mitch was my only friend. He consumed me: my time, my energy. I just didn't have time for people. I have friends now that I hang out with, mostly women, who help me laugh a lot.

Mitch used to tell me that I had the most incredible capacity to absorb pain that he'd ever encountered in his life. I think that's what's gotten me through. There's something that has, over the years and now, allowed me to transcend whatever pain I'm dealing with and continue to go on. I forgive him. That's a big part of healing, I guess.

I had a dream about a month ago; in this dream he was on the bed, and I went to him again, as I had done in a previous dream, and held him. I told him that I loved him, and then said, "Why did you leave me? I need you." And he said, "It is time for me to go. You're doin' fine. It is time for you to carry on." It was very brief and then I woke up. Maybe that's the closure dream.

The theme of abandonment played a large role in Mitch's life: in his childhood, in his relationship to his children, in the work that he did, and in his perception of abandonment by me at the end. Ultimately he abandoned everything.

Mitch chose life on his terms. He took death on his terms, too. He always had to be in control. He didn't see death as a bad thing. He didn't see it as scary. He saw it as a continuum of life and the next phase. It wasn't his broken heart that killed Mitch, but his own demons.

Suffering forces us to change. We don't like change and most of the time we fear it and fight it. We like to remain in emotionally familiar places even though sometimes those places are not healthy for us. On occasion, the suffering is so great we have to give up. We surrender the old and begin anew. Often it is the pain we experience that leads us, not only to a different life, but a richer and more rewarding one.

Charles W. Colson is the founder and chairman of the board of the Prison Fellowship Ministries, a Christian organization that ministers to prison inmates, and former convicts, and to their families. It is also an advocacy organization dedicated to criminal justice reform. An attorney, Chuck was Special Assistant to President Richard M. Nixon and later served seven months in federal prison after pleading guilty to a Watergate-related charge in 1974.

"The Most Significant Thing About My Life Was My Defeat"

Chuck Colson

I was practicing law; I was making a lot of money. I had everything, but I didn't feel good about what I was doing or about myself. I think I was going through a spiritual struggle. The good life is not the Budweiser good life; it's Aristotle's good life—the sense of virtue and worth, which is an intrinsic sense not related to success and accomplishment.

The first Watergate prosecutors told me that I wouldn't be indicted; I was not a target. Some tapes have since come out that are totally exculpatory. The *Washington Post* picked excerpts of the least attractive conversations between Nixon and myself, but there were others in which I told Nixon find out who did it, to not listen to anybody, to send everybody to the grand jury, to get rid of this thing. The prosecutors had told me way back during the Watergate investigation that if I had had those conversations, they could never indict me. As a matter of fact, Leon Jaworski said to me one night, "We wouldn't indict you; we'd give you a medal." Twenty years later, they've released the transcripts, and there it is. I really wasn't in it. I knew this, so I wasn't apprehensive about going to prison until just about the time I pleaded guilty, when I realized I *was* going to prison.

I was seeing my whole world shattered. My faith in Nixon collapsed. The administration we'd built was tumbling. I saw Washington becoming ugly. I was bored with the practice of law and not very happy with my life or who I was, despite all the outside trappings. I was asking myself a lot of soul-searching questions. I was tired of being badgered by Watergate and of being in the headlines. But the soul-searching wasn't caused by the fear of prison. Nor was it the foxhole conversion or the jailhouse religion the press made it out to be. I met an absolutely magnetic man named Tom Phillips, the former chairman of Raytheon. He told me the story of what had happened in his life and I knew what he had was what I needed and wanted. In a flood of tears, in my friend Tom's driveway, I surrendered my life to Jesus Christ. It was in June of the following year that I pleaded guilty, almost a full year later.

Paradoxically, one's greatest reward often comes out of one's most difficult experiences. There's a richness in spirituality that you can't have when you're caught up with the false values of the world.

My favorite quote is Alexander Solzhenitsyn's, which I'll paraphrase: "Bless you, prison, bless you. For there lying on the rotting prison straw, I came to realize that the object of life is not prosperity, as we are made to believe, but the maturing of the soul."

Whether your life is snuffed out at twenty or you live to the ripe old age of eighty, what really matters is that the soul is eternal. And how you react to adversities, your response to life's experiences, is more important than the experiences themselves.

Watergate and the Watergate crisis forced me to face things I was wrestling with inside. I might have postponed all of it and probably would have, because we all have an infinite capacity to put off things that we ought to face.

I accepted Christ into my life in August of 1973, and for a full eighteen months everything that could possibly have gone wrong went wrong: I saw my law practice slipping away, I saw the President collapsing, I found myself indicted, I saw Watergate getting worse and uglier; camera crews were parked outside my house. Then I pleaded guilty and I went to prison. While I was in prison, my dad died. Throughout all of this, my faith got stronger—don't ask me why. Maybe it gets stronger when you're really pressed to look at reality.

Of course nobody wants to go to prison. First of all, you're separated from your family. Then there's the shame and disgrace and the danger. And there's the loss of freedom. When I was in prison, I realized that

I must have been put there for a purpose, and it had to have something to do with helping the prisoners. I felt great anguish and sympathy for the people around me and for their families. But I also knew very well that I would never go into Christian service, because at that point I figured I'd had all the public life I wanted.

While I was in prison I thought, I'll become an advocate, or a champion for prison reform, or I'll give speeches when I'm back practicing law. The idea of going full time into the ministry gradually took form in my mind after I was out of prison. I resisted it hard, as I think people should. I don't think one should regard the ministry as a job; it has to be a calling. And so I waited a year until I was certain it was the right thing for me.

Today, Prison Fellowship is in 44 countries around the world. We're working in 800 prisons in America. We have 40,000 volunteers. We had 50,000 inmates go through our programs in the last year. Last Christmas, 140,000 children, who have a mother or father in prison, received a visit and a gift from a Christian family. We visit them as a part of our Project Angel Tree, and we continue to visit those kids during the year.

In addition, by means of my books, God has used me to touch hundreds of thousands of lives. The interesting thing is that what He used in my life are not my successes, academic awards, achievements, or triumphs. The fact that I argued before the Supreme Court, the fact that I was President Nixon's assistant, the fact that I was an administrative assistant in the Senate writing laws—He has used none of those. He used the only significant thing in my life: that I was a prisoner who was broken and went through seven months in prison.

Freedom today is something I don't take for granted. Every day the grass is a little greener, the sky is a little clearer, and the air smells a little better for me than it does for people who haven't ever lost their freedom.

Now I see that the most significant thing about my life was my defeat. I really thank God for it. What matters is not what happens to you, but how you react to what happens to you. More important than what you do is what God does through you, and you'll never find that out except in those moments when you have no choice but to surrender yourself completely.

Five years ago, I went through life-threatening cancer surgery. At one time I had severe complications and infection and almost died. Never through that experience did I say "Why me?" I figured there's got to be a purpose in it, and that God would use it somehow to help other people. I thought, If this is it, I'll walk over that line and face Jesus on the other side. My life was at peace.

Faith, Hope, and Love

Faith, hope, and love are necessary to overcome misfortune. With them, it is possible to find courage within suffering, motivation toward recovery, and a positive sense of future.

Faith, the complete confidence in something we cannot prove, is tested when we are battling for health, security, or happiness. Suffering forces people to reach out to God, and faith in a Supreme Loving Power is what many call on when they are hurting. Those who have that faith find meaning in their suffering. We marvel at their unshakable belief. The trust they have in that source of strength makes their lives flow with confidence.

Without hope, we have no reason to exist. We need a strong desire of future good and the expectation of fulfillment. Hopes and dreams spur us on through difficult times.

When one is mired in pain, love of self is difficult. Many take hardships personally: they are critical about their ability to cope. In tough times, the love and the care of partners, parents, family, and friends are a great source of strength. They support our flagging faith, give us the hope we so desperately need, and, by showing us the value we have in their lives, shore up our self-esteem as well.

Rabbi Joseph Telushkin is the author of *Jewish Literacy* and co-author with Dennis Prager of two of the most influential books about Judaism of the past decade: *The Nine Questions People Ask About Judaism* and *Why the Jews? The Reason for Anti-Semitism.* He is also the author of the "Rabbi Daniel Winter" murder mysteries. He is an associate of the National Jewish Center for Learning and Leadership, and lectures throughout the country. Ordained at Yeshiva University, Rabbi Telushkin pursued graduate studies in Jewish History at Columbia University.

"Why Does God Allow Such Things?"

Joseph Telushkin

There's certainly no coherent theology on the "why" of adversity. In Job, God doesn't, in the final analysis, say why. He says, "I am God and who are you to understand?" What characterizes that response is the statement of a medieval—I believe anonymous—Jewish philosopher who said on the issue of the "why" of suffering, "If I knew Him"—meaning God—"I would be God."

With suffering there is the real sense of mystery, although in some Jewish writings we find the assumption that suffering comes as punishment for sins. That is a major motif in the High Holy Days services. It's a recurrent theme: "Because of our sins we were exiled from our land." While on the one hand, there is something healthy in people looking first to blame themselves for their sufferings rather than reflexively blaming somebody else, it is still hard to reconcile this view with reality. Too many innocent people suffer to assume that there is a correlation between human goodness and suffering.

That's one of the reasons I have a strong belief in the afterlife.

Whereas afterlife tends to play a very significant role among both Protestants and Catholics, it's usually not discussed much in the Jewish world.

Historically, Judaism as a religion was very "this worldly" oriented. It feared that where afterlife becomes significant, it tends to distract people from the responsibility of perfecting this world. In those societies that were very otherworldly oriented, this world was often allowed to become terrible. Gandhi, I believe, made the point that in Hinduism, which has so strong a belief in reincarnation, one of the negative side effects was a tendency to think that if somebody was suffering in this world it was probably his Karma, his punishment for something he had done in a previous world. So focus on an afterlife could sometimes have the effect of taking people away from *tikkun olam*, which is a Hebrew expression that means "perfecting this world."

For me, if you believe in God and you believe that God is good, you have to believe in an afterlife. I sometimes come across Jews who don't. I say to them, "Well, in that case, it seems to me the God you believe in is immoral and inferior to human beings, because if He would allow righteous people to suffer and there is no dimension of existence in which there is a redress for that suffering, then He would be morally inferior to any human being who would reward people who had done good."

To my mind, the leap of faith in religion is the leap of faith to believe in God. Once you believe in God, I don't think you need a leap of faith to believe in an afterlife. It's a logical outgrowth of the belief in God.

Adversity often prompts two seemingly opposite reactions in people. One is an incredible sense of anger at God for allowing the suffering to happen; the other is a desire to draw closer to God, and a sense that there is a larger purpose to all that goes on, and that this world, or this terrible suffering, is not the final story.

Anger at God, interestingly, is something that is rooted in the Jewish tradition. We find in the Bible people arguing with God. It's one of the distinctive features of the Hebrew Bible. When Abraham feels that God is dealing unjustly with the people of Sodom and Gomorrah, he says to him, "Will not the Judge of all the earth act with justice?" In the same way, Job argues with God and asserts that his suffering cannot be punishment for his sins. There is a tradition in Judaism that one has the right to argue with God. As Elie Wiesel once put it, "A Jew may love God or he may fight God, but he can't ignore God." This sort of anger is an outgrowth of the belief that there is a God and that He has responsibilities to human beings.

I tend to distinguish two sorts of suffering: man-made and natural. Earthquakes and floods usually evoke a tremendous sense of sadness, frustration, and anger: "Why does God allow such things?" Yet those natural disasters often bring out human goodness as people try to deal with them, and to help the victims. The other type of suffering, man-made, is, of course, caused by human beings, and involves crime and murder. This infuriates me no end. I believe the most important obligation in the world for human beings is to fight evil. Evil causes much human suffering. Let's at least eliminate that form of suffering.

What happened at Auschwitz might make belief in God difficult for some people, but for me it makes belief in man even more difficult. It was man, not God, who built Auschwitz. The lesson I learn from the Holocaust is that the most important question in the world is how to influence people to do good. The essence of my religious belief is that it's extremely important that people believe in God, but it is equally important that people believe that God's central demand of human beings is ethical behavior.

There's a famous Buddhist legend that someone came to Siddhartha complaining about his suffering. Siddhartha said, "Go and bring me back a mustard seed from any family in this village that has not had any suffering." Of course the person couldn't find one. Pain is inevitable. Bad things do happen. I'm very aware they can happen to me. I'm not one of those people who imagine that bad things only happen to other people.

To some extent, the problem of suffering bothers our generation more because our expectations are so much higher. In the past there was much more acceptance of suffering. Many older people remember in their families or in their grandparents' families that it was common to have ten or twelve children born, and four of them die in infancy. To me, the thought of—God forbid—a child dying seems an event that alone would pain one for the rest of one's life. It's a horror of the worst sort. And yet people in the past went on. I'm sure they suffered terribly, but when it happened to many people, there was probably more acceptance of it. Losing a child in that sort of situation today seems even more horrifying, because it doesn't happen as often. When it happens to someone, he or she may feel singled out in a horrible way.

Job was a man who was very good, and terrible things happened to him. He was a man who believed and loved God and always blessed God for what happened to him. Even when his children, his money, and his health were taken away, he refused to curse God. He said, "I cannot accept from God only that which is good and not accept the bad." Job would not curse God, but he also would not say that he was being punished by God. "Because," he said, "nothing that I've done deserves such punishment." That's what our attitude should be when horrible sufferings come. Often, when we suffer in life, we don't know why. If one is suffering from ill health, one should ask, "Is there something I'm doing, or something I'm not doing, that could make me healthier? Am I in any way making it worse?" If there's nothing, it doesn't mean that God's angry at you. It means that there are things we don't know. As I said earlier, Jewish philosophy teaches, "If I knew God, I'd be God" (literally, "If I knew Him, I'd be Him").

There have been many great people who've suffered in life and have continued to love God. Even if one is undergoing suffering, it's important to remember that there are many good things in this world as well. My father had a stroke, and suffered terribly the last year and a half of his life. However, I also remember that the rest of his life had been filled with many wonderful things. One should avoid the temptation to exaggerate evil. It doesn't put a cloud over everything. It's a part of life, but it's not the entirety. It would be Pollyannaish to make it seem as if pain is not important or significant, but it is self-defeating to exaggerate its importance.

The evil and the suffering that go on in the world make up the single greatest challenge to belief in God's existence. If there were no evil and suffering in the world, everybody, I think, would be believers. Rabbi Milton Steinberg said in *Anatomy of Faith*, "If the believer has his troubles with evil, the atheist has more and graver difficulties to contend with. Reality stumps him altogether, leaving him baffled not by one consideration but by many, from the existence of natural law through the instinctual cunning of the insect to the brain of the genius and the heart of the prophet. This then is the intellectual reason for believing in God, that though this belief is not free from difficulties, it stands out head and shoulders as the best answer to the riddle of the universe."

In a paraphrase of Steinberg's argument, Dennis Prager and I wrote in *The Nine Questions People Ask About Judaism,* "The believer in God must account for one thing, the existence of evil. The atheist, however, must account for the existence of everything else." That's really the point. If there is no God, how do you account for all the good in the world? For consciousness and conscience, intelligence, emotions, love, for our sense of purpose, the very notion of a universal good and evil?

I think it was Nietzsche who said, "That which doesn't destroy me will make me stronger." I believe that's true. People who are not broken by adversity often become greater. It would be very hard for a person who has never suffered to be truly good. At most, such a person could be sympathetic with other human beings; he or she couldn't be empathetic. I am in awe of the many people who've taken their suffering and allowed it to make them better people as a result.

From the religious perspective, suffering should make one a better person and not be used as a justification for doing evil to others. The Biblical notion is a very beautiful one: "Treat the stranger well because you were strangers in the land of Egypt and know what it meant to be mistreated there." If human beings use suffering as a way to make themselves become better, and learn from it to try to reduce suffering for others, then it will mean that even though we want to avoid suffering—God knows I do—it still has the ability to teach us some wonderful things.

When things are going our way, we believe. When they aren't, we question whether there is a God who cares. "Why me, Lord?" we ask when bad things happen to us. To continue walking in faith when we are confronted with the reality of our trials is not easy. We only believe with great effort. The struggle of faith is the struggle of man.

Bill T. Jones is the co-founder of the New York City–based Bill T. Jones/Arnie Zane Company, a modern-dance company renowned for its avant-garde dance pieces, which often tackle contemporary social and political issues.

"Faith Is the Anchor"

Bill T. Jones

When Arnie died, I was in great grief and pain. I made a bunch of works. Some of them were the best works I've ever done dealing with agony and loss. One was a piece called "Absence." There was also a piece called "D-Man in the Waters," which was a kick-in-the-butt kind of piece that affirmed for me what I had always known about accepting adversity. I used to say, "To hell with you," or, "Death be gone," or, "Sorrow be gone." Now I am throwing myself into the fray and, as a result, finding some sort of transcendence.

"D-Man in the Waters" was an exuberant piece, dedicated to a dancer, Demian Acquavella, who was dying, and to Arnie's memory. They were two people I thought of as incredible fighters, incredible swimmers in the waters of life. When those two pieces were very successful, I asked, "What next, Bill? What is the next big risk for you?" I remember when Arnie was sick and dying, I said to Lois Welk, a choreographer and good friend of mine who'd known Arnie and me for almost twenty years, "Do you ever think about making a work that is a summation of your life?" I was thinking of the end of my own life, because the whole world seemed to be collapsing and I felt as if I hadn't done anything like it yet. I wanted to make a work that said everything. So I created a large sprawling theatre-dance work called "The Last Supper at Uncle Tom's Cabin/The Promised Land." The piece focuses on oppression, discrimination, prejudice, racism, sexism, poverty, and minorities. It examines the plight of the underclass and the marginalized person, the notion of hypocrisy and evil in the name of good, and how certain people have triumphed and continue to triumph. The issue of faith sits squarely in the middle of the work.

One section tells the story of Job in dance. During this section, I interview a minister from the local community, asking questions such as "What is evil?" "What is good?" "What is the purpose of suffering?" "Is AIDS a punishment from God?" I try to be a provocateur respectfully and sometimes not so respectfully. We have now given thirty performances of the entire three-hour epic in twenty-two cities. To date, I have interviewed thirty ministers, priests, and rabbis about faith and suffering.

I have come to understand there are superficial faiths and there are profound faiths. Faith is unshakable when it is true, when it is really grounded. It is something like a shield, not an armor. It is very important to sanity. I don't mean necessarily faith in God, but an understanding that there's a truth to which we can aspire, or a set of values that do not move, or that move in a way we can accept. Those ministers I've spoken with who have that faith say their faith is alive, it is evolving, it is getting deeper, sometimes changing its form or face. For me, I've come to learn faith is a reward for experience.

I'm a black American. There is something slavery taught my people that has been evident in music and art and dance. It's evident in my mother to this day. The message is life is a vale of sorrow. That's taken for granted. We're born into slavery, we die in slavery. This is how it was for the people who raised me. But you are obliged to be the best, you are obliged to run; you are obliged to be strong and brave. That was always understood. It was also understood that you would go forward because you were built to go forward. It's a survival mentality. My mother was the best worker in the field. She has had fourteen children, two of whom have died. This woman watched her mother whipped. She has pride. She only had a fifth-grade education, and yet she's trying to get, at age seventy-seven, her high-school equivalency diploma. She pulls herself onto a bus every day and goes off to school.

I heard the songs my mother sang not as songs of slavery, which is what I understand they are now, but as her spirit speaking. I heard something about humanity coming out of her. When Lyndon Johnson made an announcement one night that everyone who made less than three thousand dollars a year was living at the poverty level, I went to my father and asked, "Daddy, do you make three thousand a year?"

He said, "Oh, no, no, no." I said, "Oh, my God, we're poor." My parents obviously knew, but as a child I didn't know it.

When I talk about my life today, I realize there surely have been worse lives. I'm healthy; I had both parents. They suffered a great deal and I think they felt incredibly inadequate. I would love to be able to go back in time and encourage and help them. They had a fierceness about them in protecting us. They made mistakes, but I did have them both. I never doubted they loved me.

Meeting Arnie made me more aware of how many levels there were to my personality. The sexual commitment was a big one. It was my first serious relationship. I had girlfriends, but it was all show. He made me commit to a relationship, and through it I began true self-examination. What I saw was I could lie, I could be weak, I could be indecisive, I could be untrustworthy. Those were all things I thought I was not. So in the adversity, in the crucible of the relationship, there were insights that came out of it over time.

When I was nineteen, I didn't know how to handle the repercussions of the decision I'd made to have this relationship with Arnie, the repercussions of having left college, of ceasing to be an athlete and having come out as a gay person. When I lost Arnie, when that chapter of my life slammed shut, I learned something about what had been going on during our relationship. I also learned about what had not gone on. I was allowed to be angry for the first time in my life with a direction. I saw his frustration about the recognition he struggled for and how some of that had been denied. I could be angry about that in an articulate way. He died very young and he lived a very radical life. He was often abused for it. One thing he had taught me was never apologize for who you are and try to live by that. His passing gave me that. I don't think it was any accident that Arnie, who was Jewish-Italian, would bond with a working-class black person. He understood the desire for success and what it means to be an outsider. Arnie once said, "Dying is not the big issue. The big issue is what you do with your life."

I remember once chanting Hare Krishna in a temple and crying, yet dancing at the same time with arms outstretched. That's a metaphor for me of how I live. It's a romantic take on life. I am dying as I'm growing. I am lonely and I'm surrounded by people. I am in pain and I am ecstatic. The highest moments are when such things come together. Everything can be raised to that ecstatic level.

Ever since I was a small boy, I knew I lived on more than one level. It might sound flaky to people, but I truly believe I have. That gives me joy even when I am called a faggot on the street, or even when I worry about dying of AIDS. I know this is a great journey. I am an artist and art reminds me of what is beyond the tangible. That's why I give myself to it. I live in this world. I walk on two legs. I am black, I am gay, but George Bush and I are not in the long run essentially different, ultimately.

The dance for me represents how I look at the agony of parting from Arnie. I can see all the parts of his death now. I feel more relaxed than ever with my success or lack of success and even with the uncertainty of my future. I accept the reality. AIDS has educated me. I don't know if there's ever been a generation of people who have known that if you have this mark, the chances are that you are looking at the very last part of your life. Yet everything seems so normal. That has affected my way of thinking about the world. So I am flying high now. I'm happy. I've been given a gift that causes me to become philosophical about all things and encourages me to have courage.

A choreographer is a maker of dances. I think in dance language; that is the language I use to express the same things that a writer or a sculptor might express. Through dance I communicate to you in a way that I can't with words. I'm saying, "Look at these series of events. Do they suggest to you birth, life, and death? Do they suggest to you the dichotomy between what is right and what is wrong?" Dance, like music, reminds us we are capable of experiencing reality on different levels.

Personally I like art that is complicated and dark, full of surprises and unpredictable. Why should life be different? The pain of loss I'm experiencing at this moment is part of what was yesterday. It can very well be pleasure tomorrow. I must have the presence of mind, the centering, to be detached from both. It doesn't mean one becomes cold. I think you become more passionate once you're accepting of both pleasure and pain. You accept the wall of adversity. I am not this body that's HIV positive. I am not this body that has Alzheimer's. I'm not this body who's going through a divorce, a job loss, the death of a loved one. I am this person, but that's not all I am.

When I watched Arnie dying or when I think about myself dying, I can barely breathe, yet the message is "Hey, go past that." I'm going to be angry and dismayed unless I have the mental discipline that comes with the everyday understanding of the world from moment to moment. Then when the big test comes, I will be able to handle it. I hope that's the wisdom, the self-discipline, and faith I'm developing now. It's preparation. It sounds like something I used to hear my mother say: "I want to be ready."

In the black church they say, "Oh, Lord, make me ready." What do you mean, ready? Ready for what? For the adversity; ready for the beast in the bottom of the pit. I've been assured it's going to be all right. But, Lord, I don't know if I'll always know it will be all right. What about when I'm afflicted? It will still be all right. I'm scared to death, but feeling good. Fear is noble. Fear is what makes us human. Faith is the anchor.

To walk in faith, to have total confidence that we are in God's hands, comes with experience. Life often demonstrates to us that when we were faced with immediate disappointment, failure or defeat in the past, we experienced victory in the long run. Although, at the time, we did not like what we got, everything worked out, often for the better. How many times have we failed only to achieve success? How many times have we lost only to have won? How many times have we felt the pain of parting only to experience the joy of reunion? The confidence of faith is almost too much to expect of humans, yet many have it. Within the security of their faith, they shine as examples to all of us who struggle.

Reverend Edward Kelly, C.S.Sp., is the Associate Pastor of Our Lady Queen of Peace Roman Catholic Church in Arlington, Virginia. He served as a missionary in Africa for twenty-five years.

"Suffering Is the Ultimate Test of Faith"

Edward Kelly

If there is a God and if you believe in a God, then the kind of God that our Catholic religion is trying to present is a loving, compassionate, and concerned God.

The Son of God, Jesus, came on Earth. All He did was to come to preach about the Father, to tell us what kind of God that God really is. He kept right on going, preaching that word about God right through to death.

Suffering is the ultimate test of faith. In that faith, you might be able to find a meaning in the apparently meaningless, unexplainable occurrences that take place in our lives, such as suffering, sickness, hardship, and finally death. It's only in deep faith, I believe, that one finds that meaning. One can reject it or one can accept it. That's the struggle. One doesn't just sit down and say, "Oh, yes, I accept it. Everything's okay now." One struggles all the time in the sickness and suffering that take place in our lives. Up to death there's a constant struggle to trust and believe. I think that's how one finally goes out. According to the strength of that faith, I think, one goes peacefully or not.

Making suffering meaningful is the ultimate difficulty. The hurt is bad, the sickness is bad, the loss is bad, and the rejection is bad. The death of Jesus was bad. The abandonment of His apostles was bad. The rejection on the part of the people was bad. His physical suffering was bad to the point of causing Him to say, "Good Lord, take it away from me, I don't want it, I'm afraid of it." We don't grasp hold of the fact that Jesus was there in the garden, maybe sweating blood, saying, "I don't want this. Yet if this is to be, then I accept it and go through it."

What were the last words that He said? "God Lord God, why have you abandoned me?" Even God was gone, yet still He held on to the word about that God who had apparently left Him. That's how He died. Then came the resurrection. With that then comes the full appreciation and realization of all of the reality that had been there in struggle, in doubt, in wonderment, and in questioning. This reality was always there and was manifested finally when Jesus did rise from the dead and lives forever.

We don't say, when we are suffering, "This is good." We don't say, "Sit down and be apathetic in the face of suffering and sickness." We try to overcome suffering and sickness. We try to overcome all of these bad things. Whether we do or we don't is not important. But in striving to overcome them, we are able to go through all of the negativities, the lacks, the inabilities, and are able to work through those only because we know that there is the life, the goodness, the compassion, the mercy, and the understanding of God. God is present even in the suffering. We don't have to get away from the suffering in order to get to Him; we get to Him even while we are in it working our way through it. It's that kind of meaning that we have to strive to seek and to find in suffering, in sin, in failure, and in all the bad things that happen in life. It's when you are in the concrete actual suffering that there is the real continuing test of trust and faith in God.

Christians have heard so often: "You have to go through the suffering [see?—it sounds almost like a cliché] of Good Friday in order to arrive at the joy, the fulfillment, and the life of Easter Sunday." That's what we are celebrating. We go to church and we celebrate, and then we go out and we suffer and we ask why. We don't get to the point of taking what we celebrated and applying it to the reality in our lives. If we did, then the next step for a person who has grasped it, and continues to suffer, would be to return to church and celebrate the suffering. Can you understand that? "Celebrate the suffering?" That's what it would come to, because that's life; that's reality. If you celebrate suffering, you're celebrating reality, because we all suffer. In celebrating life, celebrating reality, in the core of that is this God we're talking about. Hidden? Oh, yes, even to the point where He was hidden when Jesus was hanging on the cross and asking, "Where are you?" But He was there, because then came the resurrection. No matter what words are said—philosophical, religious, platitudinous, or consoling—it's extremely difficult for the person who's actually suffering cancer or some other disease to say, "I understand."

I went through a heart operation, the bypass business, which brings you fairly close to the ultimate door. I went into that just as if it was a normal, ordinary thing. I didn't have to pray over it, and didn't have to seek understanding in sacramental rites. Having thought about this so much and so deeply, it was a part of me. I thought, No matter what, I know that God's there. He's there, that's all. He's there if I'm the most healthy, athletic, wonderful type in the world. He's there if I'm in bed or on the operating table undergoing heart surgery. He's there. Whatever the outcome of it is, if it's good, God is there. If it's bad, He's there. How did I arrive at all that? By the gift of faith that God gives. The only thing that I know about God is what Jesus said and did. I was born into a Catholic family, and my parents gave me a Catholic faith. That's how I got it. I would define faith simply as a trust, a belief that there is a loving, caring, forgiving God, and because He is that kind of God, then I trust that God to do whatever.

In faith, adversity—which is, in and of itself, bad, meaningless, and evil—can have a meaning. The meaning is that it is part of the reality where God is. I did missionary work in Africa for twenty-five years, twenty-two in Tanzania, and three in Ethiopia. There they can appreciate everything that has to do with being a human being, even though they're living in conditions that are not human. But it is reality. That's why in the midst of adversity they sing and they dance; they can live human relationships, and they can celebrate. They are closer to reality than we are. When you come to America, it's artificial. When you go to Africa, it's real. Those are overstatements, but they may help to grasp hold of what I'm attempting to express: the concept of reality is very important.

As your appreciation of the place of adversity in your life grows, so does your life in the adversity. Now, whether that in turn is strong enough to be carried over into the actual concrete suffering, there's where you have to struggle to hold on to it and keep it.

Can others have the same understanding and appreciation that I say I have from my Christian faith? I believe that they can and I believe that they do. If God is good and merciful and forgiving, He's good and merciful and forgiving to everyone. So I believe that somehow through the Buddhist message, the Islamic message, the Hindu message, that they who are also struggling with these ultimate questions must have the ability to arrive at a consolation, a peace, and an acceptance, which all are perhaps other words for happiness. They are equally able to be happy. Reality is so prevalent and God is so prevalent, I believe all of that exists amongst all people.

Occasionally, life's circumstances are so painful that the hope we desperately need and seek cannot be found. In such bad times, we may have to make a quantum leap of faith to grab some ray of hope. What a remarkable testimony to the human spirit it is to find hope through belief and trust in a Power that cannot be seen or proven. In life-threatening situations, mortality is acknowledged and faith becomes reality.

Richard Muldoon is an attorney in private practice in Cleveland, Ohio.

"You Wanted Hope, You Had Hope, I Am Hope"

Richard Muldoon

I remember when my longtime companion, friend, and lover got sick and was diagnosed with AIDS. I remember him saying he was willing to leave, to move, to break up our happy home. At that time I didn't care what he was sick with; he was sick and he needed me. I certainly could not have imagined in my wildest thoughts his leaving me—least of all when he was sick. I thought that if there was any hope for what the outcome might be, it was if we diminished his concerns about external things. Given my physical health, I didn't consider the disease as something I had to worry about, in spite of the fact my companion had it now.

As I look back on it now that he's dead, and we've gone through the horror and the agony, I realize I had no idea what the AIDS illness would be like. Now I compare it to trying to understand the concept of God. I struggle with it. I go as far as I can, and I believe in God. But the God thing is so beyond everything I'm capable of that while I have faith in this Higher Power, I don't really know about it. I don't know about it in the way I know about overcoming poverty. I've experienced that. I don't know about it as I know about being black in a white society. I don't know about it as I know about growing up in an alcoholic household where a father beats his wife, who is my mother, and where children run screaming in terror. I know about those things because I've lived them. Those were experiences that made me grow beyond what I could ever have thought possible.

But in each of those, including the God thing, there was a sense of a tomorrow. There was a sense that I had the capacity somehow, with the help of friends and others, not to be poor if I worked my butt off. Through the interaction of loving people who happen to be white, I understand that we can live pretty well in a society where not everyone is racist. We can overcome. When I was a little boy, I often thought, When I get big and have my own house, there won't be drugs, there won't be alcohol, there won't be fear. It will be a place where me and those I love will like to be. There was always a sense of hope. A friend once told me, "Hope is the amount of time and energy that we commit to the not yet certain."

What was different about AIDS, and all my experience up to that point, was there is no hope. The day my companion told me he had AIDS, I didn't know the desperation that would accompany this long and brutal illness. When there is a stripping away of health—a slow, agonizing, hideous, humiliating, undignified stripping away—something happens to the spirit not only of the one who is ill but of those who love that person and have to watch. And there is not the ability to have hope.

It was April of 1989. I had been feeling lethargic but I attributed it to being on the run; I'd been flying a good deal and keeping hours that were ridiculous. Occasionally I'd pop an amphetamine so that I could keep going. I figured it was time for a rest. I remember spending much of that summer lying on the floor in front of my television, and playing the usual game of daily racquetball I didn't want to play.

I had started to experience diarrhea but attributed it to eating different foods in my travels. It was nothing I had to worry about. I talked with a good friend of mine when I was in Washington around that time, and he persuaded me to take an AIDS test. So in August of 1989 I took the test and went back three weeks later for the results. The results were inconclusive; they couldn't be read as positive or negative. I said to the person who gave me the test, "Well, why don't we just say it's negative if you can't tell one way or the other?" He convinced me there wouldn't be much value in that. I took the test again, waited three more weeks, and this time I tested positive.

As I was walking out of the clinic that day, I had no idea what I would do, where I would go, how I would live—what it would mean. My friend, although not feeling up to his old self, hadn't begun literally to fall apart yet. He was a great source of strength and encouragement to me because when I could lock the doors and talk to him, I collapsed in fear and terror. He was very supportive, and we decided we would hang in and fight this thing together.

My friend had AIDS and I was HIV positive with symptoms. I was afraid to be as close as I might have been if I had not been HIV positive myself. I was always backing off for fear of what might be happening to me. I wondered if the object of my affection was the source of my vulnerability.

In June of 1990, I began to experience sore throats and fevers. My doctors weren't able to find out exactly what caused them so they gave me antibiotics. My sore throat and its symptoms would go away, but two weeks later it would come back. The saga of the sore throat, including a ten-day hospital stay, was to continue until March of 1991. At that time I began to get headaches that were so severe I wanted to put a bullet in my head.

Meanwhile my companion had been getting worse. By this time he had been bedridden for six or seven months. One of the few pleasures he had left in life was watching television. When the blindness started, it terrified him because then, he said, there would be absolutely nothing left.

In late April of 1991, I went to the hospital where I was to stay for about six weeks. Up to that point I'd been accustomed to seeing my friend every day. An important part of our life together had always been the security and trust of our relationship, our commitment to each other. When I was in the hospital, we talked to each other on the phone. Then, one day, lo and behold, he came to the hospital too as a patient.

The doctors didn't really know what was wrong with me other than that I was HIV positive with symptoms. It took three weeks before they were able to determine that it was not an AIDS-defining infection. As a matter of fact, it wasn't till three weeks later, six weeks altogether, that they finally concluded that I had a staph infection that was resistant to the oral antibiotics I'd been receiving all year.

My journey in the hospital brought things to a head for me—not so much because of how I was feeling after the pain left, but because of what I had seen happen to my friend, who at this point was still alive. Although I had been told he didn't have much longer to live, I frankly marveled at his strength of character. This man who had once weighed about two hundred pounds was now down to about ninety-seven pounds. He had lost control of his bladder and kidneys, he was confined to bed, his appetite was gone, but he was still hanging in there. Those lonely nights when I lay in my hospital bed with IVs in my arm, I would wonder whether it was worth going on if what I had to look forward to was what was happening to my friend. For the first time, I was confronted with a lack of future, a lack of hope. But it was that very same hope that made me think I should consider this some more.

One of the things that were so important was that my friends visited me religiously. Even when I was delirious with fever and chills, I knew they were there. In the middle of the night, when I'd ask myself, "Am I dying" the memories of my friends and their love for me gave me probably more hope than I'd had to that point. If I ever believed in the power of human love, I came to believe it when I was afraid and thought I was dying.

I could hear them saying, "No, no, no, not yet, you can still fight this; this isn't acceptable." My friend John reminded me of the definition of hope I was always spouting to other people. "Hope is the amount of time and energy that we commit to the not yet certain." When I was without hope, John bought it up and asked, "Do you believe it? You're the one who always says it. Do you believe it?"

During that stay in the hospital, I came to believe that it wasn't time yet. And when the doctors told me I did not have lymphoma, which they'd thought I had, I was convinced I was going to spend some more days in the kingdom. My mother, who came to the hospital every day, was a source of tremendous inspiration in my will to fight. I looked forward eagerly to her visits. She never had any doubt in her mind that I'd leave that hospital. One of my best friends, when I was in the depths of despair, said, "You can't die now—we've got to laugh some more. We're going to laugh again a lot."

It was those things that made me able to do whatever it took to join in with my doctors and fight what was happening. One of the doctors was a holy man. He said he was "born again," and wanted to know if I had accepted Jesus. "Oh, I think so," I said, "I go to Mass." He wanted me to accept Jesus more than that, though. I spoke to him about my fear of accepting Jesus under those circumstances, for I would be doing it just because I was afraid. He said, "Our Lord doesn't care what the motivation is."

Even in the face of a disease that is as terrifying as the plague must have been, there are men and women in my life who continue to encourage me to hope and to devote more time and energy to my wellness. What I don't want—and I struggle with it every day—is to lose the faith. When they close the lid on my casket, those who are important in my life will know that even to the end I kept the faith, just as my friend did. He kept the faith to the end. There are days when anger and despair and fear and sheer terror make it tough, but I'm doing it.

I absolutely hate this disease, and cannot, even on a good day, imagine why anyone should get it, but so far I can't imagine giving up. There's an old saying, "It's not how you start but how you finish." I am trying to figure out how you can finish with AIDS and still have dignity. But the courageous stories of people with AIDS, and that whole network of incredible people who help them, make it possible to believe that there's also an ingredient of humanness coming from other people that keeps hope alive. On the days I feel good, I say, "Wallow in how good you feel. You may not feel good long; enjoy it."

Every morning before I walk out the door, my mother wants to know how I feel. On one hand, it reminds me I'm not as well as I'd like to be; on the other, it's an indication of her love and concern. These dichotomies come up all the time. I go to meetings in executive suites at the top of buildings with panoramic views over a city. I enjoy the company of movers and shakers, who sip martinis and look so fine in their seven-hundred-dollar suits, discussing the construction of new worlds, both inside and outside the country. And I want to say, "Well, while we're doing all this, can't we find an effective treatment for AIDS? I've got it, you know." But it would be so devastating to all of them.

I can be sitting in on a meeting where there's an important point under discussion and I have to go to the bathroom because my diarrhea or my kidneys are being affected by the virus. I'm not paying attention, because it feels as if the diarrhea is pressing against my bowel walls so hard that if I don't go this minute, they're really going to know something's wrong with me. Can't you hear them telling their wives over breakfast, "Well, honey, we were sitting there and the most incredible thing happened. Richard went right in his chair! I don't think he's well." So I've learned to say, "Excuse me, but I have to go to the bathroom."

And the clock is ticking. Since I was hospitalized, my skin has shriveled up; little dry spots on it itch all the time. It seems almost as if the juice is being taken out of my skin. My hair is falling out. I remember my friend when he had the diarrhea, then the inability to walk, then the sores—always something. I keep playing that picture of quiet, active desperation. Unlike the God thing, where God is the great answerer of hope, I've come to think that when you get to Him God will say, "Well, this is it. You wanted hope, you had hope, I am hope." That's phenomenal. "I am hope. I am faith."

There's a journey before that, though, and it's the one that causes all the anguish. *The Thorn Birds* begins by saying: "There is a legend about a bird which sings just once in its life. . . . From the moment it leaves the nest it searches for a thorn tree, and does not rest until it has found one. Then, singing among the savage branches, it impales itself upon the longest, sharpest spine. And, dying, it rises above its own agony to out-carol the lark and the nightingale. . . . But the whole world stills to listen, and God in His heaven smiles. For the best is only bought at the cost of great pain. . . . Or so says the legend." But the thorn bird doesn't know that it's dying; we do.

People say, "Well, we're all dying a little bit every day." Yes, but you can bet on AIDS and that's the difference. The New Testament describes Jesus' pain and how He suffered. Nowhere in the New Testament does it ever say Jesus liked it. It moves beyond fear; that's why I used the word "terror." In God, what lies ahead is the fulfillment of the promise of redemption. In the AIDS illness, what lies ahead is hideous death. So when you're lying there at night or peeing for the fifteenth time that day, or there's a fever, or a sore, or you look at your head and there's no hair, you think of what lies ahead before you get to God. That's what makes the challenge of faith so severe. My grandmother used to say, "You might give out, but don't give up." We know the subtlety of the difference in terms of the dignity.

Inspirational writer Father John Powell, S.J., says the essential elements of a happy life are "something to do, someone or something to love, and something to hope for."

Without hope, the crucial motivator for taking necessary steps to ensure success, we give up. If we have no expectation of success, we remain mired in despair. We must believe there will be an end to our pain. Hope is the possibility of a brighter future.

Peggy Say is the sister of Terry Anderson, the Associated Press chief Middle East correspondent who was held hostage in Lebanon for more than six and a half years. Because of her efforts to help free her brother, Peggy became a well-known public figure. She is the author (with Peter Knobler) of the book *Forgotten: A Sister's Struggle to Save Terry Anderson, America's Longest Held Hostage.*

The interview with Peggy Say was conducted in August 1991, three and a half months before Terry Anderson's release. The world rejoiced and celebrated Terry's return to freedom on December 4, 1991. Peggy's commitment to her goal is a glorious example of a life of faith, hope, and action, and proof of positive results.

Terry, upon his release, attributed his survival to stubbornness and faith. "You wake up every day," he said, and "you summon up energy from somewhere."

David Say, Peggy's husband, is a self-employed building and electrical contractor in Cadiz, Kentucky.

"You Cannot Live Without Hope"

Peggy Say

I'm exhausted, but it's a good exhausted. There's not a fever pitch of excitement; there's a relief. We're watching the end, we can live through it, and we will have our reunions. It's not the tremendous emotional roller coaster that it's been for us other times. I've always had a deep spirituality. Terry's kidnapping was not a test of faith; it happened. I believed that God would take care of him. It wasn't: "He's kidnapped. There's no God, there's no justice." The tragedy for Terry is that he's been jailed just for being an American.

There are thousands of people across the world who pray for Terry and me every day. The hostages who have come out have told me that at different times when they were close to despair, they actually felt the prayers of people that kept them going. Terry is part of my inspiration. It's the example that Terry has set for me that drives me to do what I do. Let me tell you, there are days when I think I can't take another step. I can't do another interview. I can't get myself out of bed. And somehow the strength comes.

When hostage Ben Weir was released, he told me that they each knew there were other hostages in the building but they didn't know who they were. Unknown to one another, each had been requesting of their captors to allow them to come together to pray. For some unknown reason, even though the treatment was brutal, the captors decided they would allow it. Ben told me, "We were blindfolded and were told not to speak to each other. Dragging our chains behind us, we shuffled together into a room. We were allowed a brief hug. During that hug, we whispered our names into one another's ear, and we worshiped together."

Terry's a Catholic, and he said to his captors, "I want to go to confession with Father Jenco." Again, for some unknown reason, they allowed it. The two men were told not to look at each other, but of course they pulled down their blindfolds. Father Jenco told me, "The eyes spoke volumes." Terry made his confession, and Father Jenco said that at that moment "we expected and were prepared to die." We knew nothing of their day-to-day existence until Father Jenco came out.

I have heard Terry in his videotapes ask, "Why has my government abandoned me? Why have the American people forgotten us?" Never to my knowledge has he ever said, "My God, why hast Thou forsaken me?" If Terry can maintain his faith and strength and dignity through being chained, through being humiliated, existing in terrible, terrible conditions, I can keep my faith, too. When you're held like that, you have to reach down inside yourself and pull out the essence of what you are and what you believe. What the hostages pulled out was a deep and abiding faith in God.

I have family, and when I'm tired and depressed, they put their arms around me and it makes me feel better. Terry has nobody to do that for him. On his last videotape, the message he had for all of us who are walking around free, clean, and fed was "I will pray for you, and someday, God willing, this will end." How could I not do what I do faced with the kind of example that's been set for me by Terry? What would be my alternative? Am I supposed to say, "Well, gee—sorry, guys, it's a bad spot you're in but there's nothing I can do about it."

I have had a role to play in all of this, and I've finally come to grips with the fact that in many ways I've become a role model myself. I know that from my mail. People write to me saying this or that happened in my life, and under ordinary circumstances I would have let it destroy me, but I've seen what you've gone through, and if you can do it, I can do it.

I didn't know I could do it. At first I didn't know what to do, I didn't know where to go, I didn't know whom to see, but I was blessed from day one. I had people around me, who became my advisers, literally pushing me into meeting with people; it scared me to death. People sometimes perceive me as being in this alone. I am far from alone. So many people have been helpful to me.

What has come out of me I have had really and truly to leave up to God. I take one step at a time. I remember I was handed the itinerary for my major trip last year and I actually gasped. I was going to address the European Parliament, I had a private audience with the Pope, I was to meet with Yasser Arafat, and I was going to Syria to meet with officials there. How am I going to do this? I thought, What am I going to say to these people? I've learned now just to say, "Okay, God, you want me to do this, then help me out." On the trip back, somebody asked me, "Peggy, why do these people meet with you?" And I said, "You've got me."

I can't believe I actually grasped the robe of the Pope as if he might get away from me; I had to make him listen. He was very gracious, but I have no morals when it comes to Terry. I don't care who you are, I thought; you're not going away until I have my say. My role is making people feel emotional about this topic. These are men, these are mostly Americans. I no longer even think about the rightness or wrongness of what I do. Former hostage John McCarthy told me how much it meant to them. I asked, "John, do you think publicity prolonged your captivity?" And he said, "You know, we discussed that very topic. We were concerned at first, and then we concluded that it probably did not; but even if it did, it kept us alive." He said, "Just when we'd begin to think that the world had forgotten us, we'd hear about something you had done or something Jill Morrel had done. We couldn't have survived without that."

There's no handbook written. If we had known it was going to last this long, certainly we would have done things differently, but we forgive ourselves. I felt the thing I had to do was make these hostages real people, make Terry Anderson a face. This is a man who thinks and lives and bleeds and loves and hurts. When people go making decisions about the hostages or foreign policy—we're talking about government officials here—I want them to have to think about my brother. To ignore what these men were going through would have shamed me as Terry's sister. It got to the point where I was shamed as an American citizen and a Christian. People were telling me to ignore it. Much of America ignored it.

Today I'm seeing we have come together as a nation. There's a new empathy, there's a new commitment, there's a new awareness. We must bring this to an end. These men will be welcomed home as heroes. That's exactly what they are. Going to war and putting your life at risk is doing something valiant. The Persian Gulf troops being welcomed home was wonderful. My son was in the Persian Gulf, so we're a part of that, too. But to hold on for six and a half years, being chained to a wall, nailed in a coffin, suffering humiliation and degradation, and to come out a whole person with faith and strength and dignity—I cannot think of a better testimony to the world of what we as Americans are capable of.

You cannot live without hope. Who can? If there are raised hopes and dashed hopes, that's okay, it's still hope. The times when months and months go by and nothing happens—that's when I start sliding toward despair. Then there seems to be a Divine intervention. Just when I think I'm going to lose it, I'm going to give in to this depression, something comes out of the blue.

The period we're going through now is an agonizing ecstasy. It's tough, but it sure as hell beats giving up. It's teasing, but it's just enough to keep you going. Maybe it'll be Terry, maybe it won't. Truly, at this point I don't think it matters. The families have become such a unit. We all want Joe Cicippio to be released because his sister is dying. That's the immediate need. We all see it coming to an end.

If every other hostage family had not given me their love and support, if every returned hostage had not given me his encouragement and message to keep doing this, I couldn't have gone on. Not only has God given me the strength and the ability to do it, but I'm propped up by so many other people who believe in me and believe in God. I'm at the top of a very, very large pyramid, and there's just simply no way I could have operated on my own.

For some unknown reason I'm apparently the one who's supposed to lead this particular parade. If I had tried to project six and a half years ago what my life would be like today, or if somebody had told me I would be shaking my finger in the face of Presidents, I would have said, "Have another drink. There's no way." I cannot tell you today what I'm going to be doing a year from now. Whatever it is, it'll be the thing that I'm supposed to do. I've got to leave myself open to that. I found that every time I try to take control of my life, it's always a mistake, because my life is not in my control. I'll just wait and see; I'll be open to anything.

"My Loving Wife"

David Say

Peggy Say is, above all else, my loving wife and best friend. She has never let Terry's situation interfere in any real way with her determination to care for me and for our children. It's been very difficult at times, but we have somehow managed to emerge with an even stronger bond than we had before Terry was taken.

I've had the privilege of watching her personal and spiritual growth during the last six and a half years of Terry's captivity. Not only has she grown as a person, but we have grown as a family by witnessing the example she and Terry set for us.

She has made the world know and remember Terry Anderson and the other hostages. Without meaning to, she has also made the world aware of a sister named Peggy Say. From the letters we receive from all over the world, and from the personal experience of our family, many important lessons were learned.

Peggy has shown the world just how much an ordinary citizen can accomplish with enough faith and determination. It's never been important to her that she has become a celebrity in her own right. What has been vital to her is that she didn't just sit back and let Terry suffer in silence and abandonment.

She has been a loving and loyal sister to Terry while carrying on her devotion and dedication as a wife, mother, and grandmother. I'm very thankful and honored to be her husband, but most of all her friend, and I love her very much.

Love is that special attachment we share with others based on admiration and loyalty. Our feelings of concern and devotion for those whom we love are as important in bad times as in good. It is during bad times that the love, concern, and care of others provide us with the evidence of our value in their lives. Love in the context of hardship is a rallying around of those close to us when we are in need.

Betty Ford is the former First Lady of the United States. Mrs. Ford is President of the Betty Ford Center in Rancho Mirage, California, a drug and alcohol dependency treatment center. She is the author with Chris Chase of *Betty: A Glad Awakening* and *The Times of My Life*.

"I've Always Had So Much Help"

Betty Ford

When you've had cancer and been able to recover from it, every day has a special meaning. It's a long time before you really feel secure that you have defeated it. It's been fifteen years for me and I feel perfectly free and clear of it now, but it does take time. You have to be patient and have trust and faith. For me, faith is the belief that anything is possible, and trust is the feeling that you will be able to handle whatever is to be.

I have a little plaque in my dressing room that says: "God, help me to remember today that nothing's going to happen that you and I together can't handle." I know the word "God" is uncomfortable for some people, and that's okay; but most people, I think, believe in a power greater than themselves. That power may be the universe, the stars in the sky, the mountains, God. There is a power greater than just ourselves. It may be something people can't describe or touch, but they feel it, and that feeling gives them inner strength to do what they hope and trust they can accomplish. I believe if I have enough faith in God, I can face anything.

My faith has certainly helped me often in my life when I have been powerless to control events. Perhaps the hardest thing for all of us is to realize we are powerless in so many situations. However, without having to confront, accept, and work through problems, we would really have very dull and uninteresting lives. People say the amount of adversity that I've faced in my life is staggering for one person, but I never think of it as being in adversity. On the contrary, the adversity I have experienced has been a very positive influence in my life.

I was very young when I lost my father. I was only sixteen and I really didn't understand it. I had not been terribly close to him because he traveled a great deal, but it was like losing the wholeness of our family. He was a very important part of the family unit. The father-husband image was the masculine, powerful image, and that cornerstone was gone. When I lost my brother, I was older and more mature. That loss had more impact on me. My brother had suffered from alcoholism, and had experienced a wonderful recovery. He was living such a positive life, but he suffered from heart disease. His dying so young at age fifty-six was very sad. When I lost my mother, that was most tragic for me because we were very close. I had to work through a lot of guilt. I had just been married and it had been a very busy time. I felt that if it hadn't been for all of the excitement and activity of our marriage, she might not have had the cerebral hemorrhage that caused her death. I know now that's not true, but it's normal for people to take on that kind of guilt. We love to be responsible for everybody else's problems. I had tried to get down to Florida to be with her, but she died before I got there because the airplane I was on was held for a mechanical problem. I learned a lot when my mother died. I did go through the grieving process and worked through it to the point where I was willing to let go.

Grieving is a very long process. People die when it is their time, whether they're in an airplane accident or die of cancer. I'm a fatalist. I believe in destiny. Life is a sort of needlepoint. The life pattern is laid out; how we work the stitches is the way the pattern comes together.

Even though I have had illnesses and had to work and put myself back together, I've always had so much help, not only from God, but from the people who surround me. Our family is a closely knit unit. We're not the "Brady Bunch," but we believe in each other. We have our conflicts, but we support each other too. When anything has ever happened to me where I've needed help, my family—not just my husband, but my kids as well—has been there full force by my side. It's an unbelievably good support system. They pull for me as I go through whatever it is I'm facing. That's half the battle.

The hardest thing for me to face was not physical; it was emotional. This occurred when I was so ill in alcoholism. My family confronted me one morning with the fact that I was a very sick woman, that my illness was causing them great pain and they could no longer stand by and support me in this disease. They felt something had to be done about it. They confronted me with times, places, and experiences where I had hurt them, disappointed them, let them down, embarrassed them. They wanted me to get help, and if I wasn't willing to do so they could no longer stand by me. That's what one calls an intervention. Mine was done by the whole family, with the help of a couple of physicians who were well aware how to intervene in the disease of alcoholism.

I was shocked. They were telling me I had let them down when I felt I had spent my whole life trying to help them, guide them, be there for them. This was the greatest blow I'd ever received. What I heard was that I was failing them. For a mother and wife who thought she'd dedicated her life to her family, it was indeed traumatic. There was a great deal of emotion and tears. My first reaction was anger: "How can you say that when I've given up all my time and efforts for you?" Fortunately, in spite of the disease, I could hear them saying, "We love you too much to let you go on the way you are, because if you continue you're going to die." I heard that through my anger, and I was willing to listen to what they had to say. I was willing at least to try what was suggested to me—to go into treatment. My family had made me feel angry, resentful, guilty, and despairing, but not hopeless. I'm a person of action. When I know I'm at the wall, I don't go into depression; I take action. Often people are long on faith and rather short on action.

The only time I didn't take immediate action was when the doctors told me I needed carotid artery surgery after they had done an angiogram that showed blockage. Such blockage could cause a stroke. When the doctors warned me I could end up in a wheelchair, or I could lose my ability to speak or move, they got my attention.

I'm a nurturing person. I'm a woman, I'm a mother, I'm a caretaker, and I don't ever want to be a burden, so I took action. It wasn't so gutsy; I had a choice to make. I was asked, "Do you want to take the chance of having a stroke, or do you want to get the surgery done and hopefully avoid that?"

It was July of 1987 when I had the first carotid artery surgery. I had another the following June. In between I had heart surgery. Over a period of eleven months I had six surgeries. That was a very scary time. There was a period in my recovery when I could not read except very large type, and I couldn't think of words when I was speaking. My concern was not only whether I'd be able to walk, but also whether I'd ever be able to speak in public again.

The following September I gave an address at the University of Texas in Austin. I wondered whether I'd be able to get through it, but the talk went well enough that I was relieved and joyous. It gave me back my confidence in being able to communicate with audiences again.

My gratitude is for the quality of life that I have today in my recovery, which is very positive. I have the great advantage of not having to lean on a substance to get me through the little blips in my life. By not leaning on those substances, I can take the hills and the valleys and derive the full benefit and satisfaction of overcoming. Accepting hardship is a pathway to peace.

People say the Serenity Prayer is the answer. "God, grant me the serenity to accept the things I cannot change, the courage to change the things I can, and the wisdom to know the difference." The prayer continues, "to take the world as it is, not as I would have it." It's a very hard thing to do, but that is reality. Acceptance is important, but I guess I don't see it as the only answer. I think I live it. I truly live. Because I have been able to accept my powerlessness over people, places, and things, I have a great deal of serenity in my life. All we have is one day . . . today.

Family, linked together by a common name, ancestry, and bond of love, is a special source of strength and support during trials and tribulations. Within family, there is a sense of loyalty and goodwill that enables those in that unique circle to set aside personal and professional priorities in our time of trouble and to be with us physically, emotionally, and spiritually. The unique bond of friendship also allows those people intimate in our lives to play that specific role as well.

When there are circumstances such as age, distance, or estrangement, immediate family and close friends may not be readily available. Caregivers become an extended family; their goodness and compassion generate that same security of support and love.

Marvin Bush is a partner in the Winston Group, a merchant bank based in Alexandria, Virginia, and serves as the national spokesman for the Crohn's and Colitis Foundation of America. He is the son of President and Mrs. George Bush.

"My Whole Family Rallied Around"

Marvin Bush

At the beginning of 1985, everything was going fine. I was twenty-eight years old. My wife and I were planning to adopt a child from an adoption agency in my home state of Texas. I had been healthy up to that point in my life, never had a broken bone, never spent any time in a hospital. I grew up in a family where people didn't complain about being hurt or sick.

In the late spring, I started experiencing symptoms I later learned are very common among victims of ulcerative colitis and Crohn's disease. At that time, I thought I was having a hemorrhoid problem: there was blood in my stool. I thought I had eaten something bad. I really didn't pay much attention to it. I started losing weight and having a problem concentrating at work. I was working for Shearson Lehman Brothers, in the investment business. It was a job that required a good deal of energy and I was getting zapped of my energy.

One weekend I was up in Maine; my parents had included my wife, Margaret, and me in the group. We were very excited because we had just begun the adoption process. The head of the Episcopalian Church, Bishop John Allin, and his wife were there, too. We had been there about three hours when a special news bulletin came on television. It described some problems that President Reagan was experiencing. Specifically, it was cancer of the colon.

What happened during the next hour was rather surrealistic. My dad was on the phone. Since he was the Vice President, people needed to keep in touch with him because he might have to assume the responsibility of being President if President Reagan's illness got worse. Meanwhile a doctor on the TV explained some fairly graphic diagrams. A heart's one thing, but the whole intestinal tract quite another. Probably, like most Americans, I was a little repulsed by it all. I'd been taught as a kid not to talk about "bathroom things," and this seemed a continuation of those lessons.

The doctor, at one point during his presentation, started going down a list of symptoms that are common in people who have cancer of the colon. I think I had eight out of nine. Nausea, fatigue, loss of weight, loss of energy, and blood in the stool were on the list. As he pointed to each of the little boxes with a check next to it, I thought, I haven't scored this well since third grade.

Though I didn't mention it to my parents, I had a kind of flushed feeling and thought I'd better go see a doctor. By this time, my wife knew something was wrong with me. In addition to not feeling well physically, I wasn't really myself at home. There was a lot of uncertainty from summer through the fall. When I went to the doctor, the tests were inconclusive. He gave me a drug to try to settle the inflammation in the intestinal tract. I had an allergic reaction, and ended up being rushed off to the hospital. They attached me to an IV and the allergic reaction settled right down. For the next few months I went back and forth to different doctors with no conclusive diagnosis. Finally, they narrowed it down to a couple of different things, one of them being ulcerative colitis. So I took anti-inflammatory drugs, and that controlled the inflammation for a while. During that time, Margaret tried to get me to keep in touch with the doctor. But I was being the stubborn young guy who's never been sick before, thinking, I'm indestructible.

In the spring of 1986, while I was flying to California on a business trip, my symptoms got a lot worse. I was sweating profusely and having horrible cramps in my stomach. I'd lost a good deal of weight by then. I went from 185 pounds to about 170 at this point, on my way down to about 150 at the low point. Luckily, the plane stopped in Denver. My brother Neil and his wife live there. I called him and said, "I don't know how to explain this to you, but I feel as if I'm about ready to die. I wonder if you might come over and pick me up." I spent the night with my brother, and we talked about it. Neil said, "You need to see a doctor here in Denver." However, by that time I felt better again, so I thought, I don't want to see a doctor, I don't want to be any trouble to anybody. The following morning I went back to Washington.

I was more concerned than ever. There was more blood every time I went to the bathroom, and I had to go probably eight or nine times a day. All I thought about was looking around for toilets. I was in real pain. When you start cramping, it's just indescribable pain. My stomach knotted up and kept churning to the point where I just wanted to curl up in a dark room. For some reason, every time I went into a dark room where it was cool, I could relax.

My wife, Margaret, was in Richmond visiting her family, and I went over to the Vice President's residence to watch a video movie with my mom. I had to leave the movie three times to rush to the bathroom. I was nauseous as well; every time I sat down on the toilet, I'd throw up. My mother finally said, "Let's go." And I said, "Okay, I've had enough." So we drove over to Georgetown Hospital.

If there was any advantage I had in being George Bush's son, it was that I filled out only fifty forms before I was admitted into the hospital. Maybe others have to fill out fifty-five.

I'll never forget the nurse who said, "Just put your clothes here in this bag and we'll bring it back when you check out." My reply was "Why not leave them here? I'll be out of here in a few hours." As it turned out, I was there for three weeks before surgery.

Lying in the hospital was the most painful period of my entire life. I had tubes running down through my nose and into my throat. I was fed intravenously because I couldn't keep food down. The doctors were experimenting with medication at the time, so I was half out of it. I was losing weight, I was losing blood. I was very sick. Five or six times a day, I'd break into a fever.

It was a really tough thing for my mom and dad because they'd had one child—my older sister, whom I never knew—who died of leukemia. They'd witnessed how a disease can ravage a human body. The thought of losing another child was horrendous to both of them.

I had a ton of support from my family, which I'll never forget. My mother and I have a very special relationship. All five of us kids would say that. I'd say that about my dad, too. My mom's got a great sense of humor and is extremely loyal to all of us. I am responsible for a disproportionate amount of that white hair that sits on top of her head—from being a youngster who could be somewhat precocious to being an adult who developed a near deadly disease. Yet the tougher things get, the closer she gets. Some people cower when things get tough, but my mother is a very strong and resilient person. When things get rough for any of us, she lets you know that things will be better. She was so inspirational to me. She kept me laughing as much as she could, which was a hard thing to do at that time.

My dad's probably the most thoughtful person I've ever met. I've never seen anybody who's more concerned about more people than George Bush, and that's something very few Americans know. In our society we're too concerned with image and my dad's image is so different from what's real about him. I've seen it again and again. There's nothing phony or opportunistic about it; it's just the way he is. I would have been shocked if he hadn't come by the hospital every day. He's a loving and caring father who would do anything for any of his kids. I think my illness was almost tougher on my dad. He is so sensitive about his children that it just kills him to see us suffer in any way.

When you're as sick as I was, just three words, "I love you," mean so much. My brother Jeb, who's famous in our family for not saying a whole lot, wrote me a letter that was very short. It was three lines, but he said, "Hang in there, big guy. We need you, we love you." I recognized how important my family was to me when the most stoic guy in the family articulated his feelings about me.

I felt violated that my body had this disease and yet in another way I felt rich because I'd had confirmation of all the love of my family. Life has been a success for me already because I could die today knowing I've got all these people who care for me. My wife Margaret slept on a cot at the hospital for three weeks. My whole family rallied around; I got plenty of letters and calls.

When they told me later I was going to have surgery, it was a big relief. I just wanted to know what was wrong with me and then move forward. Whether it was life-threatening or not I didn't particularly care at that time; I just wanted to get out of pain.

That night in bed, I thought about a lot of things. The nurse gave me a sleeping pill; otherwise I probably wouldn't have slept. Early the next morning I had my surgery. And it was a good thing I had it when I did. Maybe there was a chance I wouldn't have survived the surgery, but I don't know. The doctors thought the deterioration in my intestine was so bad that there was a danger it would spread throughout my body and kill me. So there was more danger in not opening my body and doing the surgery. They took out the damaged area of my intestine, and left me with an illeostomy. I have a piece of my intestine that protrudes from my waistline. It comes out about an inch and a half and ends in a pouch that I wear on top of that, which adheres to my body, and the body waste flows through my intestine into the pouch. I empty it periodically.

When I woke up from the operation, I felt instant relief. The scar was very painful, but everybody who has surgery feels scar pain. Having the inflammation out of my intestine was like putting ice on a sore.

The recuperative stage was something that challenged me, but I like challenges. Putting on twenty-five pounds was quite easy; everybody in the family was jealous because I could eat all kinds of wonderful things. I had plenty of upside potential there. The not-so-fun part was the emotional burden of me wearing this pouch. We live in a very vain society where people care too much about the way they look. Having this thing on my waist was something that concerned me. I went through the "Why am I the guy who has to deal with this?" syndrome. I also felt pretty lucky in many ways. I recognized how much support I'd had from my family and my friends. I realized how people cared about me, and how I was a piece in the puzzle of people's lives. With that realization there comes a sense of obligation not to feel sorry for yourself and to get back on your feet. That part of me wanted to recuperate as quickly as possible and show my family and friends that their faith in me was not unfounded. Yet there were days when I felt sorry for myself for having to worry about changing the pouch, about emptying it every day. That was at the beginning, before I got used to it. That was five years ago. It's really not that big a deal now.

In our society, you tend to feel that you get judged by what you do, what you achieve. During a major illness like this, you realize people are in your corner for who you are rather than what you do.

Through all of this I think I've learned to appreciate the strengths that people have. Now, when friends experience tough times—a divorce, an illness, a death in the family, trouble with a job, an alcohol problem—they get my attention a lot quicker than they did before. My parents taught us we ought to think about other people, but when you become one of those people, and others think about you, you tend to take the extra minute to reach out and do something—like what my brother did for me by writing that short note. Just spend three minutes doing something simple; it goes so far toward making people feel better about themselves.

The recuperative process has many stages. The first is coming to grips with what you've been through. The second stage, in my case, was physical rehabilitation. The third stage for me—and it's been a wonderful stage—has been the opportunity to share my experience with other people, to talk about these insidious illnesses publicly and unashamedly.

I spend as much time as I can talking to individuals who've suffered from them or who are confronting the operation that I had. I also talk to people who have already had the operation and are going through the emotional problems I went through. From a selfish standpoint, that has been a great experience for me.

The whole thing has made me a little more thoughtful and a little less judgmental about other people. It's probably made me feel more fortunate to be who I am, not just the son of George and Barbara Bush, or the brother of Jeb, George, Neil, and Doro, but also the friend of so many good people. I'm sensitive to the fact that people have different problems and you can't always see them. Even though someone appears to be happy, healthy, and successful, that individual might have a plethora of problems that are burdensome to him or her. His sister may have an emotional problem, her brother may have AIDS.

I get a lot of letters. People mail them "Marvin Bush—White House." I know when it's a colitis letter or a Crohn's letter because they're a little thicker. People love to tell their story. I love reading them. They remind me of how lucky I am. Many of these people are lonely; they don't have a family, or a wife like mine. These are the people I try to call or write.

One hundred percent of the time I appreciate being George Bush's son; about ten percent of the time I appreciate being the President's son. There's a big difference. The good thing about being the President's son is that I can use that good name of his to help people who've had my problem.

When an article came out in the *Ladies' Home Journal,* my friends teased me; they called me "second chance Bush"—the title of the story was "Second Chance." A certain side of me believes that I do have a second chance. I feel pretty good about the first shot I had. I had a lot of fun and lived a pretty good life for twenty-eight years. I am married to a wonderful woman and have a great family, and I had a lot to be thankful for before my illness and surgery. I'm just, I hope, a fraction of the way through my second chance, and I think it's better than before. It was a humbling thing to go through; but pain can be very positive if you slow down enough to let it teach you the lessons it can.

Action

Elisabeth Kübler-Ross offers us predictable stages of the dying and death process: denial, anger, bargaining, depression, and acceptance. That these stages apply also to major adversity seems possible, although debatable. What appears true, however, is that in confronting adversity, there are common denominators for overcoming hardship: faith, hope, attitude, acceptance, and action.

While we are truly powerless in many situations, our future is more in our hands than we often believe. Self-pity and victimization get us nowhere. Decision-making, initiative, and behavior—all components of action—propel us toward personal victories in difficult times.

Activity, which takes us out of ourselves, creates interaction with others, distracts us from our upset, and moves us toward our goal of recovery. Traumatic situations present challenges that require focus, goal setting, risk, and effort. Meeting those challenges produces the good feelings of high self-esteem, the satisfaction of accomplishment, and options for the future.

Mihaly Csikszentmihalyi, Ph.D., is professor and former Chairman of the Department of Psychology at the University of Chicago. He is the author of *Flow: The Psychology of Optimal Experience* and *Beyond Boredom and Anxiety*. Dr. Csikszentmihalyi, a Senior Fulbright Fellow, is a member of the National Academy of Education and the National Academy of Leisure Sciences.

"What Can I Do About It?"

Mihaly Csikszentmihalyi

Human beings don't come with a guarantee. There are always disappointments of one kind or another. You should be able to take a disappointment in stride, and if it's something you can fix or improve on, go ahead. Don't expect that just because you are a good guy and you have blue eyes and your mother loved you, everything is going to be smooth. That's a very dangerous assumption.

Too much ease and too much smoothness in life create a false sense of security and promote sloppy habits of living. You don't feel you have to do anything in exchange. Whereas, if you start out with a lot of harsh obstacles to overcome, you may actually learn to enjoy overcoming them. You may end up taking things in stride and not letting them bother you.

Recently, I was in Europe interviewing an eighty-year-old poet who had been in jail for four years under the Nazis and then six years under the Communists. He had been beaten up and left for dead a couple of times in extermination camps. When I saw him, he had just celebrated his birthday and was full of life—happy, involved, writing his poetry, and consulting with schools. That kind of confidence and real engagement with life often is the result of harsh and sometimes even brutal conditions.

I did some experiments to get a clearer picture of what happened moment by moment in people's lives. It involved people carrying an electronic pager for a week. Every day I sent seven or eight signals at random moments between eight in the morning and eleven at night.

Whenever the beeper went off, each person carrying the pager took out a little booklet and wrote down what he or she was doing, thinking about, who else was around and then rated his or her state of mind in a variety of dimensions, such as how much he or she was concentrating, how much he or she was in control, how self-conscious he or she was, how happy or sad and how strong or weak he or she felt.

At this point, we have tens of thousands of these reports and we can study precisely and in great detail to which parts of life seem to be the most positive, the most "flow-like"—that is, when people have high concentration and at the same time feelings of euphoria and creativity. When I use the term "optimal experience," I mean an activity that is challenging, where people are using their skills, where their attention is focused, where they're having to give some energy and effort. Usually it involves a feeling of clarity of goals and of knowing how well they're doing in meeting those goals so they get good feedback. Also at those times they don't worry about not being in control; they don't feel self-conscious, they're not worrying about problems. If an activity really involves us, it leaves no room for processing other information.

When I use the term "flow," I'm talking about a state of consciousness that we've identified in people who seem to be doing things for no good reason except to get a particular experience or a particular state of mind. If that experience is so powerful, what does it consist of? How does it feel; how does it work? The one thing I discovered is that in a great variety of different activities, whether playing chess, rock climbing, or sports activities, the same quality of experience was described: one that had challenge, skill matching, goals, feedback, unself-consciousness, and transcendence of self-control. Those are the parameters that people report when they are engaged in these highly enjoyable activities. It turned out that most people got more flow out of their work than out of their free time.

Ramanujan, the great mathematician, was sick for years before he died. However, his relatives felt that even though he was suffering physically, the suffering never penetrated his mind because it was so busy doing his mathematical calculations. His mind became insensitive to the messages from his sick body. I think to a certain extent that is true.

The work of Professor Fausto Massimini at the University of Milan is fascinating. In groups that were studied in Milan, there were between forty and fifty blind people—half of them congenital; half who lost sight at some point during their life—and about sixty paraplegics who had lost the use of their limbs usually in their late teens or early adulthood. One of the amazing findings turned up in both of these groups was that those who became blind or paraplegic later in life mentioned their loss as a big change, which was tragic, but in the same breath—when asked to describe how their life had changed since then—most of them tended to emphasize that now they had a much better idea of what life was about and that they could enjoy more things in life than they used to.

Before their loss, these people had one or two things they liked to do; for example, dancing or motorcycle riding. They had a couple of things that produced "flow" for them, but the rest of life was taken for granted. Ninety-five percent of their life was "So what, I'm alive. I have these things, I have a family, I have to do a job." After the tragedy, they were suddenly confronted with a whole new set of challenges, such as how to get around a room, how to dress, how to eat. Everything became a challenge.

I'm sure that some people just give up at that point, but these were a cross section of people. Among these survivors, what they discovered was that life provided a whole lot of difficult things they had to do. By gosh, if they did anything, they felt good about it. Instead of taking life for granted, now every little thing they accomplished made them feel good. They had to plan. They had to develop a skill to do things. Instead of feeling it as a terrible bother, they seemed to feel that if they worked hard they could always improve. Somehow that effort and success boosted their self-confidence tremendously.

A good majority of these people had been rather happy-go-lucky and not very focused in their life goals. All of them now developed some life goal beyond survival. They wanted to get a degree, or they wanted to learn to play the classical guitar, or they wanted to write a manual on archery for the blind. They suddenly felt that perhaps they could do it because they had survived. They learned how to adapt back to life.

The people who get most destroyed by such a negative experience are those who, for some reason, assume that the life they had before is the only or the best life they could have. They tend to cling to the past, cling to their habits. Because newly blind people can't see the light in the morning and can't read, they may feel they are finished. That was the only life they knew, and therefore they think that's *the* life. What people who become blind discover is that there are many other ways to experience the world and to derive joy and satisfaction from it. This involves developing a whole lot of new skills, from smell to hearing to touch. Once they develop these, they are not as isolated as a person might think he would be if he just took for granted that sight is the major way or the only way to relate to the world. The same, to a certain extent, is true with paraplegics. They now focus on things that other people enjoy doing but that they themselves have not tried before.

We think of many things as tragedies because they deprive us of what we take for granted, like mobility or sight, or even money. But all of these deprivations are relative. They are relative to a "taken for granted" norm. It's true that, compared to normality, they are big deprivations. On the other hand, what we take for granted as normal could be seen as a deprivation relative to the great focus one can achieve when one can't do the normal things. Beethoven wrote some of his greatest music when he was deaf. Homer was said to be blind. There are lots of examples of people who have achieved joyful and profound things in situations that we would think are terrible.

The ability to take misfortune and make some good out of it is a real gift. I don't mean necessarily that it is something inborn, but it's something you can develop. It is a gift in the sense that it makes you richer. When one asks people whom they admire in life and why, the majority of those who are mentioned have turned around to advantage a situation that seemed very bad. Courage is seen by people as a real gift.

Adversity, unfortunately, is a fact of life. It will always be present in one form or the other. The question is, are you going to let it destroy the quality of your life, or are you going to find ways of making it a springboard for some new adventure or growth? That's a very simple issue. One way or another, you have to cope with it. You might as well find a way that will make life richer.

A passionate belief that what we are doing is right can be a compelling and motivating force in traveling through difficult times. The belief that our course is good and moral helps us overcome obstacles that would deter others. When fighting for something bigger than ourselves, resolve and strength are always there for us. Where would we be today had not brave and courageous men and women stood in the face of adversity and acted on the strength of their convictions? Where would we be today ourselves had we not acted with bravery and courage in our own past?

Jeanne White is the mother of the late Ryan White, the Indiana teenager whose battle with AIDS captured the hearts of people around the world. Mrs. White continues the AIDS education work that Ryan began. She was actively involved in securing passage of the Ryan White Emergency Care Act, a bill that provides emergency financial assistance to those metropolitan areas hardest hit by the AIDS epidemic. She also lectures across the country on the legacy of Ryan White for the Keppler Association. Mrs. White is currently involved in the creation of the Ryan White Foundation at The James Whitcomb Riley Children's Hospital in Indianapolis, Indiana, which is scheduled to open in 1992.

"The Strength to Fight Comes From Within"

Jeanne White

At the end everybody was following Ryan through the media and wanted to know how he was doing. He touched everybody's heart and made AIDS real for a lot of people. Ryan was a hero in everybody's eyes.

Ryan was very mature for his age. When the parents were picketing and saying so many cruel things about us, there was never any bitterness in him. When news reporters asked him what he thought about the controversy, he would say, "Well, they're just trying to protect their own kids, like my mom's trying to help me." That didn't come from me, because I have to say I was bitter. People were attacking me as a mother, attacking my son and our family.

The parents were calling me an unfit mother, questioning how could I allow Ryan to go to school to be killed himself or to kill other kids. They were saying he would be exposed to other diseases or would expose others to AIDS. School was so important to him. We only sued for the right for him to go to school; we didn't sue for money.

I don't care how much we accomplished, Ryan was the one who had AIDS. Ryan was the one I was going to lose, even if we won the right for him to go to school. If I'd listened to everything that was going on, I don't think I could have functioned. I had to tune it out. I had to keep faith in what I was doing. I knew I was right, and eventually everybody would see that.

Not until 1984, when Ryan was diagnosed, did the realization come that there was a problem within the hemophiliac community. It was thought that we were using his hemophilia to cover up, that he'd had to engage in some kind of homosexual activity or drug abuse to get the disease. People were saying he deserved the disease. It shows the mentality of people with panic and fear. The local Board of Health wanted to put a quarantine sign on the front of our house. A lot of people don't know this but the officials tried to make Ryan a ward of the court. They tried to take Ryan away from me. That's when I realized these people would stop at nothing.

Once, I said to Ryan, "Don't give up. Be proud of who you are. Never feel sorry for yourself." It was harder for me to take my own advice. When it's your child, when you love your children so much, the strength to fight comes from within. I look back and I think, I could never do it now.

Because Ryan was born with hemophilia, he was already different. He had lived in hospitals a lot. He had lived in a great deal of pain. He had learned to tolerate it.

I think hemophilia helped him cope with AIDS. When he was in the hospital, he saw kids so much worse off than he was. He'd be there with cancer kids, burn victims, people who were mentally retarded, people on machines, and he'd say, "Mom, I'm just thankful all that's wrong with me is my hemophilia." When he was diagnosed with AIDS, his attitude was: Well, this is just something else I'm going to have to handle. There's still people out there worse off than I am. At one point, he said, "Well, at least I've got my looks." He always liked to look good.

I was the one who had to tell him he had AIDS. Ryan was diagnosed on December 17, and I told him the day after Christmas.

I can remember crying so much at that time, but I never wanted him to see me. When I'd walk through the swinging doors to intensive care, I would dry it up. I was afraid he would be scared if he could feel that I was frightened. I prayed every time I went in: "Please give me the strength."

When I told him, his reaction was "Does Laura know?" I couldn't believe it—his nurse? Why would that concern him? But he knew all about AIDS. He had read about AIDS. He had gotten *Time* magazine since he was nine years old. I said, "Laura knows." He loved her all the more, because she knew he had AIDS and she was still taking care of him. He knew that people were frightened of it. Then he asked, "Am I gonna die?" And I said, "We're all going to die someday. We just don't know when." I don't know where those words came from. They just came out.

Ryan said, "Let's just pretend I don't have it." And I said, "Well, Ryan, we can't really do that." Then he said, "Mom, you don't know what I mean." My daughter Andrea said, "Mom, he just doesn't want everybody thinking, Poor Ryan, he's dying." He wanted to go on with his life and be a normal person. I thought he didn't want to face it. Actually, he really didn't want anybody feeling sorry for him.

They gave him three to six months when he was first diagnosed. They had no idea how hemophiliacs could tolerate AIDS at the time. But all of a sudden he got healthier than he had been for three or four years. He was HIV positive for probably at least two to four years before that and we didn't know it.

I was trying to be protective, and the doctors didn't want him to have any pets, they were afraid of viruses he might pick up. But Ryan said, "I don't care if it takes six months off my life. I want a dog, and I want a dog that I feed." It was very important to him to live his life the way he wanted to live it. I remember him asking me for a paper route, and I thought, Oh my, Ryan, there's no way. In the end he had a paper route with a hundred customers.

He watched all kinds of TV, and it got so boring for him. He wanted to go back to school. He knew he was smart, and he kept bugging me: "Mom, I want to go back to school." I can remember calling the school and someone saying, "Well, call back after spring break." When I called back after spring break, I was told, "There's just no way we would allow him to even visit school." Everybody knew Ryan had AIDS. We didn't know to hide it. I had no idea that people would be so cruel and prejudiced over the disease. I thought they would have more compassion for Ryan because he was a kid.

Ryan got AIDS through treatments he was getting for hemophilia. Factor VIII, which he needed, is made of thousands of pints of blood. We found out later that they got the blood from cities such as San Francisco and Los Angeles—the big cities. It takes just one bad doner to contaminate a whole batch. Ryan was probably exposed not once but hundreds and hundreds of times.

I always thought one of my kids would be famous—probably Andrea.

She's really outgoing and very sports-minded. She's a champion roller skater. She's quiet and shy, but she's a very good performer. She was going to national competitions all the time. It was creepy to Ryan to be so famous. But I don't think he was famous because he had AIDS. I think he was famous because of how he handled himself with the disease. We couldn't ever get Ryan to see that. Several of the news media people told me after Ryan died, "You could tell he was never on an ego trip." He fought the reporters. He didn't ever want to give them interviews. His private life was very important to him; he was never a show-off kid who liked being in front of the camera.

The loss of a child is so painful. The thing that helps me is my speaking about it. After a speech at a college several people told me, "You're so lucky because you can talk about Ryan and people listen. We can't talk about our children; people don't want to hear their names brought up, and they're afraid to speak to us about our lost loved ones." I got to thinking about that, and I said to myself, "You know, I am lucky because Ryan is such a hero in people's eyes." They want to know more and more about him. Other people lose a child; I'm not the only one. There are so many other people who feel this emptiness I feel. Some are not as fortunate as I am, but the loss is still the same. There will be a point where it will get better. I know that.

Once, on television, Ryan responded to a question of Ted Koppel's by saying that he wasn't afraid of dying, that he believed in God, and that he would go to a better place. He knew it. There was a comfortable air about Ryan; he wasn't afraid. I think he really thought he was going to be healed or cured, but he said, "If I don't, I've had a good life."

Toward the end, I felt that he was hanging on for me. He didn't want to give up. When he hemorrhaged in his brain, that's when I really knew. His whole body swelled up three times its regular size. Elton John, who had become a friend to Ryan, was with me the whole time. I couldn't have done it without Elton. As he said, "With all my money and all Michael's money, nothing can bring that boy back." When you think about that, money is absolutely nothing. Here are two of the most famous, richest stars in the world, Elton John and Michael Jackson, and they couldn't do anything for Ryan.

So when it was time to let go, I knew. I thought, I'm wanting it all for myself, for him to come back. I knew he was going to Heaven, and I knew he would not want to come back the way he would come back after hemorrhaging. His body would not be the same. I thought, I'm being selfish, I'm doing this for myself. That's when I said, "It's okay Ryan, you can let go."

He wanted to do everything in the world. He really did. I swear he would have been President. Bush and all of them would have had to watch out.

Ryan gave people hope. He had such a positive outlook to continue no matter what was wrong. That was his lesson.

Fear, a healthy emotion that signals danger, often saves us from harm. However, in the face of adversity, fear can immobilize us and cause more disastrous consequences. Courage is action in the face of fear.

There is a link between faith and courage. Those who believe strongly—even in the face of fear—take action. This action may save us from the very worst we fear.

Often immediate action leads us on a path to do the next right thing. The decision to act is in itself action.

Phil Head is a vice-president of the Manufacturers' Bank, N.A., in Detroit, Michigan. He has been assigned to the Southfield office for twenty-five years.

"I Immediately Took Action"

Phil Head

Every one of us is touched by some kind of pain. It's easy for some of us to think we're the only ones, but that's certainly not so. When I was in the oncology department at William Beaumont Hospital getting radiation treatments, I realized there was a cross section of people present, and every one of us, young and old, had cancer.

If it's your first battle with the dreaded "Big C," as it's called, you are aware of many things. You're in pain from massive surgery, radiation treatments, and fear of the unknown. Regardless of strength, all cancer patients experience this pain. And seeing all those people certainly doesn't take the burden away, but one looks around and one can say, "I'm not alone, I'm not the only one suffering. It's not just me." At that point, it's a part of life, and no one can change it. You analyze how you're handling it. You watch the ones who sadly give up. They don't walk into the room and say, "I give up, I have cancer," but in the way they accept the treatments and the way they relate to the other people, you know they've really given up. In that treatment room they are the people who can't accept the pain or won't try to accept it.

Then there are the people who try, to the best of their abilities, to spread a little fellowship and humor. From the very beginning, humor for me was a big help. As long as I was able to laugh at myself, the treatments, and my circumstances, there was hope.

After the surgery, my mouth and tongue were a mess. To make sure you don't have any infection, they feed you by machine. Moreover, it was very difficult to speak. One day, as I lay there, a team of doctors came in. There were always at least six doctors on hand because, unlike most patients who have this operation, I was not someone who had quit smoking. I was a non-smoker. One doctor looked very concerned. I glanced up as best I could, smiled, and awkwardly said, "You don't have to worry, Doctor, I'm not going to die." And he responded, "Why's that, Mr. Head?" I said, "Well, three weeks ago I wrote my last check for my fifth kid to a college, and I'm going to live just to see what it's like to have a couple of dollars in my savings account." He said, "You know, for the condition you're in, it's really wonderful you have that kind of humor."

Not long before this, I had had my physical and been to the dentist, and everything was outstanding. There was a filling that the dentist changed, and he cleaned my teeth. A few days afterward my jaw was sore, but I figured that was because of the cleaning and the filling. Four or five days later, I noticed a little discoloration. It was under or in the gum under the tooth that he had filled. The soreness seemed to have increased. Then one day I went out to lunch, returned in the afternoon, and, while brushing my teeth, thought I saw a slight discharge. I decided I had an abscessed tooth. I called the dentist and I told him about it. He said, "Your son's coming in tomorrow at six o'clock in the evening, why don't you pop in first and I'll take a peek at it?" When he looked into my mouth, he was startled because there was definitely a small tumor, which hadn't been there before. He was able to get hold of a University of Michigan oral surgeon, whom he held in high regard, who would see me the next morning. So I went in that morning and he did a biopsy. It was a malignant tumor. It had evidently been sandwiched between the gum and the bone and started moving very fast.

I immediately took action, went to Beaumont Hospital and developed a team. I was on the table almost fourteen hours at one stretch. The doctors removed half of my jaw, the inside of my mouth on the right side, and part of my tongue, and did a radical neck operation. They took the front part of my pectoral muscle—the remainder is still attached to my chest—and kind of filleted it, brought it up over my collarbone, and used it to rebuild my neck. Then they folded it in and rebuilt the inside of my mouth. It's a transplant. The beauty of using that muscle is the tissue is living and attached and has a blood supply already.

I'm one of the very, very fortunate people. The doctors did an outstanding job. Everything works. I'm in pain daily to some degree, but I have made up my mind—and I'm not a hero—that pain is a part of our lives. I must live with it, and the more I live with it, the more I almost forget that I have it. Though it doesn't seem possible, it will soon be five years since my surgery; I was a little over fifty years old at the time. Fortunately—thank God—with this type of cancer, five years seems to be the magic number. Had I not proceeded immediately that night at the dentist's office, had I been afraid and said, "Well, I'll wait a while and this gumboil will go away," I probably would not be here today. Had I waited six months, I would not be speaking now; I would be deformed, probably at home with a disability retirement.

Fear of cancer is justified; it's a terrible disease. There are many terrible diseases. However, fear causes people to ignore symptoms that can be treated. If you have faith in God, you can do it. My thoughts were: I've got it, I'm not happy about it. But I know with God's help and with me doing the work, I can beat this and I will beat it.

Two days before my surgery, after I'd had a horrible day, I got home and found a letter from my daughter Barbara; her husband is in the service in Hawaii. In the letter was a poem by John Kendrick Bangs:

> I never knew a night so black
> light didn't fail to follow on its track.
> I never knew a storm so gray
> it failed to have its clearing day.
> I never knew such bleak despair
> that there was not a rift somewhere.
> I never knew an hour so dear
> love could not fill it full of cheer.

It was as if the poem had been sent to me by God. I carried it with me in the hospital. I had it in my hospital gown when they operated on me. I've carried it with me ever since.

In all tragedies of life, we learn something and we grow from it. I learned very quickly that money doesn't mean anything. When you're lying there, it's you and God.

I have an outstandingly loving and close wife, Elaine, with whom I've been partners for thirty years. When she walked down that hospital hallway, I always knew she was coming, I was never wrong. She would walk into my room, touch my arm, and it was as if peace flowed over me. She wouldn't say anything, just touch my arm, just be there. That's a tremendous thing. A lot of men take it for granted. I tell them—and some of them don't like to hear it—that I wouldn't be where I am in my career, where I am in life, or alive today if it hadn't been for my wife. She's a strong Irish woman, and she's as close to me as God is. I have three girls and two boys, their husbands and wives, nine grand-children, and some good true friends. If you have that, it seems to me you have everything.

An experience like mine reveals who we are. Before cancer and surgery, some of me was hidden away. Today I'm not afraid to say or do the things I always believed in. We think it's a new life, but it's we who change. Suddenly we're not ashamed to walk across the room to an old person and give some love, or go to a person who's in despair and show concern. We don't worry that somebody may think we have ulterior motives. Personally, I don't mind that someone might laugh at me or think there's something wrong with me. Today I can say, "I care."

Our bank was held up a while ago, on the Saturday before Easter. Someone called me at home, and I immediately went to the bank. The afternoon wore on as we tried to estimate our loss. I phoned out and ordered some pizza and pop because nobody had eaten. When we were finally getting ready to leave, I called everyone together and said, "Before we go, I'd like to have us hold hands and say a prayer. The money doesn't really matter, what happened doesn't matter; but that we're all healthy, and no one was hurt and we can go home and have a happy Easter is what is important. I want to thank God for that, and I think we all should."

We got everything wrapped up, and the FBI and the Southfield police left. As I was leaving, a young guard walked up to me and said, "Mr. Head, I want to tell you something. That was the most beautiful thing I've ever seen." I didn't understand what he was saying. He added, "I heard what you said in there and what you did with your people. I think it was wonderful. You're a vice-president of the bank." "No," I said, "I'm a human being, one of God's people, just as you are."

Five years ago, I probably wouldn't have taken my vice-president hat off. Today it's totally different. These are my people, they're my friends, and I was thankful they weren't hurt. In a small way this is an example of how my experience with cancer has loosened me up. What-ever I went through has broken some chains that I had placed on myself.

My life is richer now. Every day I enjoy so much more the things I used to take for granted, the things I knew I had but I didn't have time to appreciate.

See the beauty of life, don't look for the bad. Look at the good things that people do. There are so many wonderful people out there to enjoy.

Self-preoccupation is probably the single greatest cause of unhappiness. The more we force ourselves to get out of ourselves, the more we benefit. Walking through adversity requires steps—the journey is not achieved quickly. Travel a short distance today; tomorrow go a little farther.

Adversity often causes us to decide who and what are important in our lives. Since our energy is more focused, our life experiences are more rewarding. We gain by re-evaluating our priorities and making time count.

When we deliver a positive message, based on our own experience, others benefit. Possibly no single human act is more satisfying and gratifying. It is better to give than to receive, to comfort than be comforted, to love than to be loved: suffering teaches us that this is true.

Missy LeClaire is a consultant with the Department of Health and Human Services. She is also on the HIV advisory committee for the Centers for Disease Control, on the Consumer Advisory Board for Burroughs Wellcome Company, the manufacturer of AZT, and on the Board of Directors for LifeLink, a coalition of persons with AIDS. In addition, she travels the country lecturing about living with AIDS. Ms. LeClaire received the 1991 Whitman Walker Clinic's Courage Award in Washington, D.C. She recently co-founded Living Strategies, Inc. Its national information service line—by and for people affected by HIV and AIDS—is: 1-900-726-4HIV.

"The Busier I Stay the Healthier I Stay"

Missy LeClaire

A month or so ago my doctor said, "We talked last year about this time and you were going to reduce your workload by half. I think you're doing four times more. Is there any way I could convince you to change this?" And I said, "Well, probably not." So he said, "Okay." I find the busier I stay the healthier I stay.

I do various speaking engagements that have fortunately taken me pretty much across the country. That's been kind of fun. When I began these speeches, I talked mainly about the experience that I'd had with my husband. My husband died of AIDS in 1987, following blood transfusions after a car accident. His psychiatrist, who has become one of my closest friends, asked me to speak to thirty-five psychiatrists he was doing an AIDS training for. This was only about two months after my husband died. I spoke for two and a half hours, and you could have heard a pin drop in the room. I thought, Good gracious, if I can make this kind of impact, and if these doctors can go on and treat people with

AIDS and their families a little differently and with more compassion, then I've done something. Since then, I've talked to every group, from the Red Cross to the Utah Board of Education and the Utah Department of Health.

It's one thing to talk about what you've seen versus what you're going through yourself. There's a tremendous difference. So when I was diagnosed with AIDS, in August of 1988, about a year and a half after my husband died, my focus shifted. I had gone to work for the Whitman Walker Clinic, so I had surrounded myself with a lot of people with HIV and with AIDS. I learned a lot from them about dealing with life and this disease.

I assumed I was positive. I couldn't see how I could possibly have escaped it. I was pregnant during my husband's illness, and miscarried. I never for a minute doubted that I was positive. I took it for granted, but when he was sick I didn't have time to worry about it. I had a very sick man on my hands, and one who didn't deal well with the disease at all.

AIDS in 1986 and in 1987 was considered a disease of junkies and gay men, and he couldn't handle that. He was not gay and he was not a junkie, so he kind of curled up and quit. He had a lot of dementia but it took us months and months to get a dementia diagnosis.

My experience taught me how to deal with the health-care system. It taught me to demand—that I'm a consumer. I learned to fight.

I was HIV positive before I was diagnosed with AIDS. I had been on vacation to Bermuda with two wonderful gay friends. We got back on a Saturday, and by Tuesday I was in the emergency room with CMV pneumonia. I've since gone on to develop pneumonitis twice, CMV encephalitis, and meningitis in my GI track and in my bladder. I've had pyelonephritis, which is a kidney infection. I have it in my joints. I've had positive blood cultures of CMV—cytomegalovirus. I take an IV drug every day for it, and will for the rest of my life. Its worst effect is that it causes CMV retinitis, which causes blindness—but, knock on wood, my eyes are doing okay. My doctor checks them every week. The minute these eyes start to go, I'm calling the Seeing-Eye dog school and I'm going to have me a dog right beside me, so I can still get around to where I want to go.

I've had so many untold infections I honestly don't remember them. I've had weeks at a time where I was doing eight and nine hours of IVs a day. I've been very fortunate in that with the help of my family I have been able to keep my insurance. I have home care as much as I need, and it keeps me out of the hospital. I really think the hospital is one of the worst places to be if you're sick, especially if you have no immune system.

The year 1989 was a terrible one for me; 1990 was a very good year. I was in the hospital only one time; I had a pulmonary embolism. Then, in 1991, I landed in the hospital on January 2; it's gotten progressively worse since then. Before I started this drug that I'm on now—amphotericin—"ampho terrible," "shake and bake," "the drug from hell," I'd had staph septicemia for twenty-eight days.

I rarely ever feel discouraged. What's frustrating is not being able to do what I'd like to do. The fatigue associated with AIDS is just phenomenal. I don't think people can understand it unless they've experienced it. It's literally as if someone pulled the plug. You can't move. I've lain in bed needing to get up and go to the bathroom, and didn't have the oomph to get up to do it.

What most people are missing is that this is not a moral issue; this is a health crisis. This is in their backyards. It's in their apartment buildings. And it will be in their families. It's been said that by 1992, more than one out of four people will know someone with AIDS. It will probably be more like one out of two. People think this can't happen to them, especially in the heterosexual community. But when you live in a large community, such as Washington, New York, or Florida, where you have a high bisexual community, or a high IV drug-user or recreational IV drug-using population, that only gets high on weekends, you have a tremendous chance of becoming HIV infected.

One of the things that I have fought with HRSA, The Health Resources Service Administration, and CDC, The Centers for Disease Control, about is that they're not teaching people how to learn to live with this disease. You can learn to live with it. I've learned. It's not easy, but you can do it. Learning to live with it means good nutrition; giving up behavioral and life-style habits that are not healthy, such as drinking, drugs, and promiscuity; getting treatment earlier; getting into a twelve-step program or one-on-one counseling; and learning to let go of anger and stress. Stress eats up the immune system. That's a scientific fact.

AIDS has actually done a lot for me, I think. It's given me the time to reflect and to look inside at who I am and what I am and what I need and what I don't need. Many people go through their entire lives and never find that out. Personally, I have found that my family is very important to me, my friends are very important to me, my work is very important to me, and to make a difference is very important to me. People will tell you I'm on a mission. I have been at meetings where I've banged the table and said, "Listen to me! You don't have any idea what you're talking about." I'm reminded of my grandmother, who died at eighty. Shortly before she died, she said, "You know one nice thing about being eighty is that you can say anything you want to say." I feel very much that same way. What are people going to do to me? Give me AIDS? I can say what I want to say, and I do.

The Bush administration has been horrid in their response to AIDS; they've made it a moral issue. This isn't a moral issue. I can remember when I was talking to the Mormons. Someone said to me, "Well, we understand that this is God's plan of ridding the earth of undesirable people." I thought for a minute, Oh dear, how do I respond to this one? And I said, "Well, to be honest, you all were raised as Mormons and I was raised as a good Irish Catholic girl. Actually our backgrounds are not that much different. My religion was very much drilled into me, as yours is also; but the God that I know is a loving God. I can't imagine a loving God saying, '*You* have to go, and *you* have to go, and *you* have to go.' He doesn't make errors, so where do I fit in? How about AIDS in Africa where it's fifty-one percent women who are dying? God doesn't make mistakes, so did he say, 'Oh, I really screwed up with Missy LeClaire and hundreds and thousands of other women and children who are infected with this'? I was married. I got it through marital sex. And we have these innocent little babies who are dying. Think about it." Well, the Mormoms did. They said they'd never thought about it that way. I said, "That's my point. We all get our minds set on what we think it should be, and we don't look at all sides of the story."

My mom sometimes teases me: "God gives you one good day, and you could conquer the world." I say, "Mom, that's all I ask for, one good day"—preferably one day after another. I'm hell when I'm well. When I'm sick, I'm really sick and I can't do much of anything. When I'm well, I'll take on the world, and I have, and I will.

I don't have any anger over my illness. I think there is a comfort level you reach when you're so used to doing things. I dealt with my husband's death. I dealt with his being sick. I've dealt with being in the hospital twelve or thirteen times. I know what this disease does. I know how it works on my body. If X happens, I know I need to do Y. If certain things happen, I know I need to call the doctor or get to the emergency room. It's my responsibility to know what's happening and to be aware of what goes on with my body and not to be too overwhelmed. My doctor sometimes says to me, "When I talk to you, I think I'm talking to one of my peers. You know as much about this as I do." I hope this disease will change doctor-patient relationships, because this is the first time in history the patient knows as much as, or more than, the doctor.

I don't fear death. I've dealt with death a lot in my life. You live your life. Hopefully, you live a good one. And you die. That's how life works. I was born. I live my life. I hope I live it well. When the Lord calls my number, it's time for me to go.

For people who are diagnosed with HIV, their automatic thought is "I am going to die tomorrow." Well, I have news for you. You are not going to die tomorrow. Don't run up the credit cards, and do continue to pay your income tax. You're going to be around for a while. We used to say there was also a syndrome called PATSS—Post-AIDS Traumatic Stress Syndrome. That's when you find out that you're going to live. When I was diagnosed, everything I read said I was going to live for eighteen months. I'm still here, more than three years later.

I think good can come out of this. Not only have I learned more about myself, but it's brought my family and friends closer. I don't think we ever end a phone call without an "I love you. I care about you." It's very important for me to say how I feel to someone. So there's deeper connection with people.

AIDS has raised my social conscience of other cultures, of other life-styles. Before my husband was diagnosed with AIDS, the only gay person I ever knew was my hairdresser. Now my father kids me, saying, "Seventy-five percent of your friends are gay, and half of them are black. I don't know what to do with you." That's been a real plus for me. What's amazed my parents has been the outpouring of love and kindness that I've received from so many people, gay and straight. "Can I go to the store for you? Do you need anything? Can I come by? Can I bring you something to eat?" I have a very hard time asking for help. But I'm learning to get over that.

I really do think God will never give me more than I can handle. Now there are a few times when I've said, "Lighten up, Lord." I've had days that I've taken fifteen minutes at a time to get through. But I think when the time comes when He gives me too much to handle, it's time for me to go. I'm starting a new business, so I'm not planning on going anywhere for a while.

AIDS is not something you can do alone. Besides the social stigma, the medical necessity is such that you can't do it by yourself. You need help, and you need to take the help that's offered to you. If it's not offered, you have to go find it. Help doesn't land in your lap. I've worked hard to build up a support system and a network of people I can call on, and I have a good medical support team and a good home-care team. I've great nurses at the hospital who take care of me and I have wonderful friends who are always there for me. One of my biggest helpers is my best friend, Dyann Frick. We've been friends since we were college freshmen. We talk on the phone sometimes five times a day. Nothing's ever too much for her to do. My two brothers, my mom and dad, my family are wonderful.

Unfortunately, a lot of people find themselves isolated. You can't deal with adversity alone. You need support. People aren't isolated just because they're isolated. They're isolated because they've isolated themselves. I've told many people in smaller areas of the country, "If you find out you have AIDS, and can't get help, sell everything you own and buy a bus ticket to a major city where you'll get the services, support, and care that you need."

Lack of action when facing adversity sets the stage for depression. Too much thought can be devastating. When the worst that can happen already has, survey the reality and then take the necessary steps to improve the situation or create a new one. Whatever seems right is probably the correct course of action for you. Trust your feelings. If you change your mind later on or discover you are on the wrong path, try something different.

Tony Bunce is a sales executive for a Fortune 500 company. He currently lives in Los Angeles, California.

"I Don't Have Any Interest in Dying"

Tony Bunce

The whole thing started about ten and a half years ago. I had a bad case of the flu. I was living in New York City and I went to see a doctor who treated a lot of gay patients. While I was there, I asked him about a little lump I had in my stomach area. He immediately checked under my arms and found more lumps and then checked my groin. The lumps were practically everywhere. He looked in my mouth and found I had candida.

I told him I also had been sweating badly at night for about six months. I thought it was where I was living. It was a loft and there was no air-conditioning. I had discounted all of these things. There was no reason to think any different, because nobody knew anything about HIV at the time. It turned out that I had what is now called ARC, which he described then as acute lymphadenopathy.

He said he'd seen about fifty gay men during the past six months who had similar symptoms; fifty percent of them were dead. He didn't give me a specific prognosis, but I got the impression I had about six months to live. I asked him, "What can you give me for it?" He said, "Nothing—just rest, eat well, exercise, and pray."

Six months later, after I got back from vacation in Puerto Rico, I was offered a big promotion at my job. So I moved to California, thinking that would be a good way to make some changes in my life. It was an important move for me, because in New York I was doing drugs, partying all weekend, and working fifteen-hour days. When I moved to California, I still worked some pretty long hours, but my home life was a lot calmer. I wasn't running around, I wasn't doing drugs, and I cut down enormously on my drinking.

In the early 1980s I got into yoga, meditation, and visualization. In the next eight years I made progressive changes. I was working out a lot, refereeing soccer games, and a person I met in Puerto Rico moved to California and we were lovers. My lover and I were in that relationship for two years and, remarkably, he is still negative.

Earlier, when I had moved from England to the States, I looked at it as an incredible opportunity. Now I started to look at dealing with HIV as an opportunity as well. I read up on it and found out everything I could.

I'd always been a big health nut and had loads of vitamins in my house. I continued to take more and more vitamins, and began taking a lot of herbs. In 1983 I met my friend Paul, who was dealing with the same problem. We decided we were going to beat it. Eight years later, he is still doing fine. He is a very spiritual person and a masseur, so at that stage I got into massage. I feel strongly that massage plays a big part in my health. I think it breaks down a lot of toxicity from the drugs I have to take, and I also benefit from the calmness I get from massage.

As soon as I moved to California, I went looking for the best doctor I could possibly find, and found him. He's now one of the world's leading researchers on AIDS. He treated me for about four or five years and I was doing fine during that whole time. I had occasional rashes and skin problems, but he was very impressed that I didn't seem to be having any major problems. In fact, the first time I got my T cells done was in 1982. I still have the test result: my T cells were 279. The last time I had them done, two weeks ago, my T cells were 245. Certainly the percentage of helpers versus suppressors has diminished significantly, but nonetheless I've still managed to keep my health in pretty good shape.

After about four or five years, I switched doctors because I moved to a different area of L.A. I saw this one for about three years. I heard about this new AIDS drug, AZT, which came out in 1987, and I didn't feel my doctor was being very aggressive in pursuing that option. Whenever I went to see him, I always had a list of questions to ask. I realized his time was valuable, but I also wanted answers. I didn't think he had them, and I felt he was getting irritated that I always had eight or ten questions while he had seven patients in the waiting room. I wasn't willing to give up my questions, so I decided to leave him. I saw another doctor, who did a test called the p24 antigen test, which the previous doctor had never done. It told not only the amount of virus in the body, but the amount of activity of the virus in the body.

If I hadn't made that switch then, I would have probably been very sick in a very short period of time, because the activity numbers were extremely high. It was at that point I went onto AZT. That was a horrible experience. The side effects that I had from it were really bad. I couldn't tolerate it, so eventually I was taken off it completely and wasn't able to take anything for a year, until ddI came out. I've taken ddI for a few years and it's worked pretty well.

Whenever something new comes along, I find out about it. I will always remember a Korean doctor I saw. He practiced some kind of Asian medicine where he walked on your back. I was impressed with him; my friends thought I was nuts. I went to his office for a session one day, and he wasn't there anymore. I guess somebody had complained he was a rip-off artist, but for the next six months I never felt so good.

Recently I heard about something else that's new called "hemispheric synchronization." They put different sound waves in each ear and create a third sound, which enables you over a period of time to do certain specific things. One of them is to enhance your immune system's functioning.

So many people don't take these opportunities. I told one person and he said, "Ah, it sounds too California to me." What's wrong with it being real California? It's another angle. I don't know what works and what doesn't. What I do know is, I'm still here after ten and a half years, and I'm in pretty good shape. I'm not stupid enough to delete a whole segment of health care from my thinking.

It's been almost a year now that I've had something called Kaposi's sarcoma, which is a rare skin cancer. For that I take extremely high doses of beta-carotene. I also take alpha-Interferon, which is an obnoxious drug that knocks me to hell. If the alpha-Interferon doesn't work, then I'll take chemo.

Last year I had a really tough year. I was in a relationship that was very destructive, and put myself through hell. I also picked up a bug while I was in Turkey called Campylobacter. On New Year's Eve I got a fever. We checked my temperature and it was 105, so they rushed me to the hospital. The doctor pressed my appendix and I just about flew off the table, so they rushed me into surgery. They rolled me out of recovery at ten minutes to midnight and there were all my friends. I was in the hospital for about six days, came out, and went back in a week later with another 105 fever. They thought I'd abscessed, so they did another surgery. After another week in the hospital, I came out; a week or two later I got the shingles, in my cornea. I'd had it once before. I was laid up with that for a few weeks. A couple of weeks after the shingles, I got diagnosed with the Kaposi's sarcoma.

I take full responsibility for the fact that I caused all those things to occur in such a short period of time. Up until then, I had maintained my health for nine years, even though I had had a few problems along the way. Fortunately, I got out of that relationship and that destructive phase. I have a network of friends who are always there for me, whether it be spiritual guidance, emotional support, or excellent medical care.

I always maintain two doctors simultaneously. If I disagree with one, I'll go see the other. I've seen nutritionists and herbalists. When I had the shingles, I went to an acupuncturist. Right now I'm seeing a chiropractor who is working on areas that we feel will benefit the immune system. It's unfortunate that I have to be so preoccupied with my condition; I keep looking for something new. I also go to a support group at least once a week and sometimes more. The people there are just wonderful. I also see a psychologist now who treats a lot of people with HIV.

I have done a lot of personal-growth workshops; I started with EST in 1974. When I moved to California, I met a friend named Robert, who was involved in an organization called Summit; we must have done forty or fifty courses. Robert and I were together for about three years. It was one of the most incredible periods in my life because he had such a calming influence on me. I've also done a workshop called the Experience and a course called AIDS Mastery, which is a workshop for people who are affected or infected by AIDS. More recently, I did a workshop called Enhance in Orange County.

There are a very few people at this stage of my life who don't know everything about me—just a few clients. My boss knows. My family knows; my friends know. It is an extraordinary release to have everyone know. My dad got a double whammy. He got "gay" and "AIDS" in the same breath. His first reaction wasn't very positive, but at this point he's very supportive. My boss has just been wonderful. That allows me to stay healthy, because I don't have to keep all the stress inside.

I grew up in England in a very poor family. This spring it suddenly hit me for the first time how much my mom had played a part in my still being alive. She'd been very sickly her whole life. She had heart problems, kidney problems, anemia, and a whole host of other things. In the last five years of her life, she spent about a year and a half in the hospital. She had two open heart surgeries back in the sixties.

When she had me, she almost died during the birth but they brought her back. They told her never to have any more children but she wanted a daughter. So she went ahead and had another child, which was my brother, and then she still insisted on having a daughter, which she did.

My dad was a little crazy because he was alcoholic. He used to abuse her, but she never moaned or complained, never said a word. Occasionally I'd see tears come into her eyes. She was so strong. I'd look at her and say to myself, "God, why doesn't she fight back? Why doesn't she tell Dad where to go?" But she really had nowhere to go. There was no way out of the environment she was in. Not until that spring day did it suddenly click that she had given me my training. I used the strength she demonstrated to me to be where I am now. I really wish I could have told her that before she died.

People tell me that I have strength and courage. I don't know that I've always recognized it. My dad taught me discipline. He was very responsible financially and kept us going. I'm proud of the fact that I've come through all this. It's hard for me to say it, but I'm also proud that I've been an inspiration to many other people who are going through this.

Right now I'm searching for a new direction. I'd like to do one-on-one counseling with people who are newly diagnosed HIV positive. It's a big gap in the whole treatment area.

I also want to facilitate support groups. Because I've been dealing with ARC and AIDS for so long, people tend to refer others to me. I've been getting calls from all over the country for years. I give them my insights. I am certainly not the be-all and end-all. If I were, I would have stopped searching. There's lots, lots more to learn and lots more opportunities.

I've been a survivor since I was a kid, dealing with growing up gay in a little town in the middle of England where it was looked upon as disgusting and terrible. Having to deal with being the smallest kid in the class from the poorest family, having the humiliation of my ass sticking out of my pants when I went to school, and never having any money—all this made me a survivor from the start, long before HIV came along.

When I was eight years old, I was selling Avon. By the time I was eleven, I'd had three jobs. When I had the opportunity to come to the States, almost twenty years ago, I didn't even have to think. I knew I had to get out. My first stop outside of the little town I grew up in was Manhattan. I fell in love with New York the moment I got there.

The worst day of my life was in February 1991, when I found out I really did have AIDS. It was the closest I came to giving up. However, when I went to see the oncologist for the first time, I had already researched fifteen different therapies that were available. The doctor was almost in shock. He said, "You know more about this condition than I do." He sat with me for an hour and we went through my notes on the different therapies. At the end of it he said, "Could I take photocopies of these?"

If you wait for the medical centers to do the studies, you'll wait a long time. I have mild AIDS dementia now. The studies are either using placebos or they've got all these wild criteria to get into the protocols. I am trying to find out now how to get a drug through the underground so I can take it myself. I don't have any interest in dying.

Attitude

Attitude, the mental position and the feelings we have toward the reality in our lives, is a big part of who we are. We take our attitude into all situations we face, good or bad. How we view and feel about what is going on plays a critical role in our ability to accept life on its terms and to lead a contented life. A pessimistic attitude about life creates unnecessary fear and worry, and keeps us stuck in a life of sadness, blame, and depression.

Those with a positive attitude fare much better at handling hardships; optimists bring a spirit of positive possibility to whatever they tackle. Meeting challenge with an attitude of "I will overcome" is half the battle already won.

Our attitude is something we can influence; what happens in our heads and hearts is up to us. To change from a pessimist to an optimist requires desire and work; but, according to Dr. Martin Seligman, it can be done.

Martin E. P. Seligman, Ph.D., Professor of Psychology at the University of Pennsylvania, is a leading world authority on learned helplessness and on explanatory style. He is the author of *Learned Optimism* and *Helplessness: On Depression, Death and Development,* and the forthcoming *Facts of Life: Understanding and Coping with Why We Are the Way We Are,* as well as more than a hundred and twenty articles on motivation. His research has been supported by the National Institute of Mental Health, the National Institute on Aging, the National Science Foundation, the MacArthur Foundation, and the Guggenheim Foundation.

"People Can Learn Optimism"

Martin E. P. Seligman

When the average person wakes up at four in the morning from a bad dream and starts thinking about what happened yesterday, it's fascinating that he'll gravitate to the most catastrophic interpretations. A tiff with my wife means divorce. My writing didn't go well yesterday means the publisher's going to reject my book. These things are unrealistic ninety-nine times out of a hundred. Typically, during the low period of our basic rest/activity cycle, we find those interpretations really magnetic, really attractive. For the most part, people spend a lot of time on the worst possibilities.

Pessimists, to me, are people who, when thinking about what makes bad things happen, habitually find the most catastrophic causes: (stable) it's going to last forever; (global) it's going to undermine everything I do; and (internal) it's my fault. Optimists either have been born with or have acquired the skill of taking the same kind of events and finding the causes that go away quickly: "This is just one situation," and, "You did it to me"—two different kinds of explanatory styles.

The glass half empty or half full has never captured much for me. It's the analysis of why the glass is half empty or half full that interests me. If the glass is half empty and you think the cause of it is "The world is in a drought; there's never going to be water again," then you're a pessimist. If the glass is half empty and the cause of it in your mind is "The waitress just hasn't come over to refill it," then you're an optimist. I don't think optimism or pessimism resides in the perception of what's happening right now; it resides in your extrapolation to the future of it, and your analysis of what brought it about.

I've spent a lot of time trying to find out where this attitude comes from, and I found four causes of it. I don't think any of them quite do the trick. The first one is genetic, an indirectly heritable source. Source two is your mother. There's a good correlation between what your mother says, her pessimism or optimism, and your own. If she gets into a fight with your dad and you hear her say "Ah, he was in a bad mood," you're learning your father's moody, but you're also learning that bad things go away. If she says "Your father's a bastard," being a mean bastard sort of stays around, so the theory you're forming of the world is that bad things stay around. The third source I found is the criticisms that adults make of you when you're a kid. If your teacher says, when you fail a spelling test, "You're no good at spelling," you're learning something about your ability; "I don't have a lot of ability." Ability's stable, global. If the teacher says "You're being rowdy. You're not paying attention," then you're learning that maybe you can do something about the situation. The fourth source is the reality of the first tragedy that happens in your life. People whose mothers die when they're young or people who are sexually abused when they're kids grow up to be pessimists.

Actually, however, I think the real source of the way we analyze the causes and consequences of bad events is something different. I think where we get our basic optimism and pessimism, for the most part, is in adolescence. It happens out of idiosyncratic defeats and victories. I think each of us can go to our adolescence and find those sorts of crucial stories that make us pessimists or optimists. Most of the stories we hear when we do clinical work are stories of rejection, rape, incest—things that give people a negative template for viewing their merits and where they belong in the world.

Childhood is not all it's cracked up to be. It's formative for some things and not for others. I believe that a lot of our emotional life is probably lodged in the transition to puberty. So we're intervening now.

We're taking ten- to thirteen-year-old kids in the public schools whose parents are fighting, separating, and divorcing—kids undergoing their first depression—and we're teaching them the skills of "learned optimism."

There are four major differences between the optimist and the pessimist when they confront a tragedy. The pessimist, by definition, when the bad thing happens says, "It's going to last forever, undermine everything I do, my fault." The optimist says, "It's going away quickly, just this one situation, not my fault." I think there are four consequences of this, three of them in favor of the optimist, one in favor of the pessimist. The first one is that pessimists get depressed and stay depressed for a long time. Optimists tend to be resilient; they get depressed for short periods of time and less profoundly so. They recover. The second consequence is this: if you look at the workplace—let's say there's a personal tragedy, like one's wife dying—the pessimist's work tends to suffer as well. Pessimists may show real problems in this domain of achievement. Similarly, if something bad happens at the office, the pessimist's love life tends to suffer as well. The optimist, on the other hand, is able to draw walls around tragedy so that it doesn't spread from love life to the office or vice versa. So achievement tends to suffer in the case of pessimists, and it doesn't suffer as much in the case of optimists. The third consequence is physical health. It looks to me as if, in general, the immune system of pessimists doesn't do very well when it's stressed. They tend to get more infectious illnesses. Pessimists—the way I see it—tend to die sooner when they contract serious illness. Optimists don't do as badly; their health tends to remain pretty good.

The one bad thing for optimism—and it may be the reason that pessimism evolved, and is still with us—is that pessimists see reality better. Pessimists are realists. They know the score. They may be sadder but they're wiser. If you want to make money in the stock market, you should get a depressed friend to invest for you. The pessimist is going to be clear-sided, closer to the truth, maybe even closer to wisdom, than the optimist.

Depression is a unique disorder, in the following way. It brings us face-to-face with existential questions, which no other disorder does. Depression is always accompanied by "What am I doing here? My life has turned to hell." People hit bottom. I think the one thing that depression does for us (and it doesn't do very much at all when it gets out of hand) is it gives us a message to change our lives. I think we're more susceptible to change when we hit bottom than at any other time.

I don't usually think of things in biological or non-biological terms. There's a lot of things that happen to your catecholamines and endorphins when you're depressed. If you're depressed because both your parents were depressives, or if you're depressed because your wife just left you, the same kinds of things are going through your head: "My life is terrible, my future will never be any better. I brought this all about." So biological depression and what's called psychological depression are pretty much the same. It's not clear that one is any easier to treat than the other.

Pessimists believe that they brought calamity about themselves, that it's their fault. The optimist generally says, "I'm a victim of circumstance." Some people must find something inside themselves when things go wrong. Not so with other people. I once lived with a woman who is the most external person I ever met. When her hair wouldn't sit right, she'd yell at me or someone else. One day I said to her, "Darling, you're the most external person for blame that I've ever met." "Yes," she said, "and it's all your fault." So there are some people on the other extreme who never look inward. Angry people, by and large, also tend not to look inward.

I believe that people can learn optimism. Even if they've learned it well—and I'm an example—they still have the four-o'clock-in-the-morning thoughts, but they know techniques for diffusing them. It's not as if you can take a pessimist and make him into a person to whom it never occurs that tragedy's just around the corner. But you can take a pessimist and make him into a person who can diffuse the feeling of impending tragedy. It doesn't go on to undermine his life. He can fight it. The crucial dimensions for pessimism don't have to do with your beliefs about yourself, but rather your beliefs about the world.

"Learned optimism" in concept is very simple. On the other hand, it's such an important skill it's not something you can acquire in two minutes. It involves something that every person has, but, strangely enough, we tend not to use in the right time and place. That is the ability to dispute, to debate.

If an external person, a jealous rival, criticizes us, accuses us falsely of something—"You're a terrible writer"—we're great at disputing that person. "What do you mean I'm a lousy writer? I had a number-one nonfiction best-seller." If someone else says it to us, we can marshal all the evidence and tell him he's wrong. The interesting thing about pessimism is that when we say something to ourselves, we treat it as if it were gospel; we don't dispute it. The very same skill that successfully turns off false accusations when others make them doesn't seem to operate when we make them ourselves. So we teach people to take this disputing skill and treat their own internal voices saying these catastrophic things as if they were a jealous rival, as if they were just as irrational as a drunk on the street yelling at them.

When people are disputing the evidence, they might ask themselves, "What's the hard evidence for the belief that I'm holding in this situation? What are some other explanations that could be attached to this particular thing that's staring me in the face? Are the implications as dire as I make them out to be? What's a less destructive explanation? What's changeable here? Where am I not at fault?" Those are the specific ingredients of disputing.

I think a good portion of the internal voices is irrational and comes out of jealous sisters, Little League coaches, and girlfriends who rejected us thirty-five years ago. Treat it as external, then dispute it, marshal the evidence against it, criticize it. That's the skill we teach. When you start disputing negative thoughts, you can see the difference right away. When you successfully marshal the evidence against it, you feel much better right away. Once people acquire this ability, it becomes a lifetime skill.

We've taught these disputing skills and relaxation to patients with colon cancer and melanoma. The preliminary results show their immune system gets a lot better. If you look at the women who have had a second bout of breast cancer, you see that the optimistic women live longer than the pessimistic women.

Greg Buchanan, a graduate student at the University of Pennsylvania, made a study of ninety-six men who had their first heart attack in 1980. Eight years later half of them had died of a second heart attack. The question is, can you predict who lives and who dies? Well, it's the pessimists who die; optimists tend to live. Of sixteen of the most pessimistic men, fifteen died. Of sixteen of the most optimistic men, only five died. So pessimism seems to predict bad outcome for heart-attack victims, and that's over and above damage to the heart and traditional risk factors.

People can become successful disputers of their own catastrophic thoughts. Unlike the early parts of physical exercise, this feels good almost right away. Disputing negative thoughts is something that's immediately apparent when you're doing it successfully. While it's not instant, it's also not a matter of months. It's a matter of a few weeks of practice.

Some people are raised in environments where they learn optimism. That positive attitude serves them well, whether in small mishaps or major disasters. Their spirit of optimism allows them to deal with setbacks quickly and efficiently. They move forward with a spirit of hope.

Challenges and change are the stuff of life. A positive attitude helps us to encounter them successfully. Fortunately, your attitude is something you can work on and improve.

Marguerite Kelly is a columnist for the *Washington Post* who has written about family issues for twenty-two years. Her weekly column, "The Family Almanac," appears in the *Post,* the Chicago *Tribune,* and the Baltimore *Evening Sun,* among other papers across the country. She is also the co-author with Ella Parsons of *The Mother's Almanac* and author of *The Mother's Almanac II,* both comprehensive books on child care. In addition, she has written for *The New York Times Sunday Magazine, Parents, Harper's Bazaar,* and other publications, and has lectured extensively on family issues.

"The Oil Well Will Hit"

Marguerite Kelly

I come from a long line of Southern gentry, which broke down when it got to my generation. Coming out of that kind of family background, one has a sense of entitlement. When I was twelve, I decided that I would be a syndicated political columnist. I read Dorothy Thompson, Brenda Starr, and Drew Pearson every day. I was going to blend the three. I went to work on the New Orleans *Item* as the copy kid when I was seventeen. It was the third paper in town and great fun. I got a daily column in about six months: a teenage-gossip column. I was assistant women's editor when I left. I was twenty-one and married by then.

My mother was killed when I was seven; she died in a fire. I was the youngest of five children. My father was an alcoholic; he was also a romantic. He talked my mother into selling her house, moving to the scrub-pine country of Mississippi near the Gulf, and starting a chicken and mushroom farm. Bear in mind, my father, who was a charmer, still wore spats. This was 1939. They had never been out of the city. They soon realized they did not know how to tell mushrooms from toad-stools, so they couldn't do that. They bought a car, but they didn't know how to drive. The chickens died, and finally the cow died. It was not a happy experience.

Our house caught fire, and my mother saved us all, including my father, but she died in the fire. I went to live with her sister, who was a wonderful, nurturing, warm person, and my next older brother went to live with my grandparents. My grandmother was the same sort. The others were all mid to older teenagers. One was in college. So we all scattered.

A couple of years ago, I read in *The New York Times* a story about death and how it affects children. I always felt a little guilty because after one year of grief I could handle it. I went on with life, and there wasn't a great deal of looking back. They said in the study cited in the *Times* that children who go into a nurturing situation do all right. The ones who don't get that are the ones that are hit terribly.

My mother was a very strong and determined lady.

Once on a very hot day, my mother was mowing the grass. We were very poor. I can remember her saying, "There must be a way to cook grass." And she tried. It was the very ultimate of optimism. She said to my brother, the chemical engineer, "You're going to be a scientist." To my brother the stockbroker, "You're going to go into money." To my brother who went to law school, "You're going to be a lawyer." I was to be a writer as she wanted it to be.

When I was twenty-one, my husband Tom and I—he was the ace reporter on the paper, and about nine years older than I—packed up our wedding presents and off we went. We would spend Christmas with his parents. He had been helping them out financially—such as we could as Louisiana journalists. The plan was we were going to work for a country paper somewhere and buy into it, because we had fifteen hundred dollars in savings, which I thought was all the money in the world. We got to Washington for Christmas, 1953.

His parents were adorable; I had met them the summer before. His father's brogue came out very strong when he talked to me. His mother, though, was senile. She had had pneumonia at the age of around sixty-eight, and now had total recall to the age of sixteen and no memories after that. She apparently had multi-infarct dementia. It's like a heart attack in the brain. It just short-circuited her. She was a very bright woman and very funny. She was always asking about her husband, "Who is that Italian fellow in my bedroom?" We were there about three days, and I had to say to Tom, "We can't leave." His mother, at this time, was running away four times a day. It was not exactly what I had in mind. On the other hand, it was not anything Tom could say we had to do, because I would be the one taking care. There were no day-care agencies for adults who were in her condition, and certainly no nursing homes that we could afford. I figured you take care of your own. So we lived there with the doors locked, the windows screwed down, and the key hidden.

I was crazy about his dad, and his mother was just a pip. One day she said to me, "Who are you? You are the worst maid I've ever had." Of course, she had never had a maid. She said, "How much do I owe you?" I gave her my wallet, which had eight dollars in it, and I said, "Eight dollars." So she paid me off, saying, "I never want to see you again." So I went upstairs. About five minutes later I came down. She threw her arms around me, tears in her eyes, and said, "Where have you been? If you only knew what has happened to me." This went on all the time. We laughed about it a lot because there's not a hell of a lot you can do in a situation like that. She'd pack up all her clothes four times a day.

The care of the elderly will teach you more about yourself than anything you've ever done. There were times when I thought, I'm not going to be able to make this. But when I did it, I thought, If I can do this, there's nothing I can't do. Grown children are obliged to care for their frail parents unless they've been really lousy parents and have not earned any respect. I do think we each have this responsibility. In taking care of elderly people, expect less, care more, and laugh when you can. You have to laugh. And we did.

It never dawned on me I could not do anything I wanted to do; I have remained extremely optimistic. To this day, at fifty-nine, I will drive downtown and expect to find a parking meter. Sometimes, if I really need something in a hurry and I don't have any change, I expect to find a parking meter with time on it.

I was raised by some nurturing people who conveyed a sense of optimism to me. In my family, it was always that somebody was going to die and leave you money. The oil well will hit. My optimism has served me well.

When we accept that life has its share of disappointments, set-backs, failures, and losses, we can move toward empowerment, which is denied to those who see themselves as victims of circum-stance. The belief that we can survive difficult times and grow in the process is crucial in navigating through life.

Accepting life is a facet of maturity. When difficult times make their way into our life, we need to feel appropriate to life and confident in our coping abilities.

Charles J. Givens is a nationally known financial consultant and author of the best-selling books *Wealth Without Risk* and *Financial Self-Defense.* The Charles J. Givens Organization, based in Altamonte Springs, Florida, is one of the largest and most successful financial education institutions in the world.

"Deal With What's Real"

Charles J. Givens

When I was in the third grade, my mother and father split up after a major fight. After that we only saw my father once or twice a year. My parents' business, by that time, was already going down the tubes. My father was great in business. My mother was great socially, but they had no experience in dealing with life. They used all the wrong strategies to deal with their divorce; the business eventually went bankrupt. My first memory of the IRS was when a moving van pulled up and took away everything that we owned to pay for back payroll taxes.

My mother, brother, and I moved to a little clapboard house on the not so ritzy side of town. It was a totally different life from the social life my parents had put together. After the divorce my mother became a bitter alcoholic. My father was a jolly alcoholic. He was everybody's buddy, no matter how sloshed he got. On the other hand, my mother's hate came out when she drank. From 1953 on, she drank a quart of liquor every night until she died. My mother and I had tremendous battles. I saw myself totally in the victim position. I was mentally screaming "Help!" and people were patting me on the head and saying, "You're just a child, you just don't understand these things."

My mother was a violent alcoholic, and her verbal abuse was unbelievable. One evening, my brother and I thought we could stop her drinking if we poured the liquor down the drain. That just makes alcoholics angrier. We were in the kitchen and my mother was yelling. We felt we had done the right thing. I turned my back and she reached into a drawer, pulled out a meat cleaver, and threw it across the room. It missed me by inches.

My brother and I also had the experience most nights of picking our mother up off the floor and carrying her to bed. "You'll never amount to anything" was what my mother told me over and over. She'd say I'd never done anything successful, I was just like my father, I was no good, I was rotten, I didn't deserve anything. I started thinking she might be right because my life wasn't working well at all.

I began withdrawing more and more. I felt that I wasn't worth much. From twelve to sixteen was a nightmare. I began spending time away from home, staying out all night and running with the wrong crowd. I decided I had screamed "Help!" long enough, and that there was one way I could get back at people. I would kill myself, and then they'd realize what they had done to me.

I got a bottle of phenobarbital out of my mother's cabinet, wrote a suicide note, and dated it for two weeks later. I guess I was a big chicken, as well. I put it in the drawer of my nightstand. That was when everything was released, almost instantly. I'd been fighting this thing, and at that moment I stopped fighting. When I stopped fighting and hit bottom, there was only one way to go and some clarity of thinking happened. I said to myself, "The only thing I ever get to be right about in my entire life is that everything is going to go wrong." Every morning I would wake up and think about all the things that could go wrong during the day. At night I'd say, "See? This is my life. It's all wrong." What I was doing was defending myself against disappointment.

After telling myself that the only thing I ever get to be right about is everything going wrong, I had a flash and thought, It's almost as if I'm writing a movie. It usually comes out the way I write it. I wonder if, by any reach of the imagination, doing all this planning has any effect on the outcome? So I decided the next morning I would wake up and create my own movie in my mind every time I had negative thoughts. "I forgot my raincoat so I am going to get soaked," or, "We're going to have a pop quiz in math, but I didn't study last night" was the way my mind had worked. I said to myself, "I'm going to write a movie in my mind the way I want it to come out."

I woke up and started having all the usual garbage thoughts, and immediately began to picture in my mind how I wanted things to come out. Lo and behold, by that night I had had one of the best days I'd experienced in years. I don't mean the clouds parted and lightness streamed down, but there was a noticeable difference. So I decided to try it again. After I tried it a few days, I began to see that I was the one designing my life, that I didn't have to be the victim. Then I got mad at my parents for not telling me the simple fact that the thoughts you have in some remote way control the outcome of your day; so I went right back into blame again. But then I realized that that was silly; the reason they didn't tell me was they didn't know it themselves.

Disputing negative thoughts by writing the movie in my mind convinced me that things could have a positive outcome. I also found that when they didn't work out, it wasn't the disaster I'd thought it would be. If something didn't work out, I had choice: drop it, or simply make a modification in my plan of attack.

When I was eighteen years old, after I'd got my feet back on the ground, I wrote a list of a hundred and eighty-eight dreams and called them my dreams list. That became my personal motivator. By having the dreams list and focusing on results, I found that the failures that happened in between became stepping-stones instead of roadblocks. My attitude wasn't "Oh, I'm a loser, this will never work." My attitude became "Here's one more way it won't work. Now let me find out how it can."

The biggest mistake you can make in life is to get caught in the process instead of focusing on the result. You must accept, if you want to win in life, that loss is a natural part of life.

Many people define their lives in what they lack or what they've lost: "I lost my spouse through a divorce" or "I lost my job." Instead of saying loss is a natural process, people tend to deal with it as something unnatural. Most people have never been taught how to deal with loss, or to understand that loss is natural. Be prepared to deal with it at any time. The objective is not to eliminate feelings, but to balance the feelings with the nature of the reality of the event.

A woman who was in one of my classes was still beating herself up emotionally for a decision she had made twenty-six years earlier to pursue a music career instead of getting married. Her fiancé had said, "Your music career is going to take you on tours. That's not the kind of relationship I want." Her music career actually lasted less than a year, and she had regretted her decision ever since. It was still the biggest emotional focus in her life, which proved to me that there is no limit to the recovery time if you keep processing the negativity over and over in your mind. You can destroy yourself for the rest of your life.

When someone says to me, "I just lost everything—what do I do?" the first thing I tell them is "Deal with what's real." What's not real is what you could have done in the past, or how you could have done it differently. People often begin to live in the past thinking they can change something by doing so. That leads to guilt and self-criticism, both of which are destructive emotions. Fundamentally, what I teach people is this: you only have one alternative, so stop pretending there are more. That alternative is to deal with what's real. Make a list of your alternatives and get on with it. If you don't, you have no chance. You are destroyed.

Sometimes people say, "Yes, but you don't realize how bad it is." The truth is it doesn't matter how bad it is. Bad is a frame of mind; it has nothing to do with the event. What's real is if you're paralyzed into inaction—that's what's real. It won't make it any less real by talking about what you could have done if it hadn't happened. If you have just gone through a breakup of a relationship, what's real is that the person's gone. That's what you have to deal with. If you have been fired from a job; you no longer have the job. You have to start from that position. So it's not "What could I have done to keep the job," or "How could I have been so stupid as to make that smart remark at the last minute." Or the blame approach that says, "My employer didn't recognize my abilities." Your only point of power in this universe is in the present moment. Where you are is where you are; where you're going is up to you.

Society's attitudes present many people with formidable obstacles. Humans can be negative, judgmental, and critical because of a need to feel superior. Their prejudicial or discriminatory attitudes and actions, based solely on ignorance or fear, are directed toward color of skin, ethnic group, sexual orientation, age, or disability and are the cause of great pain and suffering. For many who come from minority groups, the attitude of others is the real source of their frustration and hurt. Whatever they face in their own lives is seen merely as a difference or an inconvenience.

Bob Williams is a Policy Associate for the Governmental Activities Office of the United Cerebral Palsy Associations, Inc., in Washington, D.C. (Mr. Williams communicates through a keyboard and synthetic voice machine called a Touch Talker.)

"The Problem Is Not in Me, It's Out There"

Bob Williams

This machine works three ways. I can S-P-E-L-L, or there is an I-C-O-N-I-C L-A-N-G-U-A-G-E, and last, I can use both. I've had it about a Y-E-A-R and a H-A-L-F. It is like learning another L-A-N-G-U-A-G-E.

I have had cerebral palsy since birth. I am thirty-four now. CP is not progressive. It's not degenerative. What you see is what you get. CP itself doesn't have a feeling. At most it is an I-N-C-O-N-V-E-N-I-E-N-C-E for me. I am used to it by now.

What people want to know is if I feel different from others because of my disabilities. I have the same feelings as most other Y-U-P-P-I-E-S. What C-O-M-P-L-I-C-A-T-E-S things is how others see me and how over time I R-E-A-C-T to that.

I have a S-C-O-O-T-E-R to go places; if it's not working, I have a T-R-I-K-E. People along the street see me as a F-L-A-I-L-I-N-G, D-R-O-O-L-I-N-G man. Most of the time I T-U-N-E that out. There has always been a great S-C-H-I-S-M for me in that R-E-G-A-R-D. My family and friends see me as very much on the go, very much making things happen for both myself and other people with disabilities.

But the A-V-E-R-A-G-E person still sees me as someone not that C-O-M-P-E-T-E-N-T. I call it the C-L-O-A-K of I-N-C-O-M-P-E-T-E-N-C-E. Sometimes that makes me A-N-G-R-Y. But it is what I do with that A-N-G-E-R. I try to help other people and help myself.

I G-R-E-W up in two W-O-R-L-D-S. The outside world, and the one of family and friends. That is the A-D-V-A-N-T-A-G-E I have. Many just know one W-O-R-L-D, the W-O-R-L-D which says you are an I-N-V-A-L-I-D. I know that I have things to O-F-F-E-R. Since I was very Y-O-U-N-G, I have been told that by family and friends.

I have a wall poster from *My Left Foot*. The message of that film was: keeping going. I make it a P-O-I-N-T to keep going and to keep my E-Y-E on the P-R-I-Z-E. The prize is to chip away at the cloak of I-N-C-O-M-P-E-T-E-N-C-E and to have equal S-U-C-C-E-S-S in my P-E-R-S-O-N-A-L L-I-F-E. In my work L-I-F-E I have P-R-O-V-E-N myself. There are still some H-E-I-G-H-T-S I will S-C-A-L-E, but I also want more of a B-A-L-A-N-C-E. I want what everyone wants: to find someone to make and S-H-A-R-E A L-I-F-E with.

I don't C-O-M-P-A-R-E myself to others. I think it is part of the T-R-I-C-K not to let myself F-A-L-L into that thinking. I have friends without disabilities who are going T-H-R-U much the same things. I have to keep making R-E-A-L-I-T-Y T-E-S-T-S by asking myself is this because of my disabilities or is it just a part of L-I-F-E?

I think 750,000 people have CP. Whether it makes a difference is up to the B-E-H-O-L-D-E-R. As I said, I make a practice of R-E-A-L-I-T-Y T-E-S-T-I-N-G. It seems, if we all did more of the same, we would all be very much better off. When we make those kinds of calls from A-F-A-R, we do not, and cannot, know the person. It is like what the F-O-X said to the little P-R-I-N-C-E. What is E-S-S-E-N-T-I-A-L is I-N-V-I-S-I-B-L-E. To get past the surface and get to know the person is what L-I-F-E O-U-G-H-T to be.

Living with CP is no more of an A-D-V-E-R-S-I-T-Y than having B-L-A-C-K S-K-I-N or being a woman or being G-A-Y. Those C-O-N-D-I-T-I-O-N-S in themselves do not pose A-D-V-E-R-S-I-T-Y. The problem is not anything about me. It is not part of me. It is O-U-T-S-I-D-E of me.

I have my B.A. from G-W. I read a lot without being boastful about it. I majored in U-R-B-A-N A-F-F-A-I-R-S.

People say they cannot understand when I talk. For most of my L-I-F-E I saw that and was made to see it as my problem. But I am not the one who doesn't understand. The problem is not in me, it's out there.

Some people take setbacks personally. They blame themselves when things don't work out the way they want. They believe that people and events, which they have no control over, are controllable. When faced with adversity, they criticize themselves and wonder what they did wrong to bring about their misfortune. Their self-critical attitude is based on their feelings of low self-worth.

Others, however, clearly see the reality of what is happening. Confident people do not take defeat as personal or professional failure, or believe that illness is a sign of weakness. When buffeted about by hardships, illness, or rejection, these people practice what they believe: "To thine own self, be true."

The Honorable Robert H. Bork is currently a John M. Olin scholar in legal studies at the American Enterprise Institute in Washington, D.C. His distinguished career includes a partnership in the Chicago and Washington law firm offices of Kirkland and Ellis; Alexander M. Bickel Professor of Public Law at the Yale Law School; Solicitor General of the United States; acting Attorney General of the United States, and Circuit Judge on the U.S. Court of Appeals for the District of Columbia Circuit. He is the author of *The Tempting of America,* which presents many of his legal and social philosophies.

"I Don't Feel Sorry for Myself"

Robert H. Bork

I got a call from Howard Baker on the last day of June 1987 asking me to meet with the President's counsel, A.B. Culvahouse, the next morning at about six o'clock in a safe house. It was one of the row houses along the west side of Lafayette Square where former Presidents are put up when they come to town. The idea of meeting at six in the morning in that place was so that the press wouldn't see us together.

The next morning we had a conversation about bringing my FBI report up to date. He was primarily interested in knowing whether I had any scandals in my life. Interestingly, in Washington all these scandals have proper names, such as, say, "Do you have the Schmitz problem?"—I just made up that name—if Schmitz is, say, a wife-beater, or do you have the So-and-So problem. It turned out I didn't have any of those problems. I finally said, "Look, I've led a dull life." He said, "That's what we want." Then I went over to my chambers at the Court of Appeals and later that day got a second call from Howard Baker asking me if I would come over and talk to the President. He said if the President liked the idea of nominating me for the Supreme Court, then we would go straight from there to the pressroom and the nomination would be announced. So I went over, chatted with the President, and we went to the pressroom. It was moderately exciting. The truth is, I'd been talked about for that position so long that it no longer had the excitement it otherwise might have had.

In retrospect, if they had reversed Judge Antonin Scalia's nomination and mine, we'd both be on the court today. When I got there Reagan was coming to the end of his term, which meant he was losing political clout on the Hill. He had just been through the Iran-Contra business, and for the first time in his presidency the Republicans had lost control of the Senate. At the same time, opposition groups had worked up a major campaign.

The worst times in my life involve my first wife's death from cancer in 1980. She fought the disease for over nine years. That was a much harder thing to live through than this turned out to be. However, it may have prepared me for handling the difficulties this time.

The battle was really about political control of the Supreme Court. The left, the ACLU, People for the American Way, and others, have a political agenda they want the courts to legislate. They want the death penalty to be declared unconstitutional, although it's mentioned four times in the Constitution as being available. They want welfare payments turned into a constitutional right rather than a legislative grant. They have a variety of positions about sexual rights, a subject not addressed by the Constitution. Lloyd Cutler, who is a certified liberal and who supported me, said they would rather take a chance on somebody who might give them some of what they wanted than somebody who certainly wouldn't. That's what it was about.

The Constitution has various provisions that deal with very different subject matters, but there is a text there. And there is a history to that text so that you can discern what values are intended to be protected and what values are intended to be left to democratic processes. The Constitution gives us the freedom to govern ourselves democratically unless it states otherwise. A Justice has to vindicate the provisions of the Constitution. In applying them to unforeseen circumstances, he must make sure that the values the founders intended to have protected remain vital in today's different society.

"Original understanding" is the way we treat all legal documents. If you apply that to a contract, a will, a statute, or a Supreme Court opinion you ask yourself, "What did the people who made the contract, will, statute, or Supreme Court opinion understand themselves to be saying and want us to do?" The Constitution is the only one to which "original understanding" has become controversial.

The Constitution is the trump card in American politics. Once a court speaks to a Constitutional issue, whether it speaks truly or not, the democratic process is at an end. That's the last word in our politics, which is why people want control of the courts and also why they don't like the philosophy of the "original understanding" if they want the court to do things that are not in the Constitution. Both sides have tried for control repeatedly in our history: conservatives and liberals, Democrats and Republicans. Prior to 1937 we had a conservative activist Supreme Court that enacted conservative principles that are not in the Constitution. For the last half century, however, the Court's activism has been liberal. For example, look at *Roe* against *Wade*. There is nothing in the Constitution that even remotely deals with abortion either way. If we think it's a good idea, there's no problem. Just pass a law allowing it. The trouble is, we really aren't convinced one way or the other about abortion, and we keep fighting over it. If the Court steps in and says it has the superior morality and lays down the rules for us, that's improper.

There are a number of liberals, and certainly almost all of the people to the left of conventional liberals, who want to use the courts as a power weapon because they can't get their results through democratic processes. Conservatives once behaved in that way, and I'm sure there are a lot of conservatives who would like to behave that way again if they could get hold of the courts. So it's not uniquely a liberal sin.

Many liberals supported me, and many of them didn't. A lot of conservatives did. I think Reagan was sincere when he said what he wanted was judges who would interpret the Constitution and not make it up as they went along. I think he wanted to change the nature of the court, but I don't think he was asking for a conservative activist court.

There is a cultural war in this country, and that cultural war, needless to say, is reflected in the law, and the law is one of the weapons in that war. I became the focus, for a time, of that war. I knew it was happening. On the whole, like the man who was ridden out of town on rail, if it wasn't for the honor of the nomination, I'd rather not have gone through it.

My nomination became symbolic. The whole thing turned into a fiasco. It was hysteria. The groups went into a feeding frenzy like sharks.

When I was young, I got a lot of lectures from my mother about being your own person and not being swayed by peer pressure and others' opinions: "Listen to them", she'd tell me, "but don't go a way you aren't convinced is the way to go". That may have been a major influence on me.

My wife said that one of the things she thought helped me was that I saw with absolute clarity what was happening and what the problem was. I think it helps you to deal with adversity by putting it in proper perspective.

It was a straight-out political battle and I lost. I don't accept the judgment of Teddy Kennedy as to the kind of person or judge I am, so it doesn't bother me in that sense. I have a chapter in my book contrasting the charges with the facts. My public record as a judge and as solicitor general doesn't bear out the charges against me at all. I was disgusted that people would say the things they did. For example, Planned Parenthood ran a full-page ad in which it said, among other things, that I had ruled that a zoning board could properly tell a grandmother she couldn't live with her grandchildren because she was not part of the nuclear family. I know the case. It's Moore against the City of East Cleveland. It was decided by the Supreme Court six or seven years before I even became a judge. I never dealt with the case; I never wrote about it; I've never said anything about it. They just decided to throw the charge in there while they were at it. Teddy Kennedy's "Bork's America" speech portrayed me as someone who would force women into back-alley abortions, require blacks to sit at segregated lunch counters, allow rogue police to break down citizens' doors in midnight raids, and much more.

When I heard that, I thought it was so wild nobody would believe it. There was not a word of truth in it. A couple of reporters in town told me that the speech was such overkill that it would do me more good than harm. What I didn't realize was that the opposition was going to keep making recklessly false charges. It was just as wild from then on. After a while it began to sink in. To my knowledge, this was the first all-out national political campaign against a judicial nominee in our history. The accuracy of the charges being made, I thought, would have provided a good story for the press. However, the reporters just repeated the charges whether they were true or not.

I don't think judicial nominations are supposed to be political campaigns, and I don't think judges are supposed to be political. I decided I wasn't going to contribute to what was obviously a political campaign, so I stayed off the air. When I talked to the print media, I would not discuss any issues. In terms of winning the nomination, that was probably a mistake. But in terms of how a judge should behave, I think I was right. I suppose if it happened again, I might decide, Well, if they're going to play it this way, the only thing you can do is answer. Nobody else was answering at the time. I don't think my decision was naïve. It was a judgment about how judges should behave.

Some people criticized my performance before the Committee, but I don't think a judge ought to do an Ollie North. The members of the Committee would point out how terrible it was that I would vote a particular way, and I would try to explain why. Regardless of my response, they'd just, in essence, say again, "It's terrible!" I am told that the polls were much more favorable to me with people who watched the hearings on C-SPAN and much less favorable with people who saw only the nightly network news. Lichter and Lichter, who do analyses of the media, analyze tag lines on stories because they think that's where the question of bias will show. They said I had the highest score of any issue they've ever tracked: one hundred percent negative on all three networks. It certainly didn't appear that I had much of a chance.

The nomination could have been won if the White House had been organized enough to have Reagan come out swinging; but the White House staff was not prepared for an assault of such a nature and magnitude. No one had ever seen a campaign like it before. Meeting it would have been difficult because the opposition groups had been preparing and raising money for some time. The White House treated the matter as it would a routine confirmation—courtesy calls on senators, for example. Reagan did lobby Arlen Specter on an airplane ride, to no avail. But it wasn't until September that the President made telephone calls to senators. It was by then far too late. In any event, the staff kept Reagan at his ranch, probably because the administration was still smarting from Iran/Contra. The office of the President's legal counsel was the most active and helpful part of the White House staff. The Department of Justice did a lot of good work but had to keep a low profile because the Attorney General, Ed Meese, was unpopular on Capitol Hill—most undeservedly, I may add.

The Democrats had regained control of the Senate for the first time in Reagan's administration; this was their best opportunity to hand him a major defeat, and they took full advantage of it.

I don't feel like a victim. I don't feel sorry for myself. I lost a dirty political battle in which only one side was fighting. It was a pretty painful experience. I got to the point where I couldn't read the newspaper. I'd come down in the morning sometimes and ask my wife to hand me just the sports section.

I saw what happened as a rejection due to a political campaign. I didn't take the rejection as a legitimate judgment of either me or my ideas. You do your best to make sure your ideas are as correct as you can make them, and that your integrity is as solid as you can preserve it, and you don't let the rest of it bother you too much. There's no point in getting thrown off stride by your enemies if you think you're right.

The opposition put everything into question they could, including my integrity. With some people my reputation was damaged. With others it went up. The chance to demonstrate the way I think a judge should decide cases and how he should reason was denied me. On the other hand, I may have reached more people with my book than I would have with opinions that comparatively few people read. The book was a positive thing that came out of the situation. Most of it is about the law, the way the court behaves, the way the court should behave, the academic community, and so forth. I'd been meaning to write it for about fifteen years, but I never had the time. That's the reason I left the Court of Appeals. I never would have written it if I'd stayed there, for lack of time and energy to do both jobs at once.

I would rather have been confirmed—there's no doubt about that. On the other hand, I don't have a very glamorous picture of life on the Court. When I was prominently mentioned back in the 1970s when I was solicitor general I had seen enough of the Court not to overestimate the pleasures of being a Justice. For another thing, we had kids going to college at the time and it would have been a disaster financially. As my wife put it, "I don't want you to have the job, but I don't want any son-of-a-bitch turning you down either."

I heal pretty fast, though there are some people who behaved disgracefully and whom I will not speak to again. I don't go around thinking about them. I don't sit around feeling bitter about them; however, I'm not going to forget and talk to them as if we were the buddies we once were.

My opinion of Senator Kennedy did not go down during that period; it was already as low as it could be. I don't know why I should forgive him. My wife, who is extremely devout, would say it's the Christian thing to do. I have a very low opinion of the man, and I can't think of anything that would raise it. But I do have peace of mind. There's no problem about that.

You may recall the firing of Archibald Cox. That was a period of enormous stress. At the time, I recall feeling that I had a duty to something outside of myself, not just the President or the Department of Justice but to something intangible; it helped me to do what I thought was right. I never quite identified what that something was, yet I often feel it. Whether it's spiritual or not, I don't know. It's as if there is something or someone judging me. My idea is to try to do the right thing as best as I can see it. And I think I did the right thing. In the case of the death of my wife, there was nothing I could do. We were facing a disease that couldn't be stopped. In the case of the Cox firing, and in my nomination, there are things I could have done; some things I did do. Maybe I'm a little stronger than I was going in.

The quality of my life today is very good. Professionally, I'm in as much demand as I ever was, which is fortunate. Many more people know me than did before, which means that I have opportunities to speak, and that people read what I write who might not have done so before.

My second wife, Mary Ellen, was a nun for fifteen years. She didn't leave the order because she had a problem with her faith. She said she thinks one reason I came through so well was that she had everybody and his brother praying for me. She says, "Someday you're going to have to acknowledge that." She was very good throughout the whole thing. She wasn't used to viciousness of that order, but she saw the situation more clearly partly because of the way I explained it. I think my children were exceedingly hurt. They couldn't believe what was being said. They were more upset than either my wife or myself.

Pain and suffering seem to be an inevitable part of life. In practical terms, my wife says you get through purgatory faster if you behave well. I don't know what purpose adversity serves except to get you ready for the next episode. It's inevitable and we all have it coming, even if it's death. I'm hoping at least for purgatory.

Strength and Purpose

Philosophy, a search for truth through logical reasoning rather than factual observation, lends itself to a study of adversity, pain, and suffering. Who am I? Why am I here? Where am I going? These are the ultimate questions life poses. These are normal questions to ask when we encounter misfortune. Other central questions are: Where do pain and suffering fit into human experience? Do they have a purpose?

A by-product of suffering is growth. Searching within ourselves for answers, we often stumble on to new awarenesses about ourselves. In the process of self-examination, we are led to new levels of self-discovery, which in turn shape our *raison d'être* —our reason for living.

Without purpose and meaning, there is no reason to exist. We need to have a sense of not only living our own lives, but contributing to the lives of others as well. To know we make a difference, and to be recognized and appreciated for our effort, make us realize that we count.

Paul Weiss, Ph.D., is a Sterling Professor Emeritus of Yale University and a former visiting Heffer Professor of Philosophy at the Catholic University of America in Washington, D.C. He has been a visiting professor at the University of Southern California, University of Denver, and Earlham College in Richmond, Indiana. He is the author of thirty books, including *Reality, Nine Basic Arts, The God We Seek, Modes of Being, First Considerations, Sport: A Philosophical Inquiry,* and the newly released *Creative Ventures.* He is the recipient of five honorary degrees, the most recent of which is from Boston University. He is currently writing a book titled *Being and Other Realities.*

"We Need Obstacles In Order To Be"

Paul Weiss

My wife died many years ago, after a long illness. She was suffering from throat cancer. We had two children, one in college, the other pre-college. I continued a trip that she and I were planning, but I had to give up my house and take care of my children. My daughter, a freshman, was emotionally affected, a state that continued for a considerable time. My answer to all such problems has always been: "Now is the time for me to be very cool. Now I have to be in complete control." I don't allow my emotions to get in the way, but try to see what must be done. Since I'm human, those emotions were still there, but suppressed. Two or three months later, I may be walking on the street and a thought will rise suddenly and I'll fall.

When my daughter was in difficulty, I tried to see what must be done to take care of her. When my wife was thought to be dying, I got in touch with leading physicians. I was teaching at Yale at the time. We heard that the best doctors for her illness were at Harvard. I hired an ambulance to take us to Cambridge, and we stayed there for some weeks. Others took over my classes and I focused on the issue.

Whatever experience I've ever had of a so-called tragic kind, I have suppressed the emotions and had them come to expression later, without my expecting them. I did fall down when the thought of my wife's death surfaced at an unexpected time, suddenly and long after that situation was over. I am always surprised by the later expression of it. I've always thought of myself as being thoughtful and considerate of people, and concerned about them. It's when tragedy comes that I get cold, and stand away, while others are excited, anxious, and worried. I'm not recommending this. I am making an autobiographical remark.

Somebody has to know what to do in these situations. The downside is twofold: you don't have the purgation that others undergo, and you have a delayed experience. What you actually do not have, if I may say it paradoxically, is a kind of enjoyment of the emotion at that time and, therefore, a kind of a purification and clarification.

Adversity is the encounter with an obstacle too great to overcome, standing in the way of the achievement or maintenance of an objective. We're always faced with obstacles; we live in a world where there are always things in the way. Only when they become overwhelming do they constitute adversity. This is not unrelated to tragedy.

I am not only a body, I am a private being. Pain is privately felt. Adversity need not involve pain; it may end with the overwhelming of an individual and his values. It means "against": a severe case of it. Free in myself, I live in a world where I am pulled down by gravity, held in by the sun, by the rain, needing food. I am free, yet I'm stopped everywhere. When the block becomes so great that I cannot function, or when I cannot realize or maintain precious values, the situation is adverse.

Adversity can be tragic since it may result in the loss of a precious value. Not every kind of unforeseen or undesirable occurrence is adverse or tragic. A divorce may be a great relief. Sometimes a death is a blessing. The eruption of a volcano is a natural occurrence; it's one of the ways in which the earth acts, but the volcano can destroy life and property, and will to that extent be a tragic event.

Adversity is facing an obstacle you cannot overcome, preventing you from protecting or promoting the values you want. It is not identifiable with evil.

Evil involves intent; it is a form of wickedness, the outcome of a desire to reduce value or to engage in acts that will do so. An illustration, from Dostoyevsky's *The Brothers Karamazov:* a general has a dog and a little boy throws a stone at it. The boy is with his mother. The general makes the little boy take off his clothes and run like an animal. With the mother watching, the general takes his gun and kills him. That's an evil act. The general has wantonly destroyed what had great value.

There's nothing evil in a hurricane killing people. It certainly is regrettable and terrible. If you want to, you could say it's tragic.

Evil is backed by a purpose. The tragic, in contrast, involves an uncontrolled loss of value. Disease, cancer, AIDS—none of these are evil. Evil has a moral tonality to it. They are tragic, regrettable. To speak of them as evil is to personalize them. It is in the nature of things that there be pain and suffering, but not that there be evil.

This is an imperfect world; it could not be perfect without denying that God is perfect, for you cannot have two perfect beings. If there is no God, there is a just plurality of occurrences, sometimes of benefit, sometimes not. I am not religious.

Pleasure, like pain, is transient. It allows one to escape oneself. It is a kind of innocence accompanying an involvement with what heightens one's faculties and makes experience richer and more inclusive. The dominant view in the Western world has always been reason, rationalism, control. Both pleasure and pain challenge that control. Even though pleasure is the opposite of pain, it has not always been looked at favorably, because you are not allowing yourself to be controlled by virtues or your mind.

Pain and suffering are unescapable aspects of human life. They are part of the price you pay for your entrance into it. The remainder is paid by your exit.

I'm not worried for one second about my death. It's what I have to pay for my admission. I first learned that when I took elementary logic, for I was then taught that "all men are mortal." Why fuss about the fact? I ignore it.

Three years ago I had two crushed nerves in my back. The operation was a complete success. However, they let me lie in the hospital and nobody checked that I was lying there for five or six days, and the blood didn't go into my hip. So I lost my hip. The paradox is I do my exercises and I am stronger now than I was three, four, five years ago.

When I was lying in a hospital bed, coming to the conclusion that some doctor had been negligent, and with all my vital signs as low as was possible, I was still at peace. Later, when I was in terrible pain, I said to the visiting nurse, "If you had a pill by which I could end it all, I'd take it right now." She said, "It's lucky that pain can't be remembered, for otherwise no woman would have more than one child." I have forgotten that pain. I know I went through it, but it does not impinge me now. I'm willing to throw in my chips tomorrow or at any time, though I really would like to finish the book I am writing and fulfill other obligations.

All humans have the same incipient set of virtues and vices. Some of us suppress the vices more, some of us carry out the virtues a little further than others do. Our job is to reduce or overcome those vices and encourage those virtues. One man differs from another by the degree of his success in that venture.

Some things are better than others. How should one respond to the loss of the better? The answer lies in one's character: one must learn to be sensitive to the loss and to do what one can to minimize or recompense for it.

Is there good to be derived from pain and suffering? Many so-called wise men speak of pain as though it were a kind of a chastening, a way of reminding them to withdraw from temptation and folly. Some try to gain from its occurrence by treating it as part of the human condition. Or they think there are more important things to do.

It is possible to gain from pain. A drunkard finds he has bellyaches and gives up the pleasure of drinking, because he doesn't like the price he's paying and is going to pay. Many, like him, benefit from their tribulations and trials. They become a little surer, a little more aware. Some become more guarded, some retreat, and some become compassionate. Others become angry at the world while others become defeated. Most undergo pain and suffering, try to live through them, and then go on. Some say, "I'm not going to let anything get me down," and reorganize themselves. I think anybody can do this.

Death sometimes points to the value of life, just as disease points to the value of health. A smooth kind of movement will not readily allow you to recognize the nuances or even the richness of what you're living with. There are some who have all the money they need; there is nothing that they have to struggle against. I'm not recommending that they should suffer, that they be caught up in a tragedy. Still there should be some kind of struggle, if only in the planting of a garden, the writing of a book, or learning how to fence. Some would like to live from one party to another. Theirs is a boring life, with nothing to challenge them. To have all obstacles removed by others is to deny yourself the opportunity to grow. The obstacles, of course, shouldn't be so great that the result is adversity; but also they shouldn't be so minor that one becomes lax or indifferent. We need obstacles in order to be.

The universe knows nothing about our pain and suffering. Would a universe be better if human beings did not suffer? I would say yes, but with a qualification. Sometimes pain provides a notification, telling us that something may be wrong. It warns us, allowing us to prepare to overcome it. A universe without pain would not be good for us because we would then unnecessarily endanger ourselves. Pain is a warning. The degree of it, though, could well be less, and it need not be so frequent.

When people read my thoughts, I would appreciate it if they looked at them with a critical eye. By that time I might have some other views.

Some people say, "Getting older is sad, a great adversity." They don't know what they're talking about. I'm ninety. I have difficulty in hearing and I can't walk very well, but I'm thinking as well as I've ever done. My classes these last years were bigger than they had been, and I think I was teaching better than I had ever taught. I have nothing to complain about. Although I have a problem in hearing and walking, I am quite serene.

Paradoxically, I am stronger now than I was three, four, five years ago, owing in good part to the fact that I continue to exercise. I've had the same glasses I've had for a long time. I have just been to the doctor. He says my vital signs are what they have been for years, and a few are better. So I have nothing to complain about.

Still, age makes a difference. Even after a good night's sleep, I may have to nap for an hour or two. The distance from my thinking to my typewriting is greater than it had been before. My typewriting is not as accurate and my language is not as precise at first as it had been. I have to rewrite and rewrite. But the ideas are better, bolder, and freer than they were before. I think what I'm now writing is my best book.

I would like to go to the movies. I used to walk twelve miles a day. I would like to do that. I can't, but I can do other things. What am I going to do with the rest of my life? Try to be honest, decent, help the young. That will keep me happy.

Strength is a capacity for endurance. One of the dividends of suffering is the universal discovery that we possess a strength within us we never knew we had. Navigating through a difficult episode not only shows us that inner strength is there but convinces us it will always be there to serve us in the future. Overcoming gives us an assurance of personal confidence and value that far exceeds what we thought we possessed before our struggles began.

Larry King is the well-known television and radio broadcaster and best-selling author. His Peabody Award–winning radio show via the Mutual Broadcasting System is heard nightly on over 365 stations. His CNN talk show titled "Larry King Live!" is the winner of more than five Ace Awards for excellence in cable television. His books include *Larry King by Larry King* written with Emily Yoffe; *Tell It to the King*, and *Tell Me More* written with Peter Occhiogrosso; and *Mr. King, You're Having a Heart Attack* written with B. D. Colen. In 1987, he was named Man of the Year by the Washington, D.C., Lung Association and Heart Association. In 1989, he was named Broadcaster of the Year by the International Radio and Television Society. Larry also writes a weekly column for *USA Today*.

"There's a Survivalist Thing About Me . . ."

———

Larry King

There are a few "worst" days in my life. The day my father died was one of them. I was ten years old. You never forget that. He died on June 9, 1944; I learned about it on the morning of June 10. He died late at night working in a plant building ships.

Another worst day was October 3, 1951, when Bobby Thomson hit the home run off Ralph Branca. That was as sad as I've ever felt. I followed every game: I was an intense baseball nut. We were thirteen and a half games ahead on August 11 and I was already dreaming of the World Series, and there was a Giant fan in the neighborhood who taunted me. I really remember no single case of being sadder. When Bobby Thomson and Ralph Branca were on the air with me recently, forty years after the event, those feelings came back.

The day of my heart attack was a really terrible day: February 24,

1987; and the day of the heart surgery, December 1, 1987, was also a terrible day.

Before the heart attack I ate everything I felt like eating. If I liked the cheese, I ate the cheese. I was smoking three packs a day, even though I had been diagnosed in 1980. I had some blockage. I was given some beta blockers to help slow down the heart rate, but other than taking the pills, I didn't stop smoking, I didn't exercise, I didn't follow any regimen.

I had been driven to G.W. Hospital by Tammy Haddad, my television producer, because I was feeling lousy. When somebody there said to me, "You're having a heart attack," what went through my mind was a kind of combined belief and disbelief. That news was told to me by a doctor while I was lying in the emergency room. The first thing I asked him was if I was going to die. He said he didn't know, but there were some good things going for me: I was getting a new drug that stopped blood clotting; it was a right-side heart attack, which generally has a seventy percent survival rate, and I was having the heart attack in the right place. If you're going to have a heart attack, have it in the hospital.

I saw all these people running around and injecting things in me. The pain was not in my chest; it was in my arm going down the right shoulder, right elbow.

There was a feeling of me sitting on the ceiling watching all this. This was something I've seen in movies. Could this be happening to me? I had terrible pain. My immediate thought was: make the pain go away, make the pain go away. As soon as the pain went away, which was maybe ten or fifteen minutes after he'd said "You're having a heart attack," some resolve took over and I did not think I was going to die. I associated pain with "terrible," pain going away with "good," even though we were still in an emergency situation.

The doctors did an angioplasty the next day; they went in with the balloon, I was not scared. Once the pain stopped, I felt that I was going to come through it, so I remember having confidence.

I stopped smoking that day; I've never smoked since. I don't even take credit. I don't reach for them. I don't want one if I see someone else smoking; I never think about it.

However, after a couple of months I went off the exercise program. I started to eat the wrong foods. I certainly wasn't doing the right things. I told myself smoking was the reason for my heart problems, and I started to go back into old habits. In September, I had some chest pain and the doctor told me, "You're going to need surgery." I put it off; I scheduled it for December. If there's one tip I would give people who are told they need heart surgery, it's to have it—don't wait. Those months of waiting were terrible. I thought there would be some cure or something.

The afternoon I woke up after the surgery, I made a determination that I never wanted to be in a hospital again. So I became Joe Great Patient. That was from the minute I opened my eyes and the nurse told me, "You did very well." I started an exercise program that I still do every day for thirty minutes. I watch what I eat. My weight, which I think was 190 when I had the heart attack, is now at 163, and it rarely fluctuates more than two pounds. I don't veer off. Maybe I'll have Chinese food once a week and the oil in that may be wrong, but other than that I don't eat cheese, I don't eat dessert, I just watch myself. I do my treadmill every morning. You could say a quintuple bypass realigned my thinking.

When you lose a father early, you always fear dying. I still fear any pain I associate with heart. If I get a headache now, I wonder about my circulatory system. I've become very pain conscious. So any little pain, I jump.

The hardest thing to change is personality. Traffic jams bother me, things I can't control bother me, the plane circling over the airport and we're going to be up another twenty minutes bothers me. I still get anxious. But I also know that I'm doing everything else right. I'm not smoking, I'm eating correctly, I'm exercising. I know that avoiding stress is part of it. However, I have one fortunate break—work is no stress to me. Going on the air is the easiest part of my day. After my heart attack, I was back on the air in four weeks, and after surgery, also four weeks. The doctor said that's the key, because most people have a lot of stress at work and I have none. My work doesn't create an atmosphere of nerves.

Now I still have a classic A-type personality. I react to things; I look for immediate gratification; I like to have the decision now; I don't like to wait. But you can't change everything. Those personality aspects are what make me me. In every other area, I have become very aware of my own mortality—that we're only here for a period of time has become very clear in my consciousness.

I went through a time of depression, mood swings, or blues after the surgery. It didn't affect my exercise, but what happened to me is pretty common after bypass surgery. I'd start to cry and I didn't know why. Maybe it's because someone else touched your heart or maybe it's the emotion dealing with the heart, but doctors have noticed that it occurs more with heart surgery as opposed to brain surgery or cancer surgery. With heart surgery they notice, in men mostly, a post-surgical blues, where you get the weeps. I was flying on a plane to Florida with Alexander Haig and Gene McCarthy, and I just started crying. Haig had had the surgery and he told the flight attendant, "Don't worry, they all do this."

Now with my brother who had the heart surgery, it lasted in him six months. He had a lot of post-surgery depression; with me, it lasted only two months. It would occur once every three days and sometimes last ten minutes, sometimes an hour. I'd just cry. I didn't have to be talking about it; I could be at a ball game.

If I had to do it over again, I wouldn't have my daughter Chaia with me the night before the surgery. I'd have her come the day of the surgery. I don't know if it was tough on her, but it was tough on me. You know that the next morning they're going to cut your chest open. And I was thinking, Is this the last time I'm going to see her?

Nowadays I'm much more open with her, and also more trusting. I don't get as nervous about where she is. She's twenty-four now, and if she doesn't call me when she said she'd call, I don't get uptight at all. I've leveled off to a really nice father-daughter relationship. It's very easy today, but in the past it was bristling and nervous on my part.

With an experience like this, I think you're totally changed for the better. There's no change for the worse unless you're a little more pain conscious—if that could be considered worse. Just the awareness of mortality is a major change for the better that I can't even put into words. I'm just different. Everything about me is different. There's not a day goes by that I don't think about it.

I was what you would call a major-league smoker. I had a smoker's mentality. Smoke ruled me; I didn't rule it. The day of the heart attack was the complete opposite. I feel as if I've never smoked in my life. I watched people smoke and I don't know how I ever did it. Now that's a major turnaround.

I look at fat people now and wonder how could I have been overweight. I had a potbelly. Diet and exercise changed a lot of other things. When you start to slim down, you feel better. You wear brighter clothes; you take care of yourself better; you look better; and people say you look good. When people say you look good, you feel a hundred percent. You want to look even better. It's an ongoing thing.

I've had my share of adversity. My father's death, financial problems, job loss, divorce, health problems. I've had people who have a lot of faith tell me that I'm very spiritual, even though I don't feel it. People who are really believers think there's a spirit in me. I do know this: I have a comeuppance—I do have a sense of getting up off the floor. I trace a lot of that to my roots in Brooklyn, which was a special place to me. I'm doing a book now called "Growing Up in Brooklyn," and I went back and retraced all my steps. It was an incredible thing to go back through the old neighborhood where I was born, where I was when my father died, the store he used to own, the little bar-and-grill, the house I grew up in—stories and stories and memories of Brooklyn. When you think about Brooklyn and the people who came from there in that era, there's a lot of that in me.

There's a survivalist thing about me that is inherent and came when I was born. That is unexplainable to me. It could be God; I don't know what it is. I've never had proof of it, but there's something in me that gets me back up, some source of energy. My friends and family think that God put something in me that wanted Larry to help and contribute to people. Even though I don't think it's there, it's there.

S ome ethnic groups and nationalities, preconditioned by a heritage of oppression and struggle, may do better with their backs against the wall than those who have lived easier lives.

Americans, who are insulated from the rest of the world by better living conditions and by geography, fail to appreciate how people in distant lands have the strength to triumph over natural disasters, impoverishment, oppression, war. Those people seem to find whatever it takes to exist, to survive and live.

Socheat Hak is a mental-health worker for the Southeast Asian Support Center at St. Joseph's Hospital in Providence, Rhode Island.

"I Was Not Afraid to Be Killed"

Socheat Hak

My wedding was supposed to be in March 1970, but there was a coup and Cambodia changed to a republic. I came back to Phnom Penh, where I had lived before, when the Viet Cong evacuated the place in Siemreap Province where I was teaching. In June, my parents were caught in another city, so they sent a letter to my sister telling her to arrange my wedding, even though they could not be there. I was teaching elementary school and my future husband was a teacher as well. At that time the new government was looking for people to volunteer for the army, so he became a soldier. We got married in June 1970.

My husband, Hong, led a small group of soldiers and lived in another city about fifty kilometers from Phnom Penh. After we got married, I went there only once. He came back once a month, stayed for a week, and then went back. We had three children. I was not happy at that time because he was away. My mother-in-law had to take care of my babies when I went to work. She had three teenage children herself, and we all stayed together in a house I rented. In 1973, my husband moved back to the city and he became a teacher again. We loved each other and had a good marriage. We lived peacefully together.

In 1975, the Khmer Rouge took over the country. They forced people to leave all cities, including Phnom Penh. Only the people who worked for the government of Pol Pot stayed. The reason they gave was they were afraid that the government of Lon Nol was going to come back to bomb the city. The Khmer Rouge took over the capital in the afternoon and forced people to leave that night. The entire city cleared out. There were thousands of people leaving. We could not choose where we wanted to go. A few days before that, my parents, my sisters, and three brothers moved into my house because they didn't feel safe in theirs. When we left the city, we all left together; we had to walk.

We took National Route 3, but when we got to Takeo Province we saw only rice fields. But we needed a place with fertile ground to grow vegetables to help us to survive. My extended family tried several different places. The Khmer Rouge didn't want us moving around, but there were lots of people on the streets and they could not watch everybody. We finally crossed the Mekong River and we got to Kompong Cham Province. It was a place where we could grow everything and also work in the rice field. The place where I lived was called Raksmey Romdas, or Chinese Village, because a lot of Cambodian Chinese lived there. I was not allowed to work as a teacher. I didn't know anything about farming. The Khmer Rouge leader forced everybody to farm the land.

When we crossed the Mekong River, my father and mother decided to stay behind with my mother's sister. My father was seventy-nine years old at that time. My mother was thirteen years younger. The rest of my extended family, including my husband and me and our three children, continued to walk toward the village where my husband was born. We stayed with my sister-in-law, who had a house there.

In less than a week, the Khmer Rouge took my husband away. When he was in the army, he was stationed where we were now living, so they knew that he was a soldier. The Khmer Rouge came to the house in the early morning. We were eating together. Our children were four, three, and two years old. The Khmer Rouge told my husband that he had to go to study politics. Everyone knew that when the Khmer Rouge took people away, nobody came back. My husband believed that since the war had ended and only the Khmer Rouge existed, there would be no more killing and we could stay there.

The man who took my husband was the leader in that district. I believed hopefully that my husband wouldn't be killed. However, I think my husband thought he might be killed. He was very nervous; he was so afraid. There were three men that day, including my husband, who were taken by the Khmer Rouge. They just walked away. After that, I never saw him again. He was only twenty-seven years old at that time.

The old people who had lived there under the Khmer Rouge since

1973 never believed my husband would come back. They thought he would be killed. Since the Khmer Rouge had taken over and there was no other side to fight them, I hoped he might be alive. After a week, I knew he had been killed. It was painful the day he left; it is still painful even now.

When he was first taken from me, I didn't feel I could continue to live. The wives of the other two men and I kept meeting to talk to each other. Those women helped me to feel better because we talked about the same thing, the loss of our husbands. I felt that the other people were afraid to be my friend because they might be killed if they got involved in the situation.

After my husband was taken away, I didn't do some work that the Khmer Rouge wanted me to do. They wanted me to go into the fields and sometimes I refused. I was not afraid to be killed. I said to myself, "What does it matter if I am killed?" I actually wanted to die.

I stayed at this place and farmed until 1979. That was the year the new government of Hun Sen came and chased the Khmer Rouge out of the country. Between 1975 and 1979, about three million people died in Cambodia. Some of them were killed. Others died of starvation. All of the soldiers who didn't hide or lie about their position were murdered as well. There were more deaths in the upper and middle classes than in the lower class.

I started to feel better when I was busy working. I had friends to talk to and people who cared about me. I started eating better and slept better. My mother-in-law would stay home to take care of the children. The Khmer Rouge didn't let young children work, so the elderly stayed in the village to baby-sit them. In the dry season, we had to dig canals. When the rain started, we worked in the rice fields. Hundreds from my village worked in the fields.

We never had enough food to eat. A lot of children died from malnutrition. They got diseases very easily. There was no doctor or proper medicine to cure them. The Khmer Rouge had some medicines, but they didn't know how to use them. Most of the children and the elderly died from starvation. Many people got swollen and became yellow before they died.

In 1977, my three children died. My tears came out non-stop. My mother-in-law and my husband's relatives were so scared that the Khmer Rouge would take us all away and kill us because I was sobbing so loudly. When my husband was taken away, and when my children died, I prayed that they would go to the next life and go to a peaceful place.

The people who were too afraid to steal, go out, or cheat starved. I had to learn to steal and lie. I did not steal anyone's property but I did steal chicken, potatoes, and corn. Many people stole to survive. If we had gold or jewelry, we sold it to buy food, too. We ate everything that we could find; we didn't care about germs.

In 1977, I heard another group from the south was going to take over the country, so there was great hope. At that time the Khmer Rouge moved people again. Hundreds of people from about three districts, especially the families of former army soldiers were collected to be moved. They lined up in silence carrying their small sacks of clothes and their young children on their shoulders. Those people were taken by bus. No one knew what happened to them.

I heard the Khmer Rouge were killing people with hoes. They hit them in the back of the neck. They didn't shoot them. There was a prison near where I worked where they kept the people who did things against the regime. One day I saw a lot of blood on pieces of cloth lying on the ground there.

In 1979, we knew that a new group had come into Cambodia to chase the Pol Pot regime out of the country, so we chose to go back to Phnom Penh. My parents had nine children in 1975, including children from my father's first wife who had died. All of my family worked for the government so it was hard to survive. After the war, only three of us, my two brothers and I, survived. My father died a month after my husband was killed. My mother thought that he was so depressed he died at night in his sleep.

I started to teach again, and I came down with TB. One night in 1983 I was bleeding. I didn't go to the hospital right away as I should have, and I almost died. I stayed in the hospital five months.

I knew a lot of people who escaped from the country, so when I recovered from my illness I felt I should leave the country too. I didn't trust that my TB was completely treated and I also felt people were afraid to be near me. I didn't trust that Cambodia would be in peace either. I thought the Khmer Rouge might come back and take over again, and I didn't trust the new Vietnamese-backed government.

I had one month of sick leave after I was discharged from the hospital for recovery from my illness. I took this opportunity to plan my escape. One of my nieces who lived near the border of Cambodia and Thailand hid me in her house. I had forged a letter from a leader of my district allowing me to visit her. I could have been caught and put in prison for doing that. I paid a guide to lead me to a refugee camp in Thailand.

I took my other niece, Kahna, my brother's daughter, who was ten years old, with me. Kahna and I reached a border camp in Thailand called Site II, and then we moved to Khoa-I-Dang Camp in December of 1983. The camp was run by the United Nations High Commission for Refugees. That was another hopeless time. At that time, the UNHCR didn't register new refugees, so we couldn't become legal refugees. The guards were looking for illegal refugees every day to send them back to the border. At that time I didn't have much money left to buy food and I didn't have support from the relief agencies.

We were illegal for eight months. I didn't know anybody. Finally I went to live with a family and stayed at their house. I had no support from this family. One day, I found the cousin of one of my friends. I knew her from Cambodia. I went to her house every day to find ways to become a legal refugee, to find a job, and to resettle in a third country.

My goal in escaping from Cambodia was to go to France because my sister-in-law wanted me there. As I spent time in the camp, however, many people said that living in France was harder than living in the United States, because refugees could find jobs easier in the U.S. They also said the standard of living in the U.S. was better than in France. My sister-in-law agreed with that and suggested that I resettle in the U.S. I found my brother's friends in Rhode Island and asked them to sponsor me. I could not have cared less which of the two countries would take me. Whichever one would take me first, I would go. I just wanted to leave the camp as fast as I could.

After eight months the UNHCR announced that anyone in the camp could register as a legal refugee, so my niece and I did. In the camp we again didn't have enough food to eat, and also it wasn't safe at night because of robberies and rapes by people from outside the camp. At night I had to be ready to run.

After I became a legal refugee, I worked in a pre-natal clinic in the morning and taught third-grade students in the afternoon. I sometimes took English as a second language class and also used my clinical experience in the delivery room at night. In Cambodia, I had already learned English, but I never used it. In the camp, to get a job working with Westerners you had to speak English or French.

In October 1986, my niece and I were called to leave the Khao-I-Dang Camp to go to Chon Buri, Phanat Nikom, to prepare to leave for the United States. We had five months of orientation classes. Thai teachers taught refugees about going to the store, how to buy things, how to be in an airplane, and how to order something to eat. They also taught us how to go on job interviews and where to go to get help. Then we had to have a complete physical exam including immunization.

I flew to the United States. I had never flown before. It was so exciting. My niece was with me. We landed somewhere in Europe; then we landed in New York and then took another airplane to Rhode Island. From New York to Rhode Island the refugees were at the back. Three families had come over from Thailand with us. That was March 18, 1987. In 1987, there were about seven thousand Cambodians in Rhode Island. Now it comes up to almost ten thousand. There are also Laotians, Hmong, Vietnamese, Chinese, and others.

Now I am a mental-health worker. I work with Cambodians who have mental illness or other life problems. From what I know from my Cambodian clients, some of their war experiences were worse than mine. During their escape, some women were raped. A family member of someone I know got shot while trying to escape. In Cambodia, some people were arrested and tortured or they saw their whole family killed in front of them. I lost my husband, my children, my parents, my brothers and sisters, but I didn't see them killed in front of me. A lot of people saw horrible atrocities committed by the Khmer Rouge. I never felt that it could happen, but it did.

I am alive, but my sadness is buried in my heart. I need to talk about it, to let it out. I don't know how I survived that terrible time. Because of my experience, now I lose my concentration, I have poor memory, I forget easily. I miss my country. I miss my family. I can be happy for just short periods of time if I'm with friends or other people I feel comfortable with.

My clients, who went through their own traumatic experiences, are the same way. They have difficulty with their life here. They become so ill. They hear voices or see things no one else sees. They have nightmares, tightness in their chest, or have to take medicine for their depression or anxiety. Some people with relatives here cannot get along, so their new life is painful for them.

I would like to have relatives that I could visit or they could come to visit me. I feel if I had relatives here, I would be happier. The adjustment to the new culture is difficult. I still have language difficulty. It is really hard to fit myself into this new life. However, I am not afraid to ask for help and share my problems. It takes a lot of courage to come here.

Even though I have a better life today than I did under the Pol Pot regime or in the camp, I believe my life in the U.S. is harder than my life before 1975.

When I look back on my life experience, I can see that I suffered extreme stress many times. My husband was taken away and killed. I was separated from all of my family in 1975. The Khmer Rouge forced me to do hard labor and wanted to kill me. I lived for more than three years in refugee camps in Thailand. I came to the U.S., a foreign country. To help relieve my stress, I always found people who had the same stresses and the same problems. We also had the same goals: to support each other and improve our situations. I am lucky that I work in social work with therapists around who give me good advice and techniques to help me. I feel good that I have a job and money to live on. I don't want to depend on someone else to feed me. Working hard is a big step to help relieve my stress. It makes me happy to see the things I have accomplished and the people I can help. I have to go to visit my country sometime, and I might go back to live there when I get old.

Ironically, adversity often assists us in discovering our life's mission. It is not unusual for those with disability or illness to write about or lecture on their ordeal or counsel others. This new direction—an unexpected result of their calamity—spurs them to new heights. They have learned one of life's more difficult lessons: those who bring hope and happiness into the lives of others cannot keep it from themselves.

In adversity, if our being is centered only on what we have lost, then the battle is lost. If our purpose shifts to using our experience and talents to help others, then a new life begins.

Lee Lawrence is an Information and Resource Specialist at the National Organization on Disability. She served as the News and Features Editor of NBC's Dave Garroway's Today Show from 1958 to 1961, and was associate producer of NBC's *Wide, Wide World* from 1956 to 1957. Before her career in television, Lee was staff technical assistant to the renowned theater producer Billy Rose. (The National Organization on Disability's information line is 1-800-248-ABLE.)

"I Have a Value . . ."

Lee Lawrence

I had a friend, a gentleman caller; his name was Ray. There was a football game at Columbia University. He was an alumnus and a professor of art. It was a gorgeous day, a day made for football, so we went. My kids were with their father that weekend. After the game there was going to be a big cocktail party, an alumni reunion. He wanted to go and I said, "Look, I can't. I'm not up to it." "All right," he said, "but I want you to come up to the studio. I'm going to be doing a one-man show and I want you to look over my work and give me your opinion of what I've selected." He had the top floor of a brownstone house in New York City on West Seventy-second Street near Riverside Drive. We pulled off to look at the sunset, and that's all I remember. Because of the accident, I have what is called a retrograde loss of memory owing to tremendous physical shock. It's a kind of amnesia.

Ray told the police that we went to his apartment and I looked at the paintings. He fixed dinner, and after dinner, he said, we played several games of Scrabble. "Lee won every one." I had wanted to go home, but he said, "Why don't you just stay here?" This was all on the up-and-up. He had his own sleeping quarters in the front of the apartment and a couch in the studio. So I went to sleep in the studio, and he went to sleep in the living room. Because it was near Riverside Drive, he used earplugs so the traffic noises wouldn't bother him. The next thing he knew, the police were banging on the door asking him if there was a woman in his apartment. He pointed and there I wasn't. "Where is she?" he asked. "In the ambulance downstairs."

An actor in the garden apartment had let his dog out in the morning and the dog raised a ruckus. The actor went to see what was unusual, found my body, and called the ambulance. My body was found over ten feet away from the edge of the building. There was no way in the world I could have jumped or fallen. Nijinsky couldn't have done it either. So I had to have been thrown. A year or so later, some of my buddy journalists decided they were going to find out who did this terrible thing. And they discovered that there was an escapee from a mental hospital whose social aberration was to beat up a woman, not attack her sexually, and "throw her away." In the same immediate neighborhood, within two blocks, there had been several similar incidents without severe injury. The man could have been on the outside fire escape of the building, seen me asleep, come in, done a scene, and then pushed me. Ray didn't hear it because he was a hundred and fifty feet away and wearing earplugs. When a journalist asked the police why they didn't do any investigations, they said they assumed it was a suicide attempt. Suicides are more common in Manhattan than pickpockets. I don't know anything about any prosecution or charges. My understanding is that the man had been taken back into the hospital.

I was in a coma for over six months, from October 8 through the end of March. Toward the end of March, they transferred me from Roosevelt Hospital to the Hospital for Joint Diseases. Five vertebrae were smashed like pancakes. My pelvis was totally shattered. The bones in both legs were broken. My feet were all shattered—the right one very badly. Arm bones were broken. It was thought I probably landed on my feet because the injuries were upthrust. My head was not injured because I fell on grass, not concrete. Nobody thought I was going to live.

During that period of time, I had only split seconds of consciousness. When I moved to the new hospital, I was more conscious. The pain was horrendous. From 106 or 107, my weight got down to 51 pounds. I had no relationship to my body in my mind. I didn't exist. All I was was a big ball of pain. That was before they amputated my leg.

One day, the orthopedic surgeon came in and said to me, "Lee, we have decided that the best thing to do now would be to amputate your leg before the bone infection gets to your knee." Of course, I had to sign papers to give the hospital permission. I remember I asked, "Do I have any choice?" He couldn't handle that. He got up and walked out. He was crying. At one point, I made up my mind I wanted to kill myself. However, I realized I had to get well and get out of the hospital in order to do it.

Dave Garroway came to see me regularly, and finally my ex-husband allowed the kids to come. Various friends came occasionally, but I was very withdrawn. Dave had given me a television set and it was my barrier. It was just me and the television set. I didn't have to be a person.

My room faced the Triborough Bridge. I'm an early riser, always have been. That was very handy on the "Today Show." So one morning I woke up, and I was watching the daylight come. Slowly I began to realize that I did know the beauty of it, and that my mind was functioning. I thought I did have something that was still me, and maybe this was going to be a way to move on in living. That was it. That's truly what happened. It was wonderful. I didn't say anything to anybody, not a soul. It was a very private, deep-down-in-the-core-of-me kind of "whew." "All right, here you come." I could appreciate beauty. I had always loved art very deeply. This one morning it came like a streak of lightening. Morning. "Good morning." Now every morning when I get up, I thank God I'm still here.

There have been lots of big battles that I won psychologically. I had a lot of self-doubt, but I got rid of most of that. I became secure within myself. The accident and recovery had a lot to do with it. It's an acknowledgment of a strength. It had to come from somewhere. I'm alive, as the doctor said, not because of medicine.

I rejected the artificial leg. I kept it wrapped in a towel in my closet and wouldn't put it on until I went to therapy. I'd take it off when I got out of therapy and put it back in my closet. One Sunday, my kids were coming to see me, and my nurse said, "Okay, Lee, you're going to get all dressed up today, and you know what I mean." She always did my hair and fixed me up so I would look nice. She meant I was going to put on the leg; so I did. I was in the wheelchair with a little cover over my lap when my boys came in. They threw their arms around me, "See, we told you you were going to get well. You wouldn't listen, you were so depressed. It takes a lot to keep a mom down, especially our mom." I said, "You know how if you came home from school and you were worried about something, and I said, 'Let's talk about it and maybe we can figure out something so you won't worry anymore?'

Well," I said, "it's my turn. I don't like that leg, it's artificial, it's not me, and I feel frightened of it, really frightened." "Mom, there's something you don't understand. We love *you*, not your leg." "Oh." I had to find that out.

I was a very successful career person, but I was not successful personally. Divorce was the last thing in the world I ever thought would occur. My ex-husband and I had been boyfriend and girlfriend in high school. We got married, and twelve years later, a divorce. I never blamed anybody for anything that went wrong. I always blamed myself—in childhood and in the marriage. This was my fraility. If something didn't work, it was my fault. The accident and the recovery taught me differently. The fact that I lived when the doctors thought I wouldn't gave me the faith to think there was a reason I was alive. The reason was what I am, the person I am. I was here to perform and live. I have a value and it comes through in my work.

Every job I've had since I came back has been to make life conditions better for people who have difficulties. The powers that be laid it out I asked my doctor once, "So why am I alive?" He said, "He wasn't ready for you yet. He still had work for you to do, and because of your incorrigible sense of humor." We are here for a reason, and it's our duty to fulfill it. One of the things that upset me is people who abuse the privilege of the God-given right to be alive.

Since the accident, I've had four surgeries, all connected with the right leg. In 1984, I had surgery on my hip. There have been other medical problems along the way, too. However, the new me has been growing for twenty-five years now. I'm not a discard. I am wanted and I have a purpose.

NOD, the National Organization on Disability, has an 800 number that has been advertised in the print media throughout the country. The ad reads "If you're concerned about people with disabilities and you want to do something to help them, or if you have a problem yourself in dealing with your disability, call this number. That's me.

Bernie Posner, whom I first met when I worked on the *Today Show* and I'm still with today, said, "There's nobody in this world that could do the job but you." For twenty-five years I have been a purveyor of information regarding disability and its many facets to the general public and to specific audiences. There isn't one call or one letter that doesn't get responded to. One of the reasons I can do this job is that I was there.

When I got out of the hospital, believe me, I was in an alien world. I had to learn to live. I'd been in a cocoon for almost two years, and

I wasn't the same person. Certainly I wasn't physically, and a lot in my head wasn't the same either. I'm more comfortable than I ever was before in my life. I used to be absolutely terrified of being alone. Now I enjoy it. This accident made me into a person. I filled in. I do things for myself and with myself that I would never have been able to do before, because I didn't have the confidence. My identity in the past was in the people I loved, like my kids and my husband. Now it's in me. I found out that I am. It's me. People seem to like me, so I guess it's all right.

In the early days, everybody was saying, "Oh, you're a survivor." It got so I really couldn't stand the word "survivor" anymore. Once upon a time, Barney Oldfield, who was a retired Air Force colonel, called me "a gallant lady." Recently I read this definition. "Gallantry: the grace with which one survives appalling experience." After that I didn't mind the word "survivor" anymore.

I was in California with David Garroway, Jr., and we were walking. He was so proud of me. I said, "Oh, how I wish your dad could see me now." And Dave, Jr., said, "He can."

Recovery from calamity takes time. Patience is required. It is human nature to want what we want yesterday, but recovery is a journey and is traveled slowly. Goal-setting and willingness are necessary. Progress becomes our measure of recovery. Small accomplishments affirm our efforts.

The process begins with a decision. Small and large goals are charted. The work begins. The joy of meeting our challenges, a continuing spirit of gratitude, and a mission to serve others give our lives meaning and purpose.

Marie Balter, M.Ed., is a leading advocate for the mentally ill and former Director of Community Affairs at Danvers State Hospital in Danvers, Massachusetts. She is the co-author with Richard Katz of *Nobody's Child*, an autobiography that was later made into a television movie starring Marlo Thomas. She is currently writing her second book and lectures frequently throughout the country.

"I Had To Make A Decision"

Marie Balter

Mother Teresa deals with the hopelessly dying, and I deal with the hopelessly living. The latter are people who are either denied hope by others or deny it within themselves—the chronically mentally ill, the homeless, those who have lost children, those who lose hope because of what happens to them through their environment or through life's experiences. When the movie *Nobody's Child* came out, I anticipated hearing from families of schizophrenic patients throughout the country. I thought that would be the bulk of the mail. It was only five percent. So I broadened my mission. Now my message is for everyone who is in pain. I'm committed to this mission. I believe that God had His own purpose for my life, and I try to fulfill it to the best of my ability. Anybody who thinks Marie Balter could be where she is now, and have done this all on her own, would have to be out of his mind.

When I was in the state hospital, I made a very serious commitment. It wasn't just a reaching out based on pain. It was a commitment: I would not forget those I left behind. The essence of my life now is fulfilling that commitment. God and I one day had a very serious talk in the chapel, and most of it was tears. I was trying very hard to get well for the first time in my life. I was never more serious, yet I was afraid that I might fail. I wasn't looking for a quick miracle; I was looking at my efforts, and was fearful that they might be fruitless. At the time of the conversation with God, over twenty years had gone by during which I was in and out of mental hospitals. When I went in, I was about seventeen and a half.

"I will build an altar unto you, oh God, of the broken pieces of my heart." The brokenness wasn't only my time in institutions, my cancer and my husband's death; the brokenness was also my vulnerability as a person. It was all my life: the pain, the sorrow, the failures, the quarrels with family, the impatience—it was everything. I gave it all to Him to make sense out of in His own way.

My faith's gotten stronger because God has never let me down. I wasn't looking for anything in a personal sense for myself except to serve Him and His people. He's always been there during the difficult moments. I didn't expect that because Marie Balter was twenty years in the hospital, all of a sudden life would be perfect. I still live life. Because you've suffered a lot doesn't mean that you're going to have a utopian life.

A handicapped child, an alcoholic husband, a teenager on drugs, a bad marriage, a lost daughter—all are deep sorrows. When these sorrows come, there's a source that you can go to to get strength to overcome them. That's faith.

It was not foreign to me to have pain and to know that I had to find the way to overcome it, that there was something within myself. That courage within is something grand. The beauty of life is learning to overcome adversity, disappointment, and problems, and the way we do it is by not succumbing, by getting up no matter how many times we are knocked down. If you were to ask me if I would change my life because of my pain, I'd say no, I wouldn't change it one iota. Pain has enabled me to be where I am now and to receive one of the greatest gifts I've ever had. The gift of loving life. I probably wouldn't have had that gift if I'd lived a different life. And I wouldn't be able to pass my experience on. Isn't that what life is about, to be giving to each other? I wouldn't have the empathy, the compassion, the desire to help people through their struggles if I had not lived with that pain myself.

I don't talk a lot about the hospital nowadays, not only because it's difficult, but because people often do not understand that it wasn't all negative. There were some good people there. Trying to keep that fact apparent is very difficult. People want to hear the horror stories. I suppose that's okay; but they color everything by their view of what a state institution is like. There are pictures in my book that are gruesome. But that's not all it was.

My name changed to Marie at six, with my adoption. My biological mother was an alcoholic; I never knew my father. Marie did not see herself as lovable, because there was a lot of rejection in the family. I did not see good in myself. I preferred to be good rather than do anything wrong. When you're living in your home, you're internalizing everything. You're not thinking about what your father and your mother are teaching you. They become a part of you, and that's what you take with you in life. My father lived by very rigid rules, and I was afraid of him. My mother was afraid of my father as well. I can look back now and say there wasn't much to be afraid of. She was the one who taught me to be afraid of him: "You'll see when your father comes home," she'd say. She was not able to correct me herself. He was going to come home and punish me. He was a very stern man in many ways; he was temperamental, and he was abusive to her. As she'd threaten me with my father's anger, I'd remember how he behaved with her. He would strike her. I'd be in bed at night and hear it. I could see through a crack in the door what was happening. But he never struck me.

Yet I had to be afraid because I was being physically abused by my mother. Tying me up in the cellar was her way of discipline; that seemed to be the only way she knew to control a child who had done something wrong. I don't think I ever did anything deserving of such punishment. It might have been answering her back or saying no, which happened, but I was more afraid of my father than of her. Eventually I wound up as a very depressed and confused kid.

What took place back then isn't as likely to happen today, because now we have all kinds of resources for young people; we no longer even accept adolescents in the state hospital. At that time there were no halfway houses. There were no emergency shelters for kids. For the kind of problem I was showing, a person today wouldn't be hospitalized. I didn't want to live in our house anymore. It was oppressive, depressing, and uncomfortable. And I didn't have the tools I needed to make it on my own.

At the hospital I was with other kids my age, which was not so at home. I wasn't allowed to mix with other kids growing up. I was raised as an only child; my stepbrother was years older than I, was not even born in this country, and didn't live with us. In the hospital I had a large peer group. I was part of something. In addition to a peer group, there were people who paid attention to me. At home nobody cared. In the hospital there was a basic sense of love. It was a kind of illusion because the staff was being paid to take care of me. But you take that illusion of love and make it yours. That's enough to capture adolescents.

Within ten days they can be institutionalized, no longer wanting to leave. Institutionalized people have a true dependency upon a system, a hospital, upon people.

A combination of depression and panic attacks had resulted in my being at the hospital. There was a misdiagnosis, too. The doctors labeled it schizophrenia, and that almost cost me my life. Not much was known about panic disorder at that time. In their ignorance, they were giving me medication for schizophrenia, which induced a state of panic. The more panic attack I had, the more psychotic I appeared. The more psychotic I appeared, the more medication they gave me. It was like a psychedelic trip. Everybody's face was distorted. This went on for months. The more they gave me, the worse I got—never realizing that the medicine was doing it, until I got very ill with toxemia. I had liver damage. By the time they took me off the medicine, I was physically debilitated. I'd gone down to eighty-six pounds. I knew then that no matter how sick I was, I either had to die a vegetable—die physically—or fight back. I had to make a decision.

What made me turn around? The suffering was so unbelievable, and the fear of what I was seeing in that unreal world was so bad, that I didn't want any part of it. I decided I wanted to live and fight it. I wasn't able to talk to anybody about this; it was all going on in my head. I was praying. I'd say, "Dear God, I do want to live. I do want to live. I do want to live. Now, how do I do this, God? Tell me. God, give me the answer. How do I do this?" I formulated my whole treatment plan right out of the hospital.

Long before that, I underwent shock treatments, hydrotherapy, and insulin therapy, supposedly to help the depression. During that period, I was in bed for almost two years. In the last year, I started to work to get out. By then I had made my decision to want to get well.

I followed a logical procedure. I started with short-term goals. My larger goal was to get out of the hospital. What did I have to do to achieve that? First of all, I had to get well physically. I'd look in the mirror; I could see my bones. I had to develop physically, and I had to get my mind back. That started by touching things. I began by shuffling cards. The first time I made a bed, it was such an effort, but there was a purpose to it. Nobody on the wards knew what I was doing. They saw me making beds and probably thought, she's getting better. They didn't realize that this was one of my goals. My next goal was to work. I've got to support myself, I thought. I'll try to get into the hospital sheltered workshop—that will be a beginning. That will teach me to be able to go out. The other patients were taking twenty-five-cent bets that I wouldn't even get off the closed ward. That was another goal: to get a job, to get out, to get a place to live were all short-term goals. The long-term goal was getting my degree. The first step was the Associate degree. I knew there was going to be the Bachelor's degree, but I wouldn't worry about that yet. I had very clear, clean-cut goals.

When I came out of the hospital, I had to de-institutionalize myself. What really helped a great deal was going into a community college. I was now in an institution that taught me to be independent. It was all positive, all future, all hope. You do, you accomplish, you meet the challenges of the academic world. There I received the support I needed to gather together the tools I would use later on. I couldn't waste time looking for attention, worrying about whether I was loved or not. I had to support myself and I had to get an education.

It took faith, a lot of hard work, and a lot of support. The kind of hard work I'm talking about is something like forgiveness. Accepting responsibility as opposed to being dependent is hard work. Learning to develop a sense of humor is work, too. You can find a lot of things to be angry about, but there's also a lot of things that can be fun. You've got to learn to do those things, and you don't learn them overnight.

I was married for six years, and they were beautiful years. I still miss my husband, Joe. He had a pulmonary embolism, a blood clot. He had phlebitis and it traveled into his lung. It went to his heart at the end and he died. I'm still losing members of my adopted family; I've lost very close members in the last couple of years. There's still sorrow. Yet I wouldn't change life. And that's the hard work, learning to be able to say that.

I had cancer while I was in the hospital, but the doctors didn't discover it until shortly after I came out, when I was working. I had to make a decision about going back to the hospital to be taken care of—which is not what I wanted. I said, "No. I'm not going back to die in the hospital as a dependent, sick little girl. I'm going to live my life to the fullest I can. How long I live, I'll leave up to God. I'm not going to worry about that."

Viktor Frankl hits it right on target; "For those who are to survive, it's those who have found meaning and purpose." I survived because I had meaning and purpose. Faith helps you get there, but meaning and purpose are the catalyst that gets you moving and keeps you going. Frankl, in his book *Man's Search for Meaning,* found that many of the people who didn't survive Auschwitz were those who had lost their family members and whose lives were bereft of all meaning and purpose. Frankl found meaning and purpose for himself by studying the prisoners, trying to discover why some survived and some didn't.

Having achieved meaning and purpose in my life made all the difference for me. Suffering was not a negative force in my life. It was a tool for me. God gave me Frankl's book; it confirmed what I'd been thinking about my past.

For a person to want to cope with something there has to be a reason. Meaning gives the whole effort its beauty. Purpose gives you every reason to go for it.

Acceptance

Written by Protestant theologian Reinhold Niebuhr, the Serenity Prayer has been used over time by millions in confronting problems. Indeed, we analyze, dissect, and often abuse the message of the prayer, trying to change life to suit us in the face of evidence to the contrary.

The prayer says:

> God, grant me the serenity
> To accept the things I cannot change;
> Courage to change the things I can;
> And the wisdom to know the difference.

The prayer encourages us to seek peace of mind through the insight of knowing when to act or when to accept, and doing so.

The prayer continues with a very spiritual theme:

> Living one day at a time;
> Enjoying one moment at a time;
> Accepting hardships as the pathway to peace;
> Taking as He did, this sinful world as it is,
> Not as I would have it:
> Trusting that He will make all things right
> If I surrender to His will;
> That I may be reasonably happy in this life
> And supremely happy with Him forever in the next.
> Amen.

While many may fight the message of these later lines, the prayer tells us: if you take the world as it is, and live one day at a time, you may be "reasonably" happy now (and "supremely" happy in the afterlife).

Phil Buchanan, J.D., M.A., is a substance-abuse therapist at the Sacred Heart Rehabilitation Treatment Center in Detroit and Memphis, Michigan.

"When We're Upset, We've Got To Reach Out"

Phil Buchanan

I am an addict, so I've felt a lot of pain. I equate fear, anxiety, and demand with emotional pain. I've been sober fourteen years. For the first half of that time, I lived with an attitude that life was supposed to be fair. As a result, I experienced a lot of pain. I have three hundred and fifty stitches in my stomach. My "tattoo" is quite a sight. It's the result of drug abuse, alcohol, worry, and anxiety.

There's a Zen proverb that says, "When the student is ready, the teacher will appear." Pain is the teacher. Marcel Proust said, "To honesty, wisdom, goodness, and truth we make promises. Pain, we obey" when it gets bad enough. To learn to obey pain is an art form. Emotional pain has an absolute purpose in life and it's positive. Pain lets us know something needs to be fixed. Most humans avoid pain until they find the avoidance more painful than facing it.

The goal of life is peace of mind; that's number one. "God, grant me the serenity." Where do we look for God? It's got to be with people. It's other people who are going to tell us who we are, if we listen not so much to what they say, as watch the way they behave toward us. Their behavior will tell us we're important or unimportant, that we're loved or not loved, that we're accepted or not accepted.

All obnoxious behavior is caused by pain. Obnoxious behavior says someone's not getting his way and doesn't know how to ask for help. Demanding behavior is caused by self-centered pain. Did you ever have a toothache? Whom were you thinking about? If you've ever watched a self-centered person, you know he or she is full of unfulfilled self-centered demands. Fear is at the base of it.

No human agency can be the source of our happiness. It can play a part but it cannot be the source. For example, when we start demanding that some relationship be the source of our self-worth, we'll suffocate it. Many relationships are very dependent; they're very painful, too. A lot of emotional pain is tied up with trying to get needs met, making demands, having expectations and jealousy.

Ninety-nine percent of people experiencing emotional pain are so hell-bent to get out of pain they don't look at it. A relationship doesn't work out. There's a divorce. Three years later they're involved in another marriage. If the next relationship turns out to be a mirror of the past, they obviously haven't stopped to examine the pain.

Often when we're in pain we reach out to some addictive agent—work, sex, food, drugs, alcohol, sleep, gambling, exercise, shopping, watching television—to kill the pain. Action's the distraction. Then we end up feeling guilty and shameful. The only way some of us know how to relieve guilt and shame is to go back to the addiction again, which results in more pain.

We have to experience the struggle of working the Serenity Prayer backward in order to learn the value and discipline of the prayer. "God, grant me the serenity to accept the things I cannot change, courage to change the things I can, and the wisdom to know the difference." If we're hurting, there's no serenity in us. When do we think of the Serenity Prayer? When we're upset. So we've got to reach out. To whom? People. We need to learn how to say to others, "Hey, I'm hurting." People don't do that, because they fear rejection It's also the fear of being vulnerable.

"God, grant me the serenity." It's not within us, it's without. The big "I" is demanding something. We're not getting what we want, so we hurt. We need another person to point out what's going on.

If money, power, sex, relationships, or even religion becomes your god, then pain is the result. If I demand that these things make me happy, they won't; they can't. The pursuit of them dooms me. A million dollars doesn't make me happy. Power, sex, and relationships can't make me happy. Religion is worthless if we're all only tied up in rituals, like going to church. We've got to live the message of our religion.

We have to transcend our human demands with other people to gain a conscious contact with God, spirituality, some higher power.

Therein lies serenity. That's the dynamics of "God, grant me the serenity . . ."

Eventually we start to pray and begin to do some of our own spiritual work to understand what are "the things I cannot change." "God, grant me the serenity to accept the things I cannot change." We're not even going to look at acceptance until we've tried to change something. Chances are if you're hurting, something won't change that you've tried to change. Most of us live a lifetime working the prayer backward; if we could change things, then we could accept them. That's not the instruction. The instruction is, first get some peace of mind.

How do you draw the line between accepting what you can't change and changing what you can? Slowly. A person accepts something he doesn't want to accept by hurting enough. What got me into recovery? Pain. I obeyed pain when I came to treatment for my addictions. It was the "courage to change the things I can."

Life's a hell of a challenge. It's got nothing to do with fair or unfair. If something's causing you pain, it's a problem. When it hurts bad enough, you'll listen. Then somebody can help. Fear, anger, excuses, self-pity, and depression are all part of the pain. There's got to be other people who hear your self-pity, and hear your excuses. Feelings need to come out because if they go back inside, whatever's causing the pain is resented; it's refelt over and over. Depression is good because it makes reality clearer and we can no longer hide from our problems. Now you have a choice to make. "To accept the things I cannot change." Something has happened. Usually a loss is there. When we see the loss as ninety-nine percent bitter and only one percent better, we still have a choice. Ain't much of a choice. But if we start living in the one percent, we can turn that into two. The thing we can change is the way we're seeing things. That's your attitude. Your attitude about what is going on is something you can do something about.

Father John Powell, S.J., tells a wonderful story about a butterfly. Under a microscope you can watch a caterpillar try to emerge from a cocoon. It's a three-day process. They say he breaks off fifty times the legs he emerges with. It's very excruciating and painful. If you were to take a scalpel and slit that cocoon and remove the caterpillar to relieve him of the pain, you'd end up with a butterfly that couldn't fly. Pain teaches the butterfly how to get strength from the wings.

To arrive at acceptance—"to accept the things I cannot change"—is a hell of a process. As we begin to experience pain teaching us, we get hope. If we do what is necessary, we can learn from our past. Painful experience can be, in the end, a great teacher.

There is a finality to some losses that leaves no choice but to accept. The death of any special person is crushing. Most would agree, however, that the death of a child is a particularly tragic event. A child's death violates unwritten rules of life. Our grief is not only for our own loss, but for the loss of a life whose promise will never be realized. In such times, we are forced to accept the unacceptable. We share our pain with others and heal through time.

Dominick Dunne is the best-selling author of *The Two Mrs. Gren-villes, People Like Us, An Inconvenient Woman, Fatal Charms and Other Tales of Today,* and *The Mansions of Limbo.* He produced the films *Panic in Needle Park, Ash Wednesday, Play It as It Lays,* and *The Boys in the Band* as well as many television programs, including the series "Adventures in Paradise." He is a widely read contributing editor to the magazine *Vanity Fair.*

"You Have to Go On with Your Life"

Dominick Dunne

Prior to my daughter's death, I had flirted very strongly with the notion of suicide. At that point, I had a major career disaster in Hollywood. It seemed as if I was never going to get up again. I went off to Oregon where I lived in a little one-room cabin in the Cascade Mountains. I was in a state of despair and depression that was constant. To my astonishment, I had a call one day from my brother John Gregory Dunne, also a writer, to tell me that our brother Stephen was dead. We were six and he was the youngest. I asked, "How did it happen? What happened?" And he said, "He killed himself." The night before, I had almost done that myself.

I went back to my brother's funeral in New Canaan, Connecticut, where he lived. It was a terribly sad thing. He had three little boys. To this day I don't know why my brother did it. When I saw his casket and experienced the mass, it was as if I was watching myself. From that moment the option of suicide was over for me. It never would have worked after that.

I was so wounded from failure after having been successful, I just dropped out of life. This was before my writing career, which is my second career. I got an amazing letter from Truman Capote offering me hope and encouragement for my life, and saying he admired what I had done. He said, "But remember this, when you get out of it what you went there to get, you have to come back to where you belong." After my brother's funeral I returned to Oregon, packed up there, and went to Beverly Hills where I still had a place. I was broke, so I sold every single thing I owned in the world—every bit of furniture, every ashtray. I even sold my shirts. This sale in my house was both fascinating and embarrassing. Everything went. I made something like twenty-two or twenty-four thousand dollars.

With two suitcases and a typewriter, I moved to New York and started my life over again. I then literally ended all the drink, drug part of my life.

The one sustaining thing I always had through the worst part of everything was my children. Whether I was a good father or not—I hope I was—I loved my kids and my kids have always loved me. My boys are now thirty-six and thirty-four and we're very close to each other. I was closest of all to Dominique, to my daughter. I worshiped that wonderful child.

My son Griffin had an apartment on Eleventh Street. Griffin is both an actor and a movie producer, and he was doing a movie in London, so I lived in his apartment free. During this time, I joined an alcoholism recovery group. It was a miracle. It was as if I'd found a home. I finished my first book, it was published, and it was a flop. It was called *The Winners;* it was about Hollywood. I got a terrible review in *The New York Times.* Now, I'm a very sensitive person, very easily hurt and destroyed by criticism, but I thought, I'm fifty-three years old, I got a book published, I got reviewed in *The New York Times.* I kept saying, "This is wonderful, this is wonderful," even though it was a shitty review.

I had been in the recovery program for two years when I got the call about my daughter's death. Whatever happens to me, the worst has happened with that. It was five in the morning when I got the news. I called my wife, Lenny, right away and all she said was "Come, come quick." At that time I was living a block away from Griffin, and I phoned him. Alex, my other son, was then living in New York and we all got together at six in the morning and made plans. I got on the first plane out.

Dominique was an actress and she had just appeared in the Steven Spielberg movie *Poltergeist,* so it was on the news. I got to our house in Beverly Hills and there were crowds of people. Lenny and I waited for the boys' plane to come in, and then all four of us went to Cedars-Sinai Hospital. Dominique was still alive, but she was brain dead.

He had strangled her. It was just awful. The doctors said, "She's in a coma; she will not hear what you say." But I believe totally that they hear, at least Dominique did the first day. We talked to her, we held her, and we begged her to live. That went on for several days, and then they took her off the life-support systems. It was just horrible. The grief period usually starts after the funeral, but with a murder it's an ongoing process. A year passed between the murder and the trial. The man, John Sweeney, was caught right away. We all knew him and hated him.

Dominique knew Sweeney for a couple of years. They had lived together for less than a year. She became deeply frightened of him and left and moved back in with her mother. He pursued her. We didn't realize until after it was all over the extent of the terror that she experienced. She had just moved back into her house. She was with a friend of hers and they were going to go to the movies. Sweeney came by and she wouldn't let him in. He said he wanted to talk to her for a minute and asked her to come outside. Then he killed her.

The boys and Lenny and I stayed in California pretty much that whole year. It was as if the raw wound we all had couldn't begin to heal because we still had to wait for this terrible thing called a trial that was ahead of us. My wife and I are divorced, and yet the four of us became closer to each other and our understanding of each other grew that year. We watched each other's pain and rage.

There is an incredible feeling of revenge; you want to kill back. That's not the solution, obviously, but nonetheless you have those feelings. When something like this happens to you, you're either going all the way down and never get up or you're going to fight it through and go on with your life. The point is, you have to go on with your life no matter what happens to you. We wouldn't be honoring Dominique if we all quit. After a while you have to let go of the feelings of revenge.

All of us in the family are involved in groups that work for victims. I'm on the board of the National Victims Center. Lenny started a wonderful organization, Justice for Homicide Victims, in California. We see people who've gone through the same thing we went through, but for many of them it's as if their lives have stopped at the murder. They are so obsessed with getting even that they can't get past it. My son Alex had a terrible, terrible time for several years. I'm very grateful to the people on both coasts in the alcoholism recovery program who stood by me during that time. Don't think that temptations were not great to get loaded again. Those were times of such despair, but I never did. I experienced the pain of it. It's never over. It's always there, but the fact is you do go on.

This new life as a writer and the success I've had, which has really been considerable, all came after Dominique's death. I somehow feel, and maybe because I asked her for it, that she left me her talent. She was a wonderful young girl who did so much in her young life.

Griffin and Dominique were actors and funny and out there in the center of things. Alex is the middle one, the shy one, the brilliant one. Alex is a writer who is finally writing again. He's also a teacher. He went back to college and is finishing school this term. He has written his first magazine piece that has been accepted. I'm proud of my boys, they're wonderful kids. Actually they're no longer kids, they're men.

I'm proud of Lenny too. Lenny is a woman who was very privileged all her life and very private. When this murder happened, it thrust her into the spotlight. Lenny has multiple sclerosis and is in a wheelchair. So all during the trial the photographers would take her picture. She'd be on the news. I never knew how she'd handle it. She became a spokesperson for victims. Lenny Dunne is the most remarkable woman. President Bush flew her from California to the White House during Victims' Week and gave her a medal for her work in helping the victims of violent crimes. Dominique would be proud of the bunch of us

I had long been estranged from my faith. A guy came to me in Hollywood—he's dead now; his name was Bill Dozier. He was a big figure in Hollywood, head of RKO, and then later the head of CBS when I was under contract there. Out of the blue within a month of Dominique's death, he called me up and asked me to have lunch with him. He said, "There's a priest I'd love you to talk to." I said, "A priest?" We were sitting in La Scala Restaurant, I'll never forget it. He said, "Look, just go and see this guy in Malibu." So I went, and that visit got me back into a whole kind of religious life again. I don't know if that's the right word; but it was important for me to begin to pray again and I've stayed with it. So there was the alcoholism recovery group, there was the victims' group, there were friends, and there was the Church. All of them came together to provide a net for me. That's exactly what happened.

When I published my piece in *Vanity Fair,* that helped me a lot too. I first realized the power of a writer when I wrote "Justice." That egomaniacal, awful man who was the judge mispronounced Dominique's name for the entire seven weeks. He kept calling her Dominick. I thought, I'm going to get this son of a bitch. I didn't have to make one comment; I told exactly what happened in the courtroom. Just to discuss the rage I felt toward that man helped. The judge no longer is a judge.

It was unbelievable what that man did. I haven't really thought of him in a very long time, but I hated him a lot. I hated the defense lawyer too. The judge's name was Katz, the lawyer's was Adelson. Adelson was a rotten little guy with a big wig on the top of his head. He stood up in court one day and said, "Your honor, Alex Dunne has tears in his eyes!"—as if that was worse than the murder, and Alex was put out of the courtroom.

This is the kind of stuff that the victims' organizations are stopping, where the victim and the victim's family become the criminals in order to protect the actual criminal. They tried to keep Lenny out of the courtroom because she's in a wheelchair and it might get sympathy. It was unbelievable, the humiliation on a daily basis we were put through during that trial.

On the same day that Sweeney was sentenced, there was a guy who had held up a flower shop. He got exactly the same sentence that Sweeney got for strangling a girl to death. In California the whole idea of a sentence is a joke. When you hear of a seven-year sentence, it is automatically cut in half. He got six years, which meant three and a half, less the time between the murder and the trial when he had been in jail. He got out in advance, so he did about two and a half years. It made me crazed.

When he first got out, I hired private detectives and had him followed. All of a sudden, we stopped all that, and I said, "Let go. I'm not going to live my life like this. We have to let go of this obsession with the killer." We did. People ask me, "Where is he now?" I don't know. The case was lost because Sweeney got nothing; in effect, the guy did get away with murder.

Losing a child is the worst thing that can happen. I truly think it is. It's not how it's supposed to work. The parent is supposed to go before the child goes; that's the natural order. There's something so awful about a life ending before a person has experienced what she's supposed to experience. I would have gone myself in order to save Dominique.

She knew that I loved that she was an actress. The day before she was attacked was my birthday and she called up that night to wish me a happy birthday. She was doing a pilot for a series and told me all about it. I couldn't get enough. I loved to hear everything that went on behind the scenes and she loved telling it. She ended up the conversation saying, "Oh, I love you, Daddy." That's the last thing she ever said to me: "I love you, Daddy." Thank you, God. I never had the feelings afterward of "if only I had told her . . ." She knew that I adored her. I don't have that kind of unfinished business with her. There is satisfaction in that.

You go on and you have fun in your life again, too. You laugh, you go to parties, but I'll be walking on the street and I'll see somebody from behind—the hair, usually—and she'll remind me of Dominique and then it starts again. There's a part of every day that I spend with her in a way. It's not always a tragic thing, which is nice. Of course, time does help.

Dominique died without a will and she had accumulated a nice little bit of money. She was quite successful. My wife grew up on a cattle ranch in Arizona, and when her father died, Lenny inherited that ranch. Later on she sold it, but kept fifteen hundred acres, five hundred for each of the three kids. So Dominique had five hundred acres of a ranch in Arizona when she died. When a child dies without a will, everything goes to the parents. Lenny said, "You take the residuals and I'll take the land." The boys got the money. I think that was how we worked it out. So all these years I've gotten checks from TV shows. One came about a month ago, and it was for ten cents. The residuals had run out. I sobbed so; I felt as if she was really going away. She was saying goodbye. I thought, I'm never going to cash this check. I have it up in the country house, behind a pillow.

I am much more at peace with myself than I have ever been before. I have become a better person through this. Lenny said to me one day when we were driving in the car, "Do you have any idea how much you've changed?" It was a nice comment. A lot of things that were once important to me are no longer important. After something like this happens, everything somehow comes into focus. I used to have a lot of phony goals and I don't now. I have had a huge success in the last few years and I've made a lot of money. There was a time in my life where I wouldn't have handled this success well, but I think I have.

I'm happy. I have never in my life worked as hard as I work now, but I love to work. That all has come about since the tragedy. I have a new house up in the country, which I enjoy, along with my New York City co-op. My son Griffin is married to the beautiful actress Carey Lowell, whom I really love. They have a wonderful child, my only grandchild, my first grandchild. I worship that kid and she knows I do. I have a lot of love to give, and I'm not afraid to give it now. My daughter-in-law Carey said to me, "Does she remind you of Dominique?" I didn't say it to Carey then, but I said it to Griffin, "You know, I don't want Carey to think that Hannah is a little Dominique substitute. Hannah is Hannah and I love her for that." I thought that was very important for me. I told Griffin and he told Carey. You can't make one child a substitute for another child.

Pain, suffering, and adversity are absolutely part of life. I think everybody gets his own version. Everybody gets something that's bigger than he thinks he's able to cope with. It's really the making or the breaking of people. I truly believe that. Terrible things happen to people. But it's kind of relative, isn't it? Everybody's got his own version of the worst thing that's happened. I believe it's part of the process of life.

When we have suffered profound loss, acceptance requires experiencing very painful feelings. Often we do not allow ourselves to feel the hurt, anger, hopelessness, and fear that accompany traumatic events. The rage and depression we feel are torturous. We wonder if these powerful feelings will ever go away. In time, however, we comprehend the loss and we accept it. While life may be different because of our loss, we know we have been touched deeply and have survived. When our focus shifts —and it will—from what we have lost to what we have, life once again may be exciting and positive.

Margaret Chanin, D.D.S., is a retired Associate Professor of Dentistry and former Director of the Preventive Dentistry Clinic at Meharry Medical College School of Dentistry in Nashville, Tennessee. She is also a fellow of the American College of Dentistry. In 1970, she was the first recipient of the Professional Handicapped Woman of the Year Award from the President's Committee on Employment of the Handicapped and Pilot International. In 1985, Dr. Chanin received the Distinguished Alumni Award from Baylor University.

"I Needed to Learn to Live with What Had Happened"

Margaret Chanin

I had hoped to work full time until I was seventy-eight. My mother did. My father didn't retire until he was eighty-five. I retired my dental license December 31, 1990. I am completely retired now at seventy-four, but I stay busy. I'm actually busier than I want to be, with church activities, the home for the indigent aged, programs for handicapped people, and social functions.

I don't like the word "handicapped," because I think of the handicapped as being people who are so severely disabled they can't function at all. I've never looked for a job in my life; every job has looked for me. I think of myself as really just being inconvenienced even though I'm classified as handicapped. I feel I've had such a normal life.

The young man I would have married was killed in the accident I had in 1941. Well, five years later I was married. I got a job with the Mott Foundation in Flint, Michigan, before I even got my degree, and the people there came looking for me. At Meharry, a woman called and asked me if I'd come out for an interview. So I feel I have lived almost a charmed life. I have had many honors; I never asked for any of the things that came my way. God has opened all the doors for me; I don't feel I have anything to complain about.

I can't bathe and dress myself or comb my hair, but I do put on my makeup with the aid of a prosthesis that has a hook, and I can function at home by myself. If I'm not going anywhere and don't have to be dressed, I can get up, take my gown off, and get a brunch coat on. I'm so blessed. I have a paid person who comes and bathes and dresses me. I have a whole retinue of friends I can call and say, "The ox is in the ditch." Some of them will phone me on Monday and say, "Do you need me this week, any particular day?" I'm very fortunate.

Even though my marriage did not last more than twenty-three years, it was a good marriage until my husband's health fell apart; we've remained good friends. I was his project for those twenty-three years; everything centered around making me independent. I would never have driven a car without him. I would never have had a usable prosthesis if it weren't for him. In 1953, we sold the house, he resigned from his job, and we struck out for California with two babies and nothing but the fact that UCLA wanted me as an experimental amputee. They were the ones who fitted me with an arm that I could use comfortably. My husband said, "I'll dig ditches to make you independent." I admire him for what he did for me, and I appreciate it tremendously.

The owner and her brother-in-law were in the sailboat. I was outside the boat holding on to the chain with my hands. I said, "Oh, something's pinching me." Lew, the young man I was with, said, "It's shrimp biting." He had reached down into the water and pinched my leg—just cutting up. When he did, I threw my feet against the prow of the boat. I was not grounded but he was. Apparently, at that instant, the boat drifted against a high-powered, 12,000-volt electrical line that crossed Goose Creek bay. The wire touched the metal track that the sail goes up.

They said the current only went through my arms—that I acted as a shunt—and then, seeking the ground, the current killed Lew instantly, electrocuted him. I have vague snatches of memory of people getting me to a hospital, and then transferring me to Houston that night. For about three weeks, I don't have much memory. The doctors did not amputate until four days after the accident. It happened on a Sunday, and for medical reasons it was Thursday before they could tell where to cut. They had four good surgeons working together, including my brother-in-law, who was a general surgeon. I had the best care that was available at that time in Houston.

For three weeks, I didn't know my arms were gone. I didn't know that Lew was gone either, except I sensed something was wrong because I thought if he was all right, he'd have been at my bedside. I was alone in the room one day and there was just a napkin across the top of me. The wind blew it back and I saw the arm was gone on my right side. When my brother-in-law and my mother felt the time was right, they told me that Lew was dead and that my arms were gone. I don't have anything at the shoulder on one side, and I only have three and a half inches on the other side.

During the last weeks in the hospital, when they tapered off the drugs and weren't giving me pills to sleep, I was overwhelmed by the fact that I'd never be a dentist, but as soon as I was conscious, the dean of the dental school, Dr. Frederick C. Elliott, came and said, in answer to my fears, "Oh, yes, you will. We've got a lot of dentists with hands—we could use an extra one with just a head." I later found out he had already been in touch with the board and asked them if they would license me. They said, "If you graduate her, we'll license her." So the Texas Board of Dentistry licensed me.

I had the accident on the 29th of June, and I re-entered school in September with my class. I had to have a hired dental student as an assistant to help me. While I was in dental school, my goal was to get through. Before I graduated, the dean recommended that I go to the University of Michigan or Johns Hopkins for a master's degree in public health. When I applied at Michigan, they wrote me that I had to have a bachelor's degree. I had only done the requirements for dental school and trained as a medical technician. So I had to back up and go to Baylor. Now I had that goal to work toward. Then, when I graduated, I went on to Michigan to get my master's degree.

The first year, I had gone straight from the hospital to live with my sister and brother-in-law. My brother told my sister, "I will pay for you to have a full-time maid so that you will have plenty of time and energy to take care of sister." My mother was with me the year I was at Baylor, the year I was at Michigan, and the year I was at the Mott Foundation.

I sued the Houston Lighting & Power Company for not having warning signs posted on the bank, saying: "High-Powered Line Crossing Body of Water." A photograph showed the line was eighteen inches below the legal limit. I think I sued for $150,000, which would have been my lifetime earnings at that time, based on dentists' income. We settled for $37,000. My reasoning was I needed to learn to live with what had happened to me and to feel I was financially independent enough to finish my education without being dependent on my family. If I'd sued for a million dollars and gotten it five years later, and wasn't adjusted to what I had to face, what good would it have done?

You grieve for a limb just as you grieve for a person. I won't say there aren't times now that I'd give anything to reach up and run my fingers through my hair, or to feel my skin, or feel my face, but when those moments come I concentrate on something else. I can remember wasting a lot of time thinking that if I prayed hard enough I could wake up with my arms, that God could perform a miracle. I don't doubt that He could if it served a purpose, but it would be upsetting the laws of nature to do it. I can remember saying, "I don't see why God let me live. I'll be a millstone around my family's neck and a burden on society." I had periods when I was overcome with grief and weeping. I went through that for several years.

I don't think it was my faith in God that got me through. I wasn't mature enough. It was my faith in my mother's faith in God. She had such a strong faith. When I'd be dissolved in tears and grief, or quit crying and verbalize my fears, my mother would say, "If God spared your life when twenty doctors said you couldn't live, there has to be a reason for it. You may be old and gray before you ever know it, and you may not know it until you get to Heaven, but it's your responsibility to keep looking, keep searching for it."

After the accident, when Dean Elliott came to the hospital, the first thing he said to me was "Margaret, don't think that God is punishing you for something." And I said, "Dr. Elliott, it never occurred to me. I think of God as a heavenly Father, a loving Father. Why would He punish me? We pay for breaking the laws of nature, but He didn't make me do what I did. He will help me."

I was in the wrong place at the wrong time. I don't think it was God's will that I'd go through life without my arms. It happened: a pure accident. If we're faithful, He plays a part in opening new doors for us. It was my business to avail myself of whatever came along, which was to stay there in school. I don't have hands, but I've had a thousand hands of other people to help me.

I don't think of myself yet as elderly. I don't guess I ever will either. When my mother was eighty-four, I said to her one day, "Mother, I don't believe you'd ever stay home if you had someplace to go." She said, "I wouldn't. I may have to sit in a rocking chair someday, but I'm not going to sit there until I have to." She often said, "The way to keep from getting old is to have new experiences, have new ideas, and make new friends."

I had a girlfriend, and one day I walked into her room while her back was turned to me. She was putting polish on her nails, and she asked,

"Margaret, what kind of polish do you use?" Then when she realized what she'd said: "Oh, I'm sorry." I said, "But that's a compliment!" Often people will ask me questions that they'd ask somebody with hands. They don't realize it until it's out. I consider that the highest of compliments. I would hate to think when my name came to somebody's mind, the first thing the person would think was "She's armless." If I haven't made any more impression than that, I've made a poor one.

When we see people from afar who are wrestling with illness, disability, or loss, we tend to view them as victims. Surprisingly, these same people often do not hold a similar view of themselves. They have accepted their lives.

Self-pity diminishes a person's spirit, while acceptance is the key that opens new doors for living. When a person has experienced a major loss and totally accepted it, he moves ahead with life.

I. King Jordan, Ph.D., is the first person who is deaf to become President of Gallaudet University, in Washington, D.C., the nation's only liberal arts college for students who are deaf. He served the university previously as Dean of the College of Arts and Sciences and Chairman of the Department of Psychology.

"I Can't Hear; So What?"

─────

I. King Jordan

I was on a motorcycle without a helmet. This was 1965; helmets weren't required at that time. I ran into a car, went off the front of my motorcycle, and crashed headfirst through the windshield. My head cracked open like an egg. I had two fractures. The lateral fracture was really bad, but it was the basal fracture that caused the deafness. I have virtually no hearing in one ear and a tiny bit in the other. That helps me modulate my voice. The worst damage was the head injury, and for a long time I was in a coma. The physician said to my father, "If you can pray, pray for him to die." Two or three times they gave me the last rites.

I went to a meeting in Vermont once, and Senator Patrick Leahy introduced me as one who, when he was young, liked pretty women, fast cars, and didn't like books. That's a pretty accurate description. We had a contest among some of my peers in high school to see who could go for the longest stretch without taking a book home; I went for months and months. Somehow I managed to pass all my courses without doing any work. Later on I had conversations with my son when he was in high school and I was concerned about his study habits and his behavior in the school. He once said to me, "If anybody can't tell me about those things, it's you."

My years in high school were really good years. I enjoyed them thoroughly. I was a clown, but I made a lot of friends. I went back to my twenty-fifth reunion, a few years before I became President, and it was great fun to see my friends again. They were proud of me but they were very surprised. I'm sure if they'd had to vote for the least likely to become an academic, I would have been on the top of the list. My wife Linda was at the reunion with me. She's a very skilled interpreter; she can hear. It would have been quite frustrating if I'd been there without an interpreter and tried to communicate directly. I'm not a very good lip-reader. I had the bad habit when I first became deaf of filling every vacuum with speech so I didn't have to lip-read. People who become deaf later in life tend to do that. If I'm talking, I don't have to worry about trying to understand you. But when I have a good interpreter I don't do it.

When I went to graduate school, I was without any support. I studied in a department of psychology that had never had a deaf student before. Because I'd only been deaf for three and a half years, I didn't know what things I needed. So I behaved the same way that everybody else behaved, except I didn't understand anything. What I did to compensate was to spend most of my life in the library.

I also compensated in another way. I would ask two or three students in each class if I could borrow their notes. I ended up with the best notes in the class. They learned quickly, too. When it came time to study for final exams, people wanted to see my notes.

When I think about my graduate experience, I realize how much I missed in the seminars, the lectures, the interaction with students. If you're in a class or just having fun and you have an interpreter, you can understand everything that's going on.

There has been a steady progression in positive changes for deaf people over the last twenty-five years. Each year things are a little better. When I was an undergraduate student—and I'm speaking for myself—sometimes we'd go out in groups. Perhaps we'd be standing in line at a movie and signing to each other. If someone looked at us, we'd stop signing, or sign less obviously. If we were in a restaurant and people were looking at us, we'd be embarrassed! Consequently we stopped signing big and started signing very small. We even began talking to each other without signing, and trying to lip-read each other. Today I'm really embarrassed to tell you that I was one who behaved like that, but I know a lot of other people who did it too. That was in the 1960s; there was a stigma to showing your difference.

I didn't grow up deaf, so I can't speak for people who have, but back then it was almost as if I was sorry to be deaf, didn't want people to know I was deaf, didn't want to be open about my deafness. If I sat quietly and didn't sign, people wouldn't notice me. If I signed, people would talk about me. I'm sorry to say that's true. Now fortunately you don't see that. I don't mind people calling me different now; I am different. I do mind if people think I'm less able. I think that's probably what was in my mind back then.

I didn't think I would stay deaf. Again and again the doctors told me, "It's a temporary thing; it will go away as your system recovers." For a year they told me that, and I kept waiting for it to happen.

At the beginning the focus is on the loss. It takes time to change the focus from what you can't do to what you can do. That's the big challenge. Once you change the focus, it's not very important anymore that you can't hear. Many people experience Kübler-Ross's stages when they lose their hearing. My anger was directed at the woman who was driving the car I hit, then was directed at the doctors who kept telling me that I wasn't really deaf and my hearing would come back. My anger didn't last very long, and I've never had any depression—that's supposed to be one of the stages, too. I think I'm smart enough to recognize it if I experience it.

I was interviewed for *60 Minutes* by Meredith Vieira. She asked me, "If there was a magic pill and you could swallow it, would you take it?" I was really shocked because she interviewed me for a total of about fourteen hours. That meant that in all that time, I still hadn't convinced her that I felt all right, that I didn't feel the need to be a hearing person. I can't understand why people who can hear can't understand that. I think they're focusing on what it would be like *not* to hear. I might ask a hearing person, "What would it be like to be deaf?" Immediately that person would probably say that she couldn't do this, she couldn't do that, and she couldn't do this, she couldn't do that. Honestly, you just stop thinking about it after a while.

Last night my wife and I were going out, and my daughter was going out too. We walked out to our cars together and she put down her car top and started to sing and sign, "I'm a coooool rider, I'm a coooool rider." When we had lunch today, I asked her about the song. Never until just now did it occur to me to think, Wow, I don't know what the music is like, or I've never heard the song, or I wish I could hear the song. These days that does not enter my mind. Twenty years ago, if someone had signed and sung a song, I would have said, "I can't hear that, I can't appreciate the music." But I stopped that kind of thinking. I shared the joy that my daughter was having. She was just really a happy kid and that made her daddy happy, too. I didn't miss anything from that moment, that experience. The whole thing was based on a song; it was based on music, and I can't hear music. The focus for me was not on what I can't do; the focus for me was on the beauty and spontaneity of the moment, how much I enjoyed it, and how much she enjoyed my enjoying it.

Whereas people might see deafness as a negative, a loss, it seems to me that some special perceptions, a depth of experience, a new kind of life opens up. If people say, "Oh, King can't hear." So what? When I speak to groups, I use that expression often. "I can't hear; so what?" I'm fed up with people asking me about hearing. I can't hear. It's as simple as that.

I'm so happy that I chose to learn sign, and that I have friends who do sign. I could leave here in my car and take a trip across the country. If I made the necessary phone calls first, I would never have to stay in a hotel. If I'm walking on a street in Europe signing and a deaf European sees me, he'll come up and introduce himself.

Once, when we were in York, England, we got off the train and started walking, looking around and signing. A man came up and signed, "You know, there's a deaf club here and we meet on Thursday." Well, it happened to be Thursday. We ended up going to the deaf club and had a wonderful time. We see more when we travel than many people outside the deaf community because we meet people all over the world.

People talk about my kids and ask, "Wouldn't you have wanted to hear your children's voices?" I say it would be nice, especially when they were little kids. But be that as it may, you know, I can't. Then they sometimes ask me about our relationship. My kids are really much richer for my deafness. My daughter is a skilled signer, both receptively and expressively. She can hear but she can sign well enough to join a group of deaf people and communicate. I think it's expanded her world.

My son signs, too. When he went to the University of Colorado, he joined a club called I Hear, without saying anything to me or his mother. It's a group of deaf people and friends of deaf people from the university. He was very active in the club. Someone else told us he had joined. It helped him make contacts in the town and make new friends.

The notion that my life is different, that my communication style is different should intrigue you. It should not put you off. Sadly, in the past it did turn people off. They didn't want to become involved. Their attitude was "There but for the grace of God go I."

If there were a thousand consequences from the accident, nine hundred and ninety-eight were good ones. It changed my life. Who knows how long I would have remained a "free spirit," where that would have led? Often you read about people who become disabled and then take off. Disability forces us to re-examine what we're doing. I think I may even have overcompensated for a while. I was a little afraid that, as a deaf person, I would have to be better. With blacks, women, disabled people, and other minorities, maybe it's a good motivator.

Being deaf is not such a terrible thing. When I had my accident, my mother, my father, my friends—all of us were so grateful that I was alive. I don't think there was a lot of attention paid to the fact that I couldn't hear. We had to write, and I had to lip-read as best I could. It was all an inconvenience and not a lot of fun, but we were delighted that my health was coming back. I never thought of the deafness itself as the worst thing that could have happened.

Basically, I define myself as a normal individual whose ears don't work. The only thing that doesn't function the way bodies are designed to function are my ears. If you look at a person who needs glasses, it's the same thing. His eyes don't function the way they're designed to function. That's not a big deal. Hearing aids are not as big a deal anymore. I say to people, "Look past my deafness and look past other people's deafness. See what's inside."

When I was asked "the magic-pill question" for the 60 Minutes interview, my answer pleased me immensely and was spontaneous. Often you think, If only I had said so-and-so. If only I had told her this. But when the interviewer asked me, I just answered right away, "Would you ask a black person if he would take a pill to become white? Would you take a pill to become a man?" Really, that's the same question. But even when the interview was over, she couldn't understand why I responded the way I did. She told me both on and off camera, "It's completely different." She said, "I never was a man. You used to be hearing." That was a different life. I'm forty-eight years old and I became deaf when I was twenty-one. I don't have a lot of adult experience as a hearing person. Almost my entire adult life is as a deaf person.

My life before the accident was a lot of fun. I had many friends, but I had a very superficial life. I had no really deep relationships with people. After the accident I learned who my real friends were. Most of the superficial friends had other things to do. My really good friends became better friends. I met my wife and established the most important relationship in my life. I learned to think about other people—something that had never occurred to me before.

A dear friend of my wife's came to the house and she'd brought me those little rollers that you massage your back with. She said she looked and thought, and looked and thought. "What can I buy for you? You really are a person who has everything." And she's right. I have everything. My family, my job, my friends; I have it all. I can't imagine a fuller life, a happier life. I wake up every morning before five o'clock. I wake up because I want to wake up; I'm ready and there are a lot of things that are going to happen that day. I want things to happen. There were times in my life when I would stay in bed, and not want to get out. I haven't felt like that for years. I love my life.

The subject of death is fraught with denial. Our own mortality is terribly threatening for us to acknowledge on an emotional level. How we will die is frightening to most of us; we struggle with the question "Is this all there is?"

Death is the ultimate lesson in acceptance. For those who believe strongly in an afterlife or that life is part of some ongoing, larger process, the spirit of possibility helps to achieve acceptance of death.

Those who acknowledge death as a part of life place greater emphasis on enjoying the moment, nurturing significant relationships, helping others, and absorbing life's beauty. Out of the ultimate "bad" comes the ultimate good.

Donald AuCoin is the former Executive Director and Resident Manager of the Triangle Club, a clubhouse and meeting place for recovery support groups that serve the lesbian and gay community of Washington, D.C.

"Once You Get that You Die, How You Die Is Not Such a Big Deal"

Donald AuCoin

Sometime in December 1988, I looked at the bottom of my foot and there was a bruise. I didn't think anything of it at the time. In April—you don't look at the soles of your feet very often—I looked again, and it was still there. I pretty much knew instantly. I went from optimistically hoping I hadn't been exposed to the virus to knowing I was fully diagnosed with the disease of AIDS. On some level it was a relief because now I knew. It was something that I'd suspected, so it was no longer a dread. For some people a diagnosis means six months and that's it. But by fall I realized I was still here and was going to continue.

I really needed to be around people, so I sought out HIV groups who were in the same boat, made new friends, and gradually realized I wasn't going to die "today." On a spiritual plain, I think we are greater together than we are alone. Not asking for help, relying on the ego, feeling alone—all are part of the problem. Saying "I'm part of a community, others are like me, and this is a shared experience" is part of the solution.

I probably have had less denial about AIDS than most people I know. It's really hard to have denial when people who used to be in the groups aren't there anymore. Death is okay, letting go is okay. Disease is okay. It is and it isn't. There's nothing we can do about it.

At least half, if not more, of my closest friends are HIV positive or have AIDS today. How I deal with the issue of death and dying has to do with lessons learned in my recovery from alcoholism, which focuses on living in the real world. If I'm already working on letting go of the ego in my program of recovery, then dying is just the next step. It's a dramatic step. It's a big jump, but it's qualitatively no different. I don't know what I believe regarding an afterlife, but I do believe it's all going to be okay.

When I was diagnosed, I started seeing my therapist again. One of the things I asked her was if I was denying that I'm really going to die. Am I just a little boy whistling in the dark with my hands behind my back, saying, "Ah ha, it's okay, it's okay, it's okay, it's okay." Recently I went through a depression, but I don't think it had to do with dying; it had to do with certain things I want in this lifetime that I don't think there'll be time to achieve.

AIDS means that I will probably or absolutely die sooner than I would normally have died. I have a damaged immune system. There's probably no way other than a cure, which we hope for but which I'm not counting on, that will restore my immune system. Because of my damaged immune system I try not to wait until tomorrow to do anything that I want to do today. I tell people that I love them today because there is no guarantee of tomorrow. I don't seem to have much patience for discussions about the material side of life. I try to do something enjoyable each day; there's no waiting until I have a vacation to do something that's fun. I really try to live in the moment. I only have today.

Sure, I find myself slipping from that perspective, but the predominant time frame is to live in today because I could wake up tomorrow— and I'm well aware of it—and not be able to swim fifty lengths in the pool, as I'm now doing. I wouldn't be able to do the crew rowing that I'm doing. Yesterday I swam and I was absolutely in the strokes. It was an incredible experience. Many people never get to appreciate the moment because they're anticipating the future with some sort of fear or regretting the past. One way I have an impact on people in my life now is to ask them the questions "What are you doing today? Are you happy today?"

A person with AIDS or a person facing death is not worried about a straight-line résumé. I'm totally beyond what I do and how people perceive what I do. I'm leaving a job soon, and people ask me what I'm going to do next, meaning, what will I do to earn a living. What I hear them saying often is, "How will you define yourself next in terms of your job or your career?" If I never do anything again in terms of job or career, I will be totally content. I had a career in advertising, direct marketing, and public relations. The Triangle Club drew on all of my management and creative experience. I'm in contact with literally a thousand people a week. It's been a wonderful and rewarding experience.

Everybody in my alcoholism recovery support system has dealt with the "death" of themselves on a very real level. I've already experienced through my recovery having a life I didn't expect to have. With my HIV diagnosis, I say, "Thank you for that life." It is truly a second life for me. I empathize strongly and feel for people who get sober and find out they have HIV. My recovery prepared me for having AIDS in an incredible way. There wasn't a radical changing of my life. I was leading the life I wanted to lead when I was diagnosed. I wasn't anchored in the material world. I had been making my decisions based on a life that was not grounded in fear, but grounded in risk, new experiences, and letting go.

I feel as if I am a miracle. The miracle was changing from a person who hated himself to a person who loves himself. That has allowed me to love a lot of other people. The more I love people, the more I'm able to love myself. The more I love myself, the more I'm able to love others. I definitely feel that I was dead, and now I'm alive, fully alive. The sober life I have been living for the last twelve years in recovery has been a gift.

It was the offer to do the work I've been doing for the last year and a half that pushed me into the medical program I'm in, which is a study of three different drugs: AZT, ddI, and ddC, in rotation. It comes with some good health-care support from the National Institutes of Health. I'm continuing to be in the study, and they say at NIH that I'm doing very well. The only symptoms I have are the continuing spots of Kaposi's sarcoma on my body. I have this skin cancer that is never going away, and it keeps growing. In the AIDS world that's minor.

My body is not fighting AIDS. I'm not fighting AIDS. I'm living, I have AIDS. It's probably going to kill me, but I'm not fighting it. I think my immune system responds well to a spiritual and emotional letting go.

Death isn't scary; the dying process is scary. There are people I've seen who are weak and can't get up stairs. I don't know how that kind thing is going to affect me. I may find that there's a lot of reading I want to do, and I may not mind being pushed in a wheelchair. I will take it a day at a time when that time comes. All I'm having to accept today is I'm going to die. That seems acceptable. It seems life is about acceptance and living.

Once you get that you die, how you die is not such a big deal. Once I've gotten that, there's a lot of good stuff that comes. There's a lot of living in the now.

Change

Adversity often conjures up mega-events with tragic consequences. Our attention is easily captured by famine in Ethiopia,
floods in Bangladesh, a seven-car accident at rush hour, the killing
of soldiers and civilians in a gulf war bombing. However, when
Thoreau said "The mass of men live lives of quiet desperation," he
may have identified the greatest ordeal of all.

It is the job of parents to teach their children that they are good,
lovable, capable, worthwhile, and important. Sadly, to the contrary,
millions have been taught the very opposite: they are bad, incapa-
ble, of little value, and unimportant. Perhaps the most damaging
message some children receive is that they are unlovable. In search
ing for love and happiness, life for them is a never-ending emotional
struggle to overcome self.

The most profound change a person can undergo is the change
from self-hate to self-love.

Lonnie MacDonald, M.D., is a psychiatrist in private practice in New York City specializing in the treatment of addictive disorders. He served as the first Chief of Community Psychiatry at Harlem Hospital.

"Underneath Was a Child Wanting to Love and Be Loved"

Lonnie MacDonald

The sense of aloneness, disconnectedness, and detachment from other people may be the most painful experience for humans to undergo. There have been a number of experiments that confirm this. The most classic was René Spitz and his research with newborns who were brought up without human contact and developed severe depression. The absense of early human contact has grave consequences. My own association to the importance of this is in studying not only the consequences when separation from human contact occurs, but the lengths to which we go to maintain contact—or if it's lost, to try to re-establish it.

The first separation from a human that we experience is at birth: separation from the mother. What some researchers have called "birth trauma" becomes the precursor for subsequent repetitions of the separation anxiety that we later in life find in broken relationships, divorces, and losses through death.

The history of humankind, certainly modern humans, can be found in variations on the theme of our deep human need to love and be loved, and what happens in the process of our growth and development that can deform and distort how that human need is or is not met. If I use myself personally, a consequence of my having been the first boy in my family after five girls, the bond of my relationship with my mother was extremely strong. When my mother was pregnant with my brother-to-be, William, I was two years old. My mother went to the hospital for delivery. I had a cold that morning and was placed in a chair near the stove to get some heat. While being dressed, I was told to raise my arms to put my shirt on, and in lowering my arms I tipped a pot of scalding hot water onto myself, and was severely burned. I ended up in the very hospital where my mother was. I was so severely burned the doctors wondered whether there would be some deformity in my legs. This was an extremely physical and emotional experience. The separation for me, not only from my mother but from the family as well, with me being in the hospital alone and in pain was so traumatic that for most of my life the experience was completely blocked from my memory. Yet it became one of the motors driving my behavior without me being aware that it was doing so. The "accident" of spilling the water on myself was an attempt to rejoin my mother at the hospital.

The lengths to which we go to reunite and reconnect can be astounding. Unconsciously that desire was operating in me in such a way that I was attempting to reconnect with my mother.

All kinds of conflicts can occur when the yearning to be close, to experience the sharing of feelings, and to bond becomes linked to pain upon closeness or pain as a consequence of closeness. It can become a powerful motor in influencing later experiences of intimacy or connectedness.

If somebody walks into my office who has had difficulty in giving and receiving love and finding an appropriate partnership on some level of attachment, that person probably has incidents in childhood that have greater depth than just normal separation—for example, when a mother goes off to work. Someone who has repeats of these traumas and no outside source of help, comfort, or healing will experience profound struggles with relationships.

If there is a chronic situation of abuse in the form of neglect or physical abuse, the effects are even more damaging. Usually when we're in an ongoing environment with humans, there is a perpetuating pattern of behavior. Consequently there are varieties of self-protective and defensive coping mechanisms and survival patterns that children develop, such as submissiveness and people-pleasing.

Patterns of physical or emotional neglect or abandonment and patterns of verbal or physical or sexual abuse set in motion a lifetime scenario of struggle, of feeling inappropriate, less than, alone, and not connected. When I work with my patients, I say, "We will try to be as open-minded as we can to observe and understand how things work," referring to how humans come to be the way they are. "We'll particularly be interested in self-esteem—how our sense of self is developed and affected by those things that help in the positive development of self-esteem, and those things that can interfere, undermine, and corrode it."

There is an apparent paradox in how some humans, yearning for that sense of connectedness and closeness, are driven nevertheless, to become more and more self-involved, self-reliant, and self-protective. In their attempts to survive, they resort to self-defeating behaviors, of which there are many.

Feelings, which are there for the purpose of telling us about ourselves in our environment, enable us to have information as to how to deal with that environment. A number of my patients have had the childhood experience of blocking off feelings in order to survive. In adulthood they used chemical substances to numb their feelings, and became addicted. Minimally, their dreams, aspirations, and accomplishments became undermined. More dramatically, the outcome of running away from feelings can be running into death through overdose, automobile accidents, or behavior in which the addicted may be killed or end up in prison. Often patients who were not taught earlier how to deal with feelings of frustration, anger, and rage will take the experiences and feelings in, stuff them, and become increasingly depressed. They may even end up committing suicide. Often the person who develops submersion of angry, violent feelings turns them inward, and becomes an overachiever. The person who is acting out externally, trying to escape from looking into self, may end up in jail.

What is hard for most people I've had as patients is facing the result of their childhood experiences. They may be left to feel "less than" and not worthwhile if they've been told they're "nothing" or that they "will never be anything." Assaults on the sense of self in childhood can be so painful that we come to believe what we're told about ourselves. We are such objects of loathing we feel that no one would want us.

Feelings of isolation, of being rejected and alone are very, very painful. Running away from looking into self is what the behavior motor is fundamentally about. It leads to feeling awful, unacceptable, undesirable, unlovable. In the therapeutic process the person is encouraged to connect with those feelings so that he can undo the falseness of his beliefs.

Varied reasons bring people into therapy. Whatever may be the dynamics in each case, a breakdown in the psychological security system that a person has developed causes the painful feelings to emerge. It can be triggered by any number of things, such as a relationship that doesn't work out or the loss of a loved one through death. It could be the loss of a job. Some people who are workaholics get fired and their psychological security system is pulled out from under them. "Hitting the emotional bottom" is usually caused by a failure of old methods to block off the pain.

However, there are survival means and techniques that we sometimes develop and use. Some people go through all kinds of life's traumas but have developed relationships that provide comfort, support, and assistance. While they may be deeply wounded emotionally or even physically, a gathering of those healers may get them through.

Often individuals in therapy who continue to grow are able to sustain emotional wounds or traumas, and have more capacity, flexibility, and mechanisms to explore options. They have more freedom of choice. In the past the choice possibly had to be immediate gratification or avoidance of pain through chemical substances or acting out in some way with food or sex or relationships. The new capacity to experience feelings enables the individual to move through the situation rather than avoiding it or acting out self-destructively.

When we talk about the sentinel value of feelings or sensations, we are beginning, though only in recent years, to understand the subtlety of language that goes on among some species in the wild animal kingdom. In humans the unconscious picks up information much faster than we're able to register consciously. Often there is a delay relating to repression. We know there are instances when we meet someone for the first time and have the feeling "I shouldn't trust this person." But sometimes we may discount that initial reaction. We think we're being silly or the person may be particularly disarming. Only later do we come to realize "My gosh, my first impression was right. I should have trusted my feelings."

Having to protect ourselves against painful stimulation leads to the dulling of the sentinel value of our feelings, which give us information about ourselves, others, and our environment that is not only useful, but might result in the difference between life and death.

If I were still teaching, I would use the film *Fatal Attraction* as an instructional tool to demonstrate the way that the discounting of earlier feelings by the character Michael Douglas played led to his getting deeper and deeper in the entanglement with the Glenn Close character, who was exceedingly disturbed. The process of therapy helps uncover the buried, blocked-off feelings, and leads to a heightened awareness where there is increasing capacity for self-awareness rather than self-neglect.

Pain is a part of the human experience. There are ways of allowing a child to experience pain without having to repress the sensation to such an extent that he ends up blocking off sensation awareness, thus setting himself up for increasing detachment from the world of feelings, his own feelings, and connection with the feelings of others. Detachment from the world of feelings will cause great pain later on. What number of people do I see so damaged that some of this struggle will be part of their lives? In the United States, I certainly believe, the majority of the population.

Most parents are loving. They bring to parenting their own childhood experience, so it's a mix. Different family members and friends can also be mediating and moderating forces and provide resources along the path. For me, personally, there were many along the path who helped to offset, to some extent, an undertow toward escape from self, which became the ambition to overcome no matter what. I was looking outside myself for a sense of self-appreciation through accomplishments. It can't work that way.

Compared with most people in the world, I had a charmed life. Yet the damage was done and I had to respond one way or the other. I'm not surprised, now that I understand more, that I had to block out the awareness of the enormous pain I felt when I moved from an all-black school system to a racially mixed high school. I had been brought up in an environment, back then in the early thirties, in a segregated Jim Crow town where not only was there the message that being black "you're second class" and "you're not worth as much as the white person," but there were boundaries set and penalties for violating those boundaries, on segregated public transportation, in movie houses and stores. The threat in those days was that if you violated enough, you could lose your life. There were lynchings back then in Pennsylvania. I was voted the most popular black male student in high school because I was in the mode of disarming and people-pleasing.

A number of my black peers at the time, in the tenth grade, dropped out of school for a variety of reasons: they had to work to make money, got pregnant out of wedlock, got married, or got involved in crime. I realize now I was driven to overcome even more strongly as I moved through life. But it finally caught up with me because I was running away from facing myself. The sentinel feelings were blunted. The psychological security system worked for many years until I arrived at the crossroads. Dangers were there, and if it hadn't been for some guiding protective force, I could have gone either way.

The effects of racism were deeply influential in my parents' lives. Both my mother and father were born in Georgia. My father's side of the family was white. My mother's family was quite dark. Because of my father's relationship with his father in the South in the early 1900s, he became strongly anti-white for a good part of his life. The mixed messages in my family were there all the time, expressed in many ways. Characteristic of the time was that old ditty "If you're white, you're right. If you're yella, you're mella. If you're brown, stick around. And if you're black, jump back." Those things were recited and became a part of the experience of blacks calling one another "monkey" and "nigger." The contamination was there, outside and in the family as well.

Another important experience that was traumatic for me was that my sister Helen, my favorite sister, died when I was ten. That really left me bereft, with a great feeling of loss. Two years later my middle brother, William, was murdered. He was murdered by a group who had apparently wanted him to engage in some kind of sexual behavior while he was with them in a rowboat. He had refused and they tied his hands and feet together and threw him overboard. As his older brother, I've had profound feelings of guilt about that ever since. For most of my life I never talked to anyone about any of those feelings. At the time, back then, I pushed them under.

My mother and father were real battlers, not physically but their arguments with one another would often drive us kids crazy. There was admiration and love at the time, too. It was not one note. Certainly a predominant-sounding note was their struggle financially.

My parents had eight children. They loved us, were responsible, and worked hard. They had many problems and obstacles to overcome. I know that they did their best. Of us all, only two are still alive: my sister Alice, four years my senior, and I. Alice has been a tower of love, strength, and support for me and we are closer than ever now.

We here on Earth share so many things in our experiences, despite all the differences, because we are human. If we don't come to acknowledge our mistakes of the past, we will just be doomed to repeat them. The wonderful side is the discovery of self-extrication from that kind of bondage and perpetual victimization caused by the need to remain a deeply defended, self-protected, wounded little kid—as I was, living behind barriers without understanding what the motives driving me were. I was at the whim of those motors, being carried where those motors drove me without choice. Today, rather than running away from myself, I can move increasingly toward extrication from destructive control to positive self-appreciation and self-acceptance, and to the discovery of aspects of myself creatively and my capacity to experience love.

The damage done that blocks the capacity to love and be loved can be diminished and opened to healing—as opposed to bringing more tragedy and destructiveness into our lives and the lives of others. We can come out at the other end, and begin to bring love into our lives and the lives of others. The good news is that this is possible. If we have some spark of openness to the possibility of help from outside ourselves—rather than remaining locked into the belief that we can only trust ourselves and must stay disconnected and isolated—we have a new opportunity to utilize the adversity, including our own backgrounds, to build more strength, character, and tools for dealing with whatever life hands us. We can use adversity to overcome, rather than to be overcome.

As a psychiatrist, I find the process of therapy wondrously incredible. I enjoy the feeling of closeness with another human being who trusts me enough to allow us to visit together with the wounded child within and to experience the joy of increasing reunion of the child with the grown-up. Rather than having the grown-up hate that little child, which is usually the case in my experience (it certainly was with me personally), we come to know and better understand why the child might have been so self-distorted and deformed that to survive he acted out in all kinds of destructive ways. Underneath was a child wanting to love and be loved. To experience the increasing acceptance and love by the grown-up of the child within is an incredible journey.

We hate change that is thrust upon us against our will.

The loss of a job, the death of someone we love, illness, disability, divorce, separation may produce guilt, anger, hopelessness, despair. Feelings must be felt; losses must be grieved.

Accepting radical change necessitates summoning up all of our coping skills. It appears that our world has come to an end. Hopelessness is a normal human reaction; it is the way we comprehend, for the moment, what has happened to us.

We know that others have coped with similar difficulties. However, even with that evidence, we doubt our ability to survive.

In our despair, we hold on to life with white knuckles. We are forced to examine self and look for options. Others help us. Then, amazingly, we recover as millions have done before us. We grow. We become different. We live a new and different life. It's okay again, often better.

Traumatic events set the stage for transformation. When we are suffering, we are often motivated to seek assistance to relieve our pain. Mental-health professionals and clergy report that emotional pain is usually what leads clients to them for therapy and counseling. Support and guidance often help those who are hurting to find the short-term relief and the long-term happiness they seek.

Pat Pomarici, M.A., is a counselor in clinical psychology and currently a treatment coordinator at the Mary Lee School in Lockhart, Texas, a residential treatment facility for girls needing out-of-home placement. She is a former associate counselor at the Marina Counseling Center in San Francisco, where she facilitated support groups for dealing with post-earthquake trauma.

"Adversity Sets the Stage"

Pat Pomarici

The normal reaction to a quake is shock; it comes out in many different ways. Normally you don't see people collapsing and crying. A lot of activity can come out of that shock. People go into action. If it's not heroic, it's some other kind of movement.

After the earthquake of 1989 in San Francisco, I heard many stories from the people who came to our earthquake support groups. People would come to the groups who had lost their homes. They'd be angry. People who had suffered lesser things would be angry or sad or depressed. The horrors take a long time to process. There's the flight-or-fight syndrome. That's normal. A major event such as an earthquake can be a time for transformation; it's a good time to take a look at the things that come up.

Post-traumatic stress disorder that comes out of a quake is acute; it usually ends in about six months. It's not comprised of the ongoing problems that many Vietnam vets experience. After the quake I saw old emotional issues getting triggered really hard. Fears and insecurities that were deeply rooted in the character of a person surfaced. Things that were kept at bay before the quake came tumbling out: anxieties, fears, depression, terror about crossing the bridge.

If you are familiar with tarot cards, you know that the Tower in the Crowley deck is a beautiful card. It shows a building tumbling. There's a lot of reds and blacks in it; there's lightning. It's all very much like a quake. The main theme of that card is transformation. You can change in a positive way. Or you can go the other way; you can become angry or bitter. A traumatic event can change you radically.

Adversity, I believe, makes a person look deeper. Someone who has lost a person close to him through death or divorce often experiences despair. Early-abandonment issues surface. A child can't understand the experience of a leaving. A loss in infancy is devastating. It sets the stage for emptiness and a hunger. Self-recrimination can surface: "It's all my fault." A positive thing that can come out of a loss is that you learn about the parts of you that were never attended to when you were young. A positive transformation after the loss of a job may be that you get a better job or decide to go back to school. Adversity sets the stage to make a constructive and positive transformation or to do destructive and angry things that are self-defeating.

People who are bitter and those who really hold on to their anger are crying out. Friends often say, "Oh, come on. That was ten years ago. When are you going to get a life?" There may be some wisdom in that, but those who are in pain need someone to say, "It really does hurt." We don't ever get enough of that. If you realize you're stuck in that anger, find safe places to express it. Don't hold back. Try not to dump it on your loved ones. Have murder fantasies, throw bottles, scream and cry. Find support groups where you can talk about your anger and bitterness. One person cannot shoulder a lot of bitterness.

Any predominant feeling can be a gateway to growth. One-on-one therapy is excellent. People should consider therapy if they're in a lot of pain and can't seem to get out of it.

You can go into therapy because you want to grow, but for most people it has to be something fairly drastic to motivate them to seek help. When hope dies, it's very scary. Hopelessness is another entry trigger into a therapeutic situation. Hope is crucial. Some people, when they're beginning to have suicidal thoughts, call a suicide line and get channeled into a source of help. There's the beginning of transformation.

Lives of quiet desperation can with help transcend horrible events and losses. The ability of humans to recover is awesome.

Life tries to teach us some lessons over and over again. Being human, however, we resist and must relearn them many times. What life is trying to tell us when we are in pain is that change is necessary. Yet we continue to repeat the same old behavior that produces the same old negative results, and we stay stuck in the same old misery.

Occasionally, a major life event will come along that shakes us to the very core, prompting profound self-examination, self-discovery, and change. The apparent negative experience turns out to be a tremendous growth experience.

Devin McCoy is a laborer for Tri-Valley Growers Container Division in Fremont, California. He is working toward a nursing degree at Ohlone Junior College in Fremont. For two years he worked as an Emergency Medical Technician for Patient Care Ambulance in Alameda County.

"I Like Myself Now."

_____

Devin McCoy

I was working two jobs at the same time. I was fueling airplanes and working in a machine prototype shop as low man on the totem pole. I was going to school, too. When the earthquake hit, I was at Chabot College Library.

I was on the second floor of a two-story building, which started swaying side to side. Instinct told me "under the desk," and under the desk I went. People were running around and around. I grabbed one girl by the hand as she went by me. At the same time, I was yelling at the top of my lungs, "Find a desk, get under it, and cover your heads!" After I grabbed that girl's hand and told her to get down, the fluorescent tubes from a light came down. They came down so slowly: frame, frame, frame, frame, smash. We were still swaying, and I said to myself, "This building is going to fall." Impending feeling of doom.

After the building stopped moving, I shouted, "Everybody out, everybody out, out, out, out, out!" Then: "Walk, walk. Walk quickly, but walk." There was a lot of screaming, a lot of high shrieks. The building was evacuated with the exception of a few people who were too scared to leave. I was too scared to stay and talk them out. Then I went around the other buildings in the quad area, looking for people who were hurt.

Chabot College is in Hayward, along Mission Boulevard. It was closer to the epicenter of the quake than San Francisco. A lot of people had radios, and somebody yelled, "The bridge fell! The Cypress fell!" I knew Cypress.

After I graduated from high school, I went to EMT school, emergency medical technician. I did emergency response ambulance work for a short time but didn't like it. Then I found out about a special unit dedicated to Children's Hospital of Oakland, and joined a company called Patient Care Ambulance. But I wanted to get out because I needed time to go to school. I had let my EMT license expire.

When they said that Cypress had fallen, I knew what it was. I knew it was a two-level freeway and that cars would be in between them.

It was a major catastrophe. Everybody was running around like Chicken Little. So I got on my bike and rode. Everywhere I went there were lights and sirens. On my way, I stopped at my house and I picked up my jumpsuit and my ID, which still looked valid.

I showed up at the scene wearing my emergency response uniform, my jumpsuit with EMT nightglow on the back. I looked as if I belonged there, and I jumped in. People from all walks of life were working side by side pulling rocks off the Cypress. The structure had fallen and there were piles of debris. The rocks had to come off. So I started throwing: pebble, pebble, pebble, rock, rock, rock. If there was anybody alive in there, we had to get them out fast; there wasn't time to move in heavy equipment. One level fell onto the other: an automobile sandwich.

I sweated away, lifting rocks, lifting rubble. When I got tired, I'd take a break and somebody else would start where I left off. It was getting dark, and some people set up a little booth to pass out supplies. People were going to need water. People were scared, beyond panic.

About seven o'clock, when I came down from the bridge, ministers were talking with frightened people and offering them hope. I listened to the words of a minister talking to a lady. He said, "Worrying isn't going to help you." He said the person she was worrying about was "a potential victim, not a victim. He might be delayed on the other side of the bridge." The World Series was going on, so there weren't as many people on the Cypress as there would have been during rush-hour traffic any other day. The minister went on: "There's a lot of hope. He might have stopped off in a bar to watch the game. He might be a million places other than on the bridge. Worrying isn't going to help anybody. What you have to do is pray."

I listened to him, and I said to myself, "Giving these people a little hope is going a long way." So I found a lady who was sitting down crying. She was really worried about her son, who was with his best friend in the city. I repeated almost the same sermon over and over again, to her and to other people. This went on all night long.

I didn't sleep that night. I couldn't get a call through to my wife, and she didn't know where I was. I panicked her and my family terribly, but what I was doing had all my attention. It was so important to me at the time that everything else was irrelevant.

After the quake shook me at the college, I was terrified. Then I thought: that could have been it. It could have ended your whole life, and you have accomplished nothing. Life gone in a blink. I said to myself, "I've got to help." I was really compelled to help.

Early in the morning, bodies started being brought out. The bodies would come down in a bag. I'd open the bag, see the body, look for identification, then close it up, and tag the bag. Zip and tag, zip and tag. I talked a lot of people down, too. I zipped and tagged, and talked; zipped and tagged, and talked. I helped out in any way I thought I could. I think I tagged thirty bodies. I don't have any idea how many people I talked to. I know I talked to somebody constantly during my time there. A talk-down might take two or three minutes; it might take an hour.

I worked there for eighty-four straight hours; three and a half days. I caught an hour nap here or thirty minutes there, but I didn't take very many breaks. What I was doing was very important to me. I had a certain amount of authority. I carry myself well and people respond to that. Give them information with assuredness and calmness and they respond very well. Give them information that's accurate. Sometimes I just turned up my radio. I'd have two or three people with me and I'd say, "Here's what I know. Feel free to hold my radio for a little while, but you have to be calm, don't break it, and I'll be back to pick it up a little later." I'd just go off and talk to somebody else.

About day two, I called a bunch of numbers a lot of times, and finally got through to my wife. I said I was on the Cypress, and told her then and there, "Things are going to be different when I get home." I meant it, and I stuck by it.

Cinnamon, Brendon, and I were three people living in the same house. I was working two jobs and going to school, and I was an ass. We got married in 1988; we'd been together for five years. I treated her nice right up until the day Brendon was born; then I started going to school. "I have to graduate, I've got to graduate." My grades were failing anyway. Pregnancy, child to come, your fellow students don't know, you're keeping it all a big secret. Whenever we were together, we'd fight. Sometimes I'd get so angry it was like looking through a red balloon. My wife's not the type of person who backs down, and neither am I. One day I got physical. It was a mistake and it was wrong, but I lost control. I put her to the wall. I wanted her to shut up. That gives you a picture of what my life was like. I wasn't doing well at all. I felt pressure all the time. I remember headaches. Everybody was always calling me to bitch. I was mad all the time.

I worked Saturday, Sunday, Monday, Tuesday, and Wednesday at one job. I worked three overlapping days, and the other two days would be just one job. On the two days that weren't overlapping, I'd go to school. I was beyond angry, and nothing was mine.

Now that I look back on it, I had a lot—a lot that I didn't choose to take advantage of, and I saw that the night of the quake. How long does it take a caterpillar to become a butterfly? It didn't take me any time at all. I had a metamorphosis right then and there at the bridge. My son has never been sick a day. He is smart. He is everything that a perfect child could be. I started thinking about how lucky I was. I never saw it before. I saw sick kids every day. I saw death every day when I worked Patient Care. I never took the time to appreciate what I had. I didn't see the time I took to go to school as being my time. I saw it as something I was doing for somebody else. I felt like a rat running around a maze to get a piece of cheese. The night of the quake I realized, I'm not a rat, I'm not a rat. I can be anything I want. It was an amazing revelation.

When I came home, I changed. I was pleasanter to be around, I was more understanding. My wife was "amazed"—that's her word. She wouldn't buy it at first. She was so suspicious she didn't know whether I should go see a psychiatrist or whether I'd just flipped out. We even started making pancakes on Sunday morning. I'm quite good at it now.

As hard as it had been before, it got a lot easier. I quit both jobs. I got another job where my dad and my wife work. The more time we spent together before, the more friction there was. The time we're spending together now is quality time. I'm not saying it went from rough seas to smooth sailing, but everything started getting better. We paid off old bills. The car, which was nothing but problems, I just gave away. I said, "Get it out of here."

During those eighty-four hours, I got a brand-new perspective. The perspective was that people are people. Nobody's out to get me; nobody's out to hurt me. My family, who hadn't been important to me before, was important to me now. I am dedicated to my family now.

Before I don't know if I'd have paid a ransom on them. Today I'd sell my soul to get my family back.

When I was working for Patient Care Ambulance, I picked up a quotation, "If I were to die today, would everything in my life be the way I wanted it to be?" At the time, I thought it was a really neat statement, but I didn't put it into my heart. That statement came to life that night. Nothing was as I wanted it to be. I said, "I've got to change this." To coin a phrase, "I saw the light."

I used to be angry a lot. People didn't like to be around me because if I was offended, I'd tell somebody, "Goodbye, you're gone." I don't do that much anymore. I am convinced that without this quake I would never, ever have experienced what I'm experiencing today. I had no self-esteem at all. It was hard for me to look at myself in the mirror. I laughed and I smiled, but I wasn't happy. Fueling airplanes? Big deal. I didn't want to be a grunt. I didn't want to live and be average and die. I wanted to be something.

I'm going to school to be a nurse. I also teach dance now to small children. It's volunteer time. My son Brendon and I started in February of 1990. He had seen the movie *Tap* and would come into the kitchen clomping around. "What are you doing?" I asked him. He answered with authority in his three-year-old voice, "I'm tapping," and I said, "Okay, we'll give it a shot." Up until the quake, dancing was something I never did. I took an adult class and he took a child class. I've worked at it every week since I started. I give it no less than four hours a week, and it's usually double or triple that. We've even done a few performances. My relationship with my wife is excellent. We talk and we have dinner together. It was never a family before the quake, but it's a family now.

The day of the quake I realized I had a skill that will be with me for the rest of my life. When I was standing there talking to people, or zipping and tagging, I realized there aren't many people who can do that. After the quake, I felt I had performed well. I went to a call that I wasn't even called for, I just went. After the quake, my self-esteem was restored. Every time I look inside myself today, I see a person who can help. I see a person who's worthy. I see a person I can appreciate. Probably a lot of people like themselves, and I'm one of them now. I didn't like myself before, but I like myself now.

Sometimes we are so unhappy that we need to change. Our suffering tells us something is wrong. Pain is the motivator.

The causes of unhappiness may be self-preoccupation, low self-esteem, self-centeredness, failure in relationships, resentments, trying to meet someone's expectations, blaming others, victimization, addiction. Through the process of therapy, counseling, group support, and personal inventory, we change; life itself may stay the same. Our internal changes create the freedom to be ourselves and we experience a personal vitality we never dreamed we had. Personal growth requires willingness, hard work, and patience.

Susan Warner is an accounting and computing consultant who owns her own management support business, WarnerAccess, in San Francisco, California.

"I Knew What Counted and What Didn't"

Susan Warner

I had come back to San Francisco the summer of 1988. My husband and I had separated, so I was in a big third-floor flat in the Marina area doing nothing because he was paying the rent. Having grown up in an alcoholic, rage-a-holic home, and having had a dysfunctional and abusive childhood, I didn't know how to do anything except take care of the needs of other people in order to be allowed to be around them. I see my workaholism as a way that I kill pain. When I've got my nose buried in a computer screen, I'm perfectly happy because I am completely invisible to myself. My eating behavior is the same kind of thing. I used to go grocery shopping and I would get a panic or diarrhea attack in the store because there were so many choices. I wanted everything. It became easier not to eat at all. I do everything in extreme except chemicals.

I watched my mother do everything around my father. Nothing in my mother's life was about her having any sense of a life separate from him. I've never seen my mother have a close female friend at all. My father traveled a great deal. When he was away, my mother's attention centered on me. When my father returned, my mother's attention returned to him. Where some people feel abandoned when a parent goes away, I felt abandoned when my father came home. It took a long time for me to sort that out.

I had no experience of myself as somebody truly separate and apart from everybody else until I came into recovery and did two years in Adult Children of Alcoholics. I had no concept of having been a child, having had fun, having been silly, having climbed a tree or gotten dirty. I can remember when I was a child being at drunken brawls in bars with my mom and dad, hiding under the table, watching furniture and bottles fly around the place. I could try to describe it to you, but the terror that a four-year-old child would feel at that scene was something I couldn't feel.

That summer in San Francisco, I realized that I was still repeating old patterns, that I was still choosing people who were needy. I was needy, too. The way I took care of my needs was to find somebody more needy than I was, and then I could be powerful. What I'd done all my life was to make myself useful to other people. I would talk in meetings and attract people with what I said. They would come up to me, and as soon as they gave me their attention, I was right there focused on what they needed to say. Then I would make myself available on the phone, and if for some reason they couldn't stay in their apartment at night, they could come and stay with me.

What attracted me to such people was that they paid attention to me. As soon as anyone did so, I zeroed in to get more attention and keep the person around. I had no idea that I could participate in a relationship on any kind of balanced basis or that it was okay for me to have needs similar to other people's.

On the Fourth of July, I told someone I had been available to—a young woman—if I was going to spend time with her that day, that what I needed was not to be her big sister and concerned with her feelings, but I needed to be the little sister for a change. She got very angry at me and stomped out of my flat. So I pulled back from people at that point, and I was pretty much alone. I was reading a lot, I was crying a lot. But for the first time in my life I was spending time with myself without experiencing real depression. For probably six weeks I didn't go to a single recovery meeting, because I couldn't trust myself not to tie myself right back in again if anybody came up and talked to me.

When I finally started going back to meetings, I met a woman who gave me a set of tapes on child abuse by Pia Melody. Among other things, Pia talks about how most adults would treat an expensive vase more carefully and preciously than they would a child. It had never occurred to me that I might be precious until I heard those tapes. Listening to them was a tremendous breakthrough.

On the afternoon of the earthquake, I had lain down to rest in my spare room with the TV on, and had fallen asleep. I was lying on a futon, and when I woke up, it was moving across the room toward the television set, which was coming at me, and the chandelier was flying up to meet the ceiling. The first thought I had was I wanted to be dead and gone before "the big one" happened. It was terror and anger at the same time. I had to get out of that room because one whole wall is windows. Since the flat is a long Victorian one, I had to run about fifty feet to get to the middle of the house where it would be safer.

I remember the noise. It sounded as if all the wood in the house was in a big basket and a giant was shaking it. The next thought I had was: If this is as bad as it's going to get, I'll be okay.

The actual quake lasted approximately fifteen seconds, but I had no concept of time. Most people felt that it lasted forever. I started throwing things into a big shoulder bag. I knew I wouldn't come back to the house that night; I didn't want to be alone in a third-floor flat if another quake happened—with no lights, no water, no telephone.

My flat was three blocks from the first building that fell down and two blocks from the Marina Middle School where the Red Cross put the homeless people after the earthquake. With the exception of the Bay Bridge, the Marina was the hardest-hit area. It looked like a war zone for months afterward.

When I got outside, people were walking around as if it were any other day. I managed to cross Lombard Street to get to my therapist's office. I was fifteen minutes early. There was an aftershock, and I crouched with another person in the office. I noticed how scared she was, but I really wasn't scared anymore. I waited until 6:15—my appointment was for six o'clock. Terror went through me when my therapist didn't arrive. Somebody said she had gone to Oakland, and I was terrified that she might have been on the Cypress structure or on the Bay Bridge. It was actually the fear of a small child being afraid she'd lost her mother.

I had learned how to play in the back of the bar, and that's what I did the night of the earthquake. A friend of mine owns a bar here in the city, and he kept it open that night. That's where I went. I sat in the back, listened to the radio, and watched the people at the bar. That was familiar.

The next day, when I got back to my flat, I called and talked to my therapist's husband. He told me the last time he'd seen her, which was about fifteen minutes ago, she was just fine. She phoned me the next morning, and we talked for almost an hour.

Most of my friends suffered greater emotional trauma after the earthquake than I did. I had a completely opposite response, and wondered what was wrong with me because people were edgy and I wasn't. I spent the first four days after the earthquake putting together a thousand-piece jigsaw puzzle. It just seemed like the right thing to do. I was rethinking all the things that had happened and going through a lot of feelings. For me, the whole experience of the earthquake was about being able to see how I had been shedding chaos in my life and about getting things organized. With a jigsaw puzzle you can get some pieces to fit together because they look as if they're supposed to fit. But if you hold them up, you'll see light come through and you know they're not the matching pieces. My life was like a big jigsaw puzzle. It was as if the picture was all mixed up. I'd pick up hunks of it and hold them up to the light and realize the pieces really didn't fit. The picture of my life never looked right until after the earthquake.

At first I felt ashamed that nothing really horrible had happened to my flat; not a single piece of plaster fell in my house. The kitchen cupboard doors that didn't lock tightly opened up, but nothing came out. In the restaurant next door, the kitchen fell apart, but nothing in my house broke. In fact, two things were fixed. My toilet used to make a terrible noise. After the earthquake, it was quiet. The front door lock used to stick, and it didn't anymore.

The Marina Counseling Center was doing earthquake survival meetings for people to discuss the effects of the earthquake. One woman talked about not being able to get to her job. Others talked about their fear. They talked about things they lost. Some were homeless.

When it came my turn to talk, I said that I didn't understand why I wasn't as upset as everybody else. I knew that there was every reason to trust what I was feeling, but I couldn't because all around me people were so frightened. Finally, the facilitator of the group told me that for most people who have reasonably orderly lives, it's as if they've cleaned out their closet. They've taken the clothing they're not going to wear anymore, folded it all neatly, and put it in a box up on the shelf. They thought it was all dealt with, and that the order they saw was what they could believe in and trust. When the earthquake came along, it opened the closet door and threw the box out into the room. Now those old clothes were all over the place again, and they needed to be sorted through once more.

Because of what I had been doing that summer in coming to terms with how the picture of my life had become skewed, growing up in an alcoholic home, acting out much of my mother's behavior in focusing so much on other people and not enough on myself, the facilitator said,

"It seems to have happened in reverse for you, Susan. You had all these old pieces of clothing lying around on the floor, and when the earthquake happened, it just folded them all up neatly and put them in the box, then put the box up on the shelf, and closed the doors." That was exactly my experience. Now I knew what counted and what didn't.

All that counted for me after the earthquake was to be kind to myself, to stop badgering myself in any way, to stop letting people be around me who were badgering themselves, to stop allowing myself in any way to have negativeness around me, and to stop abusing myself emotionally.

I made a commitment to a little five-year-old girl named Susan that nobody was going to matter more than she did. I give first priority to my relationship with God, my second priority to my relationship with myself, and my third to the relationship with whoever happens to be in front of me, and that person changes all the time.

My business is successful today. My relationships are unbelievable. I have several women friends, and I'm starting to date in a moderate way. I always held on to people, and they would go away, usually angry. I don't hold on to anybody anymore, and more and more people keep coming back. The earthquake had a profound effect on my self-esteem because I knew God wanted me on the planet.

I had lived through a major automobile accident and lost my little brother in a plane crash. On some level, I always had the feeling that I was just barely escaping. The profoundness of it all was realizing that I wasn't meant to be homeless, that I wasn't meant to be dead.

I kept wanting to go over and "rescue" somebody with a child from the Marina Middle School shelter because that's what "I'm supposed to do." Friends who were living at the shelter said, "Don't bring anybody home, Susan. Take care of yourself." Even those who had lost everything were supportive of what I had to go through, which was so different from what they had to go through.

It was my own earthquake. It's an addiction to need to help somebody. That's what co-dependency and love addiction are all about. I had to break the pattern.

I'm filing for divorce. He's not my father, he's my husband, and I was using him the way a child uses a dad. I can't use him as a dad anymore because I'm more mature. I'm outgrowing my need to have daddy figures. It's as if I were about seventeen or eighteen years old and about to move away from home for the first time.

S ome people claim to live a totally different life after a traumatic event or an ordeal of pain. Not only do the externals change, but the very essence of the person is altered. The greatest personal change a human being can undergo is the transformation from being self-centered to becoming unselfishly focused on others.

There is the triumph over personal hardship and the discovery of goodness and compassion as well. We find our very essence; we discover who we are. By putting others first, satisfaction is the dividend; happiness is the result.

Bill Russell is the President of Nish-Nah-Bee Industries, Inc., in Traverse City, Michigan, an assembly operations plant that supplies products to General Motors and other automotive companies.

"I'm Finally Starting to Get Happy"

Bill Russell

My greatest achievement was escaping my own environment. I was brought up in a family of thirteen children. My mother is a full-blooded Ottawa Indian and my father is a half-breed Chippewa Indian. My father, when he married my mother, moved our family to Traverse City, Michigan, and we were the only Indian family in an all-white community. My mother and dad were very much alcoholic when I was young. I don't remember a lot of my childhood but I do remember getting swatted at and beaten up on. I left home when I was eleven years old because of the physical abuse. I had received a bad beating. My father was very drunk, and he said some terrible things to me and I said some terrible things to him. I was eleven; my father was fifty-five. The eleven-year-old lost. I packed my little belongings and lived on the beach in Traverse City for over three months. I was finally taken in by one of my sisters who had recently been divorced and needed a babysitter. As I remember all this, I can feel my head getting warm.

What I really had to fight was not only the fact that we came from a very poor, uneducated, alcoholic family, but to top it off, back in the thirties and forties Native Americans, or American Indians, were treated as blacks were, so we experienced a lot of discrimination. The neighbors across the street from us would not let us play with their children; I was not allowed, when I was a young man, to go out with girls; people called me "chief"—all things that caused me a great deal of anguish.

I had learned physical abuse from my parents. When someone made fun of me, the only way I seemed able to react was to retaliate. I flunked two or three grades in elementary school because I wouldn't go to school. I still couldn't read when I was in the sixth grade. I was thrown out of several elementary schools in the city. My getting in fights in grade school and high school was the reason I got transferred so many times. In those days, the punishment for getting into a fight was a whipping; the janitor would hold you and the principal would spank you with a razor strap. One time I got in another scrap after I'd just had a spanking. The principal, who'd just spanked me, separated us. There was a good-sized rock on the ground and I grabbed the rock and hit him right between the eyes with it.

I remember many instances of being physically abused by my father and my mother, by the school system, and by other children. My response was to be physically abusive to other people; that seemed to be the only thing I knew. I was a very small person but very strong. People used to call me ugly, which also caused me a lot of grief. When I was young, I got my front teeth knocked out in a hockey game. We could never afford to have our teeth fixed, so I went around for years with holes in my mouth and my teeth. I didn't get them fixed until I was fifty years old. I had no dental care at all from the time I was born until the time I was fifteen or sixteen.

My mother ended up being the worse of the two alcoholics. We lived in a house with no heat, no electricity, and no running water. We had outdoor johns. We had a pump out in the yard. We had a garbage room at the back of the house, and it was absolute filth. The health people came and condemned our house and made us move. In the wintertime—we had no beds—I slept on a mattress on the floor with Salvation Army coats for blankets. There was little food. My parents spent their money on alcohol. My dad abused everybody in our family, especially my mother. Many times I can remember being flung across the room and hitting the wall. I'd stand back up and get it again. I was the twelfth of thirteen children, and by the time the alcoholic abuse got to me, it was unbelievable.

When I left home and lived at my sister's house, I had several jobs and became intent on getting through school. I'm a fairly determined individual; I have no idea where it came from. I get fixed on a course and, like a bulldozer, I keep pumping and pumping until I finally accomplish what I set out to do. It's either black or white in my life, no gray at all.

Believe it or not, because I was such a rarity, one of the very few

Native Americans in northern Michigan to graduate from a high school, the Ottawa Indian Association sought me out and gave me a scholarship to Michigan State University, in Lansing. I was given room, board, tuition, books, fees, and spending money. It was wonderful. So I went to college and screwed up. I was accepted, and I soon forgot about school and started getting into relationships. I went to Lansing in September and the university asked me to leave in December. I knew it was coming, so I actually left before they dismissed me.

I went into the Marine Corps. The reason I joined was that somebody told me they were good and tough, and I considered myself one of the tough boys. I broke thirteen pairs of glasses in boot camp; somebody would say something I thought was offensive, and naturally I would hit him.

However, in the Marine Corps I started eating properly. I got some good medical care and had some of my teeth fixed. The Corps was really good for me; it gave me the opportunity to get some of my anger out, with the encouragement of the drill sergeants. I took quite a bit of advantage of that, until I really hurt somebody. Then I stopped, and I have never done it since. I put a man in the hospital with broken ribs and a concussion, and it was all over a cigarette. Finally, when I hurt that man so badly, a bell went off. I had to figure out how to get through life without being physical. The Corps gave me some tests and decided that I was a halfway decent student. They sent me to Naval Justice School where I became a court recorder.

At the Naval Justice School I was in a class of thirty-eight students, and I came out the highest of all the enlisted men in the class. I was asked to go on a special legal team in the Marine Corps because of my scores. It was the first time I'd received a reward for doing something, but I figured that if I didn't get either a college degree or some special training, I would end up doing the physical work I'd seen my parents do and living like them. So in the second two years of my four-year hitch, I went every night to the library on the base, and I read and read and read. I took all the courses I had screwed up in and taught myself how to get going. I finally took an entrance exam for college, got an early discharge, and, with the GI Bill, went off to college. I ended up getting a bachelor's degree and a master's degree in accounting, and I also have a teaching certificate for high-school education. In 1961, I graduated from Michigan State University with very good grades, something like 3.6 in my course area, and 3.3 or 3.4 overall. Meantime I'd gotten married, but when I went to the university I worked in the hospital seventy hours a week, went to school full time, and studied full time. When I finished school, my wife divorced me because I was never around. Then I got hired by the Ford Motor Company. But at Ford I did the same thing again; I started to work eighty, ninety, and a hundred hours a week. I ended up bouncing a little for about a year, until I met my present wife. We got married, and I settled down again.

Up until that point, I had not done any drinking at all. I had made the typical vow: "I will never do what my parents did." When I quit working the wild number of hours and quit being so concentrated having to go to school, even though I was still working eighty or ninety hours a week, there was somehow still time left, and that's when I started to get interested in drinking. After we were married for about five years, we moved into Traverse City and then I really got into it. I discovered the party scene, got into a terrible group, and just took right off. I made myself a real ass. I drank every day and poured myself into bed. I'd come home at eight or nine o'clock from work and start drinking.

I was getting wild with my drinking. A lot of my business was downstate, so I'd say that I had to be downstate more often. I'd buy a bottle when I got there. Sometimes I didn't even have sales calls to go to, so I would drink in the motel room. I'd drink every day and I'd drink until I was drunk. I began to act like a boisterous fool in restaurants.

On one of my trips, I went out to dinner with an old friend of mine and his wife. We drank before going to the restaurant. I proceeded to get so inebriated at the restaurant that when his wife said something about the light being too bright, I got up on the table and then fell off trying to turn the light off. Though I was to pay for the dinner, I could not read the bill. My friends later told me that I went outside and grabbed hold of the wooden arm on the parking gate and ripped it off, because I didn't want to put in the thirty-five cents to raise the arm. I didn't go home then; I made them drop me off at another bar and I have no idea what I did. I was doing similar things quite regularly.

My last drunk was February 14, Valentine's Day, 1981. My wife and I went out to a restaurant with another couple. We had cocktails and four bottles of wine before dinner. Then we went to their condominium and they opened a fifth of Jack Daniel's. I wouldn't leave until I had finished the bottle. Naturally, I didn't get up the next morning until eleven-thirty. These same people came over to have lunch with us. We were on vacation and they said, "Well, why don't we have a drink?" I was still sicker than a dog from the night before. They put that sucker in front of me and I looked at it. I was so green and felt so awful that I pushed it back. I never had another one. That's when I stopped.

I wasn't drinking, but I was still a complete ass at home and doing the things I had done before. I didn't have any friends. I would railroad everything. I can't imagine how my wife stayed with me. I would pile-drive and hurt and be angry and say terrible things. People in the plant who worked for me hated my guts.

In my aggressive stage, I thought that if I made money my life would be wonderful. Everybody would love me—my kids would love me, my wife would love me. My goal, because of my beginnings, was to find out how to make money, and that's really what my life was about. I was very good at it. I'm still not bad at it. Making money was not one of my problems; my real problem was about me.

We were visiting friends, Betty and Ree Lasker in Eau Claire, Wisconsin, and Betty told me a story about a man who was an alcoholic. He had been sober for a long time. The guy retired, and he was fishing in the lake one day and thought since he was retired he could have a drink. He popped open a can of beer, and six months later he died from alcoholism. That story really struck me. I finally figured out that I was still an alcoholic; I just wasn't drinking. And I realized that someday down the road I would think it was okay for me to drink again. She said, "If you could, you ought to go to an alcoholism recovery meeting, see if you like it." When I arrived home, I phoned and asked where there was a meeting. I went to my first recovery meeting six years ago. I've been going ever since.

Today my wife and I get along well. We've been married twenty-nine and a half years. My son—he got thrown out of high school; I can't imagine where he learned that—didn't graduate from a local school. We had to send him to a tutorial school to get him into a college. In December he'll graduate from the University of Michigan with a Master's degree in human resources. He's doing very nicely. My daughter is now a junior at Eastern Michigan University down in Ypsilanti and she's doing very well, too. I'm pleased at how my kids have turned out. I think they're both going to be good responsible citizens.

What's changed for me is the quality of life. I have a terrible drive, and I absolutely want to be right. It's caused so much trouble, strife, and disharmony in my life. It's also done some good in that it's given me motivation to become educated and to do well in business. At my stage in life, I need to take it easy and be good to myself. In learning to be good to myself, I am finally learning to be good to other people. I run our company today on principles of honesty and kindness to others. If you were to ask my employees, I think most of them would tell you they've probably never had a boss like me. I show my emotions. I try to be good with the people. I listen to them. I look at them when they're talking. I also tell them about me. We share, and when we share we become part of each other. I don't mistreat them. The people on the floor know as much about this company as I do.

I'm fifty-five years old, and I'm finally starting to get happy, a state I've not achieved before in my life. The best is yet to come. I'm proud to be a Native American; I'm proud to be an American Indian; I'm proud of who I am today. I was a mean son of a bitch. What is interesting is to take a look at the pictures of me ten years, fifteen years ago. Recently, my wife and I went to a family reunion in Sun Valley, Idaho. All the family was there. There were lots of pictures of me, and the most interesting thing is I'm always smiling. I'd never seen myself smile before. The best one was a picture somebody took of me in a kayak going down the Salmon River. We were whitewater rafting and I'm going through a great big wave in this kayak with my oar, and I'm smiling. They took about ten pictures of others going down the river, and I was the only one smiling. They were all a bunch of young guys; I was the oldest one there. The rest of them were all serious. They wanted to do it well, and I was just sliding through the rapids. I was having a hell of a time.

We now live in a three-bedroom ranch and I do my own lawn. I've gotten rid of my boats, I've gotten rid of the cars. My change of view in the value of money has gone from number one to probably seven or eight out of ten. I finally figured out that I am not the important person; you are. As soon as I understood you are, then I began to get better. It's taken a long time for me to do that.

Support and Wisdom

Helping Others

_____

The primary source of support for those experiencing adversity is family and friends. Through their care, love, time, and attention, value is affirmed, hope is offered, feelings are released, and recovery is achieved. Those who suffer need not suffer alone if family and friends are there for them.

In order that we may support our loved ones better, and so that others may know how to support us more effectively when the time comes, the contributors who had faced traumatic times were asked to recall what kind of help from others was most effective for them when they hurt, and the experts were asked to give their advice on what constitutes effective support.

Dr. Robert Buckman on Supporting Others

A young physician who died of testicular cancer wrote an article in the *Lancet,* which was published shortly after he died. He described his illness as a prison cell. He said there are different kinds of doctors—you can use this to describe family as well. Some doctors just look through the peephole in the door and walk on past to the next. Some open the door and exchange a few comments with you. Others open the door wide and come and sit on the bed next to you. I'm adding a little bit to his analogy, but both you and the patient, the prisoner, know that the prisoner has to stay and the visitor is free to leave. However, the act of opening the door wide and sitting on the bed is perceived as support and sympathy. That's what family members, friends, doctors, and nurses should be trying to do within whatever time availability they have.

There is a deep urge in us that makes us try to support others. I know I sound like Desmond Morris here, but he does talk a lot of sense. He says, "Man is a very cooperative animal." When one of us is wounded, we tend to try to help and support. We have the desire to help, but most of us haven't been shown how to do it properly and our sense of propriety gets in the way.

One aspect of this is the fear of being tainted. Rationally, we try to withdraw from a person who is sick because we are so frightened that it could happen to us. But if we realize—I pick my words carefully— "there but for fortune go I," it actually strikes us that random fortune could cause this to happen to us. We will pull away from that person because we don't want to acknowledge that fact.

In helping someone who is going through a major adversity, the first thing is to establish whether or not you're in the right position and whether you're wanted. If you're not wanted, try not to take it person-ally. Something happens to old Fred and you rush round. It may be that you're exactly the person that old Fred wants to talk to because he doesn't like his family, or it may be not. The first thing to do in supporting somebody in adversity is to make an offer, leave it, and then come back and see whether you're wanted or not. Quite a good idea is to, as it were, leave your emotional calling card with another relative, or with somebody who isn't in the first circle of supporters and say, "If I can help please let me know."

However good and well-equipped to help you think you are, try not to thrust yourself at the patient. The second rule is, make your offer specific. There's absolutely no use saying to somebody in adversity, "If there's anything I can do, please call." That's completely pointless. Say, "Look, can I come round and see you Tuesday?" Then ring up on Monday and say, "Shall I see you tomorrow?" In that way you give the person a chance to exercise control and options. The person might respond, "No, I don't want you to cook me dinner, but I'd love to go to that movie I've been dying to see." It is useful to have some pragmatic suggestions. With gifts, don't go and buy someone a car unless you're the kind of person who normally gives cars to people. Offer to baby-sit.

The rules of good listening make up about eighty percent of good supporting. First, however, get the physical context right. That means sitting down, eyes level at—and I now quote from intercultural relations expert Edward T. Hall—"a distance of twenty-one to thirty inches between you." If the person is angry, not necessarily with you, it's also very helpful to have your head lower than his. It's very interesting how lowering the head diffuses anger. You want to look as if you're there to stay, so undo your coat and take it off. People do sit with their coat done up because they're so frightened. Get physical stuff like the bedside table out of your way, create an area of privacy, and shut the door.

Having got the physical context right, you just need basic rules of good listening. Number one, don't interrupt. If the person is talking, you don't talk. Number two, when he says something, show that you've heard it. One of the most important techniques is using a word or some variation of a word that the person has used in a previous sentence, to show that the sentence has been received. Then roll the conversation along with what we call facilitation technique. It's a grand phrase but it actually means saying, "Yes, uh-huh," and "Tell me more," and "I see," nodding and smiling and encouraging, making sure that when you say something it is partly set, or the direction of it is set, by what the person just said.

If you say A, and she says B, and you say A again, that'll show you haven't listened. If she says B, and you say X, it'll also show that you haven't listened. If she says B, and you say yes, not only B, but also C, it shows that you've heard and are in a way being molded by what the person is saying. That is most valuable. That is what listening means: being changed by what the other person has said.

The most important bit of what goes on inside the patient is ventilation. We really underrate this. Allowing somebody to say something he thinks or feels, and staying there while he says it, is an incredible therapeutic action in itself. Simply staying in the same room with somebody who is deeply depressed or intolerant or self-sympathetic, and showing, by staying in the room and not recoiling, that you accept that as an attitude and as part of the person is amazingly helpful to him.

A lot of support has to do with giving permission. One thing you should really try to do is, if somebody is feeling lousy, give him permission to feel lousy. You don't necessarily do it by saying, "I give you permission to feel lousy." The subtext of what you're saying is "You're still Derrick or Fred or Susan despite the fact that you're feeling lousy."

You don't want premixed foods and dishes thrust at the person. You don't want to offer any "one size fits all" kind of philosophy. Certainly you don't want any moralizing. The tendency to draw lessons and moralize is very high. The listener is trying to protect himself from the thought that this illness might happen to him, so he says, "Now, you should never have done that. I told you not to go to Africa and get near those funny mosquitoes." The tendency to moralize is the listener's defense.

Part of the action of listening is to lower your own defenses and accept that the act of listening may be painful for you. You may actually hear things that link you to the patient: "There but for fortune . . ." The kindest things you can do are to avoid moralizing, drawing lessons, pointing out how much better you are. Probably you're not much better. None of us are really any better than anybody else. A very small number of us are worse. What you are is not necessarily better than the other person; you are just luckier at that particular moment. We absolutely do not need spiritual and religious judgments. I'm afraid there are people who do make them. People really do think, Great, he's sick, he's in bed, he's immobilized—this is just the moment for me to go over and convert him.

A lot of people, many more than are recognized, feel very guilty about illness. If they're sick they have the feeling that they oughtn't to be, that somehow they ought to be at work. They shot both legs off: "Well, I should be back at work Friday." We really admire and enshrine health, youth, and beauty. That's terrible. If somebody has shot both your legs off, you really needs some time to adjust to it.

Giving a person permission to be ill was a fantastic lesson I learned personally. I was walking around with all kinds of things going wrong. My nerves were failing in my hands and feet. I had skin blotches and bad arthritis, and it affected my bowel at one stage. A doctor looked at me and said, "This must be terrible for you, Buckman. You've got all these terrible things going wrong with you; your skin, your peripheral nerves, your joints, and now your bowel. It must be awful." That was the first time anybody had said such a thing to me. I almost hugged the bloke. I thought, God, this is amazing; I now feel legit, I now feel it's okay to feel as awful as I do.

When eventually I got back to work, that was a device I used quite often with my patients. In one patient, it turned her instantly from an unapproachable, angry, withdrawn lady into somebody who was completely outgoing and calm when I told her that she was judging herself much too harshly. She was really sick, and any normal person would have taken to bed two months before. She'd been up and out and at work and compelling herself on for months to the point where a lot of people would have given up completely. I acknowledged that she was really terribly ill and that she had no grounds for blaming herself or feeling guilty. Within a few minutes she was almost transformed. The next day she was just amazing. It was extraordinary.

Georgann Fuller on Being There

What helped me was that people were there. They'd call and say, "Let's go have lunch," or "I'm coming over just to be with you," and they would let me talk. I feel very strongly that people who are grieving a loss need to talk, not only to go over the same material, but to choose what they want to remember about the lost person. Eventually many memories will fade away. So they're trying to find those memories they want to hold on to. Oftentimes a friend or relative who knows the person can remind you of things.

I was lucky because most of my friends didn't tell me to "get on with my life" until about a year after Jim died. But I still get a lot of "it's time for you to let go." If people really thought about who I am, they would know I'd get on with my life.

Rabbi Joseph Telushkin on Waiting to Speak

I'll tell you an interesting law that is known by traditional Jews, but not widely by non-traditional Jews, and certainly not known by non-Jews. When someone dies, Jews observe mourning for seven days. It's called Shiva. When you visit a mourner's house, you are not supposed to speak until the mourner speaks to you. There is a very specific reason for this. You don't know what the mourner needs at that moment. You might feel you must speak to him or her about the dead person, but it's possible that at that moment what the mourner needs is not to focus on that.

Likewise, you might walk in and feel your job is to take the mourner's mind off the deceased, so you'll talk about sports or world affairs. This may be a mockery because the person does need to speak about the dead person. Maybe you simply don't know what to do. The mourner might really just want to sit in silence.

Interestingly, the rabbis claim to have learned the tradition of not speaking first in a mourner's house from the Book of Job. When Job's three friends, who turned out not to be totally great friends, heard about what happened to Job, they came and visited him, and it says they sat near Job, on the floor, for seven days without speaking.

What one is supposed to do is wait to hear what the mourner says. Then respond to that, to that need.

Richard Berendzen on Hearing from Others

When I was in the hospital, Gail would come to visit every day. We would also speak on the phone when she was back in Washington. She would tell me about what mail and calls had come in and about people on the street stopping to say hello. They were the life ring tossed from the boat. When I felt I was going down for the second, third, or last time, she would say, "Let me read this letter. Let me tell you about this call." So-and-so had called and left a message on the answering machine. And she'd play it for me. Out of the ocean of despair it would pick me up.

Later we met people who said, "I just didn't know what to say." I know they were absolutely honest in that. I know they were with us all the way, but they felt they would intrude, that we were busy, that we had a crisis, and to call or write would be the wrong thing. I understand that. I might have done the same thing. Gail's message in her speech to a luncheon of concerned women who had come together to support us was "dare" to write.

Gail Berendzen on Reaching Out

It doesn't have to be a tome, you don't have to write a long letter. If you know somebody is having a problem and you react to it, then get your reaction out to the person. In our case, each letter was different; each one reflected the person who sent it. That, in itself, was a treasure. Some people we know have a rather strange sense of humor, and they'd send a joke. I'd think, Here I am, my life is falling apart in front of me, and here's this stupid joke. Yet somehow there was an endearment about it.

One woman drove over and gave me the rootings of a plant that she had cut. It was in a paper cup and was the scrawniest weed, probably about four feet long. I got home from being at Johns Hopkins and walked into the kitchen and there it was with a note saying, "I've been growing this for months and thought you might like to have it." What it did was say to me that she didn't know what to do, but she wanted to do something so she gave me this cutting.

I would encourage anybody who reacts to do whatever comes from within. As Richard said, "It's a lifeline"—it's one more person who is speaking to you. The quality of what the person says isn't important; it's that somebody did something. There are levels. Some of them are thoughts and prayers. Someone would say, "We just want you to know we're thinking of you." If you know somebody who needs support, you might have a feeling of not wanting to intrude on their lives. I urge you to overcome your doubts and reach out to that person, say what you're thinking. Your silence might be interpreted as disinterest.

I told the women at that talk to reach out no matter what. After that I got letters from women saying, "I'm one of them you were talking to who wanted to write, but didn't. And now I am writing to say . . ." At that luncheon I got the largest number of thank-you's that I've ever received for any event I've done, and I was the guest of honor.

Dr. Josefina Magno on Love

When someone is experiencing an illness, love is the most important and consoling thing we can offer. When you feel a loss or are in pain or sick, it's a great help to know that people around you care about you and love you. The pain of loneliness is almost as excruciating as physical pain because the pain of loneliness cannot be alleviated with drugs.

People who care about you and love you can make suffering and pain much more bearable. That love is best expressed by being present for the person who is ill. The feeling that someone is available to you at any time of the day or night is so important.

In our society, when somebody is sick, you go to the hospital for fifteen minutes or send flowers, and you feel you have fulfilled a social obligation. That's nice, but it actually doesn't do much unless the patient knows you can really be present to him or her. A lot of us don't know what to say, especially when we're visiting somebody with a serious illness. We are very uncomfortable; we feel we should be saying something nice or something witty. We don't have to say anything. We just need to be there. I could write a fine script on what to say when you visit somebody who's terminally ill; but if you don't care in your heart, no matter how beautiful the words are, they won't mean anything. Even if you don't do or say anything, if the patient feels that you care, that sense carries more meaning than anything else. Being loved means that you are accepted unconditionally.

When there is true love, people can give it unsparingly, and the person who is loved feels no sense of indebtedness. If we don't have love in our hearts, we cannot be gentle, we cannot be caring, we cannot be sensitive to others. If we have love, all these things come naturally. When there is love, it affects everything we do or say.

Betty Ford on Prayer

My own experiences have given me a great understanding of what people go through when they're suffering from breast cancer or alcoholism or heart disease. Having been through those myself, I can relate to those people. I hope I've been a support by being there and letting them know I'm concerned and I care. People I know who are suffering are in my prayers. Prayer is one of the most powerful things we can offer when somebody is ill or in adversity. Prayer is thoughtful consideration. Prayer is letting your heart go out with concern to other people through a Higher Power.

Helping Yourself

During the interviews for this book, the participants—in order to help those experiencing adversity—were asked, "If someone were going through a personal hardship right now—divorce, death, chronic illness, job loss, disability, major setback—what advice, based on your own experience, would you offer?"

Many of their encouraging responses are included in this section. While actions may speak louder than words, these bits of wisdom are eloquent and inspiring.

Betty Ford on Attitude

I don't think we fully recover from anything unless we have a positive attitude and the upbeat feeling that we can make it. We have to believe in ourselves and ask for help from those who are close to us and can be supportive. So often people don't; they're afraid to ask for help.

If suddenly I were stricken with a terminal illness or even paralyzed, I would try to keep going. In the first place, I'd ask God for help. I know my family would be there for me, but I would also figure I had to do the footwork. Believing in your own ability is very important. You can't just sit around and not do anything.

Jeanne White on Pride

A difficult time is hard going, but it will get easier. Try to focus on the things you have accomplished in life, and the things you still want to accomplish. It's easy to feel sorry for yourself, but you have to go on. You have to turn disaster into something positive. It's okay to wonder, Why did this happen to me? But when you start losing pride in yourself, that's when you go down. Be proud of who you are. Look at the people who have had catastrophes in their lives and see how many have made something positive from them.

Peggy Say on Not Surrendering

There is nothing in life that can defeat you faster than giving in to defeat. If you want to live, fight to live. Shame never killed anybody. Grief never killed anybody. Humiliation never killed anybody. Sometimes you probably wish it had. Life is tough. Learn to deal with it. But don't give in to it. Never settle. Don't be a bystander. Participate in life.

Devin McCoy on Answers

I can identify with the person who's at his wit's end. It's a very real thing. However, I know if you look hard enough inside yourself, you'll find hope. I found answers. They weren't clear at first. I didn't know how things were going to change; I just knew they *were* going to change. If there's a negative side to something, then there's a positive side to it somewhere. You might have to look hard and deep, but you will find it.

Lee Lawrence on Life

Resign yourself to something that hurts. It's part of life. Do whatever you can to ignore it. You can give in to it, but then you become nothing.

Tony Bunce on Survivors

You can always tell the people who are going to do well. They're inquisitive. They found out three days ago they're positive and they've already read the encyclopedia of HIV. They're terrified, they're frightened, but they are doing something about it. People who just accept the way things are—who feel sorry for themselves, let their doctors do the talking, and don't take any steps—will not do well.

Larry King on Being Optimistic

Focus on the pluses. You can't know up unless you've been down. "The sun will come out tomorrow." That's a hackneyed song but it's true: the sun does come up tomorrow. You think it won't, but there it is. Just when you're down, the lottery number pops up. Life has a way. Some nature or force has a way of resolving things. You also play a part in the process. Someone once told me, "It's not that your house burned down, it's how you react to it." You can say, "My house burned and I'm ruined," or you can say, "My house burned down and now I'm going to build a better one."

Phil Head on Action

Some people feel God will take care of them because they have faith. You have to have faith, but then you have to take action too. He's not going to come down and do it for you. He can help us. By being inside of us, He gives us the added strength. We have to do it. We have to say, "I'm going to have an attitude that will make my body heal faster." Dwelling on pain only prolongs it.

A client told me this story. A fellow who was very charitable decided after praying to God that he should win the lottery. He kept praying to win the lottery but he didn't win. He was getting agitated with God, so one night he said, "I think I should win the lottery, God, and you're not helping me out." Suddenly there was a clap of thunder and a voice spoke, and it said, "Bill, meet me halfway. Buy a ticket!" You've got to meet Him halfway; He can't do it all alone.

Margaret Chanin on Focus

When you start thinking about what you can't do, you have to make yourself stop and think about the things you can do. Don't focus on what you can't do. There are a lot of people who can't do many things.

If you're thinking of others, are concentrated on a goal you've got in sight, and are working toward it, you don't have time to turn inward and analyze. If people are concerned and caring for you, how can you let them down, crying in your soup in a corner?

Robert Weiss on Getting Feelings Out

The ways of dealing with a trauma or severe reverse that seem to promote recovery are very few. One is to talk to somebody. Talking to yourself doesn't seem to work. Therapy and support groups are very helpful. Another technique is to write a journal. Some people use a tape recorder.

The trauma is so painful because all you have are feelings. Journal writing permits you to think about the trauma, get it out, and see it at the same time that you're feeling it. The combination of seeing it and feeling it is what's effective. Talking to somebody does that as well, because you have to find a way of structuring your words so that the trauma will be meaningful to the other person, and will at the same time capture your feelings.

Some people who have gone through a divorce or a death write letters they never mail. Writing angry letters is great; the process of writing is a process of taming.

Polly Schechter on Coping

During the process of separation, one of the things I did that helped me get through the sense of loss was to put my thoughts on tape. It helped me by verbalizing them, playing them back to myself, listening to them. It helped me work through some of the really hurtful times.

Dr. Robert Buckman on Humor

Humor is a frame we draw around what frightens us to show us and the rest of the world that there is more to the universe than what frightens us. We're making a joke and we're saying, "Look, there is more to me than this fright. I can rise above it and I can see outside it. I can see outside the frame. The fright fills the frame on the wall—but look, there's more wall outside it." That's what humor does. It's an extremely important coping strategy.

Father Ed Kelly on Embracing Reality

The deep message of the Gospel is that resurrection is there, life is there, reality is there—all are there, even while you're suffering. Embrace reality. If the reality is an illness, a job loss, the loss of a loved one, embrace it. It's your attitude in it that becomes important.

Richard Berendzen on Abuse

I don't think the American public has the vaguest notion of the extent of sexual and physical abuse in this country. It is probably the largest, ugliest, most hideous secret in America today. It's one that nobody wants to face. Approximately one in four males and females have been abused sexually, if not physically or emotionally. Males now may have an abuse level close to that of females.

I might not have believed that even after my experience at Johns Hopkins if I hadn't received the phone calls and letters that came after I was on ABC "Nightline." It was mind-boggling—so many hurting people wanting to reach out to me or to tell me their story.

I hope that people who have been abused as children will learn not to make the mistake I made. Don't assume you can control everything yourself, regardless of whatever abilities, education, or other attributes you may have. Realize the depth of the fault line that was caused way back, years or decades earlier. The child still lives within the adult.

Gail Berendzen on Isolation

There are many adults who were abused as children, and many of them, I am sure, have told nobody. I hope that somehow they can get a sense that they must seek help. They should not try to handle it alone; reaching out is a healthy step.

It's remarkable the strength that you can find within yourself; however, human connectedness is profoundly important. There are professionals around. If you need one, find one. There are also people who are willing to help you and guide you who are not necessarily psychiatrists or therapists. There are social workers, pastors, rabbis, and priests. Perhaps your helper may be the next-door neighbor or a person who works with you, perhaps a friend or a relative. There are a lot of people to help you. The issue is to find the right one; the wrong conclusion is to assume that you don't need anyone.

Georgann Fuller on Grief Work

The grief process takes a long time. It doesn't just take six months; it takes two or three years, sometimes four or five. It's not just grief from death; it can come from divorce and a host of other traumatic situations as well.

To get through loss and grief you must be determined to work through it. If you sit back and do nothing, you're not going to succeed. You'll continue to have the pain for a long, long time.

About six months after Jim died, I was having a really bad day. I kept thinking about loss: I not only lost him, I lost a husband. I thought about loss of income. Then I made a list of over fifty things I felt I'd lost, and I have since added to that list. I've lost hundreds of things. Now, in order to make some peace with that, I've got to take those losses, look at them, integrate them, and decide what I'm going to do with them. How am I going to think, feel, and act about each of those losses? I have a tremendous job to do. It's as if I am a spoke of a wheel to Jim and I have all these connections. What am I to do about the connections that aren't there anymore? They have been ripped away and yet I've got to do something with that. What do I think about the fact that I'm no longer a wife? What does it mean to be single? I used to say, "I am exhausted all the time." Do you know why I was exhausted? I was trying to understand what all this meant. Every time

I thought about it, something triggered feelings.

I'm an advocate of support groups made up of people who have gone through what you're facing. I had that in my Pan Am group. I can still pick up the phone any day or night and call twenty-five or fifty people. That has been very helpful to me. Grief support groups, widow and widowers groups, parents of murdered children, MADD—those sorts of groups are wonderful.

A person who has suffered great loss may need therapy. Somebody who cries a lot, who won't get out of bed or doesn't want to get dressed for days, someone who cannot handle the basics of daily functioning, who has difficulty eating or sleeping, who talks about suicide—all are candidates for therapy. They should seek some kind of professional help.

Dr. Robert Buckman on Loss

If it doesn't hurt when people are lost to you, then clearly you've got no investment in those around you. Unless you are prepared to risk hurt when someone goes in any sense, then you will not have had any value from that relationship.

Better to have loved and lost. I use that as a consolation. I've been through a few really monstrous messes emotionally. I've been through a divorce and the odd relationship where you get dumped by somebody you thought really liked you. You feel dreadful and loathed. You feel, Oh, God, I'm worthless. Then you more or less pick yourself up. It is the desire to risk that kind of pain that actually makes you what you are. Nothing comes guaranteed, nothing is risk free. The desire to take emotional risks of loss is exactly what makes emotional ties and interlocking worthwhile.

Jim Brady on Pain

It's amazing what your physician can do. If you're in pain, schedule another appointment with him. Go back and say, "Look, this can't be right. Isn't there something that you can do or that I can do about this pain?" Generally there is.

Dominick Dunne on Support Groups

You've got to keep on; you've got to; you can't give up, you cannot give up no matter what happens. You've got to keep on with your life, keep on with whatever you're doing. If you do, you will come through.

Our case was so publicized at the time that Parents of Murdered Children came to us. Of course, we resisted it, but finally we went to one of their meetings. The boys went for a while but Lenny and I kept going.

Your friends who love you get glassy-eyed if you continue to talk about something such as we went through. If you're sensitive at all, you understand that and you stop. In support groups like ours there are people who've been through the same thing you have and who understand. They allow you to express your grief or your rage or whatever is gnawing at you that day. It was very, very helpful. The people were fabulous. I'm not the joiner type at all, but I would encourage people to join one of these support groups. At least give it a try.

Phil Buchanan on Why Groups Work

Anybody who's going through a major adversity has to connect with other people. I think the best place to start is in a group. Someone who's really hurting responds more quickly to somebody who's been there. Identification is the antidote: "I identify with your pain, you identify with my pain."

You need the commonality of a group. Seek out a group of people who have your kind of problem; within that group you will find the hope you need. Accept your pain. Talk about how it feels and what happened that caused it. Being able to let out the pain will help you feel better. A well-structured, consistent, faithful group is terrific.

Marguerite Kelly on Marriage and Divorce

I see divorce lessening; people are rethinking it. They are saying, "I'm not sure I should have done this," or, "Maybe we can work this out." Romantic notions about the joys of being single or being a single parent seem to be fading.

The qualities of a good marriage are congeniality, respect, laughter, and communication. By communication I mean talking so honestly that the listener really understands what you say, and not bottling up feelings until you want to scream out some totally wrong things. It's important to know how to argue, negotiate, compromise, and accept. When you start seeing your partner making a complete ass of himself, you have to recognize that the same could be said of you on some other occasion. You've got to give as much mercy as you would like to get.

The biggest cause of divorce, I think, is a lack of communication. Perhaps "connection" is a better word. I am amazed at how much people love, and how poorly, oftentimes, they express it. It takes guts to say, "I love you." Many people shut down when they're hurt. They should know that it's important to say, "I don't know if you realize it, but my feelings are really hurt." If you can't or don't have the courage to get across to another person how you feel, you're not being honest. It takes courage to say, "Here's what I am, here's what I feel."

Signs of a marriage in trouble are: not being considerate, not being glad to see each other; not needing to talk to each other daily even before you see each other; triangulating by using a child instead of confronting directly. Children are a terrible stress on a marriage. The lack of them can be, too. The only things kids want are time and thoughtfulness from their parents. Everything else is negotiable.

Parents don't nurture their marriage the way they nurture their kids. A marriage is an identity of its own. It has to be petted and babied and protected if it's going to be kept safe. That means getting away for at least three or four weekends a year—even if you don't have money enough to do more than camping on the beach from Saturday morning to Sunday night—just the two of you. The marriage will go on, but the kids are, in a sense, temporary. Lack of time, privacy, money, and the fact of the relentless daily grind are other things people come up with that cause problems in their marriage.

Everybody in a bad marriage gets hurt. Children are terribly receptive to the vibrations. They sense the discord even though they may not know what it is. But, being children, they're very egocentric, so they naturally think they have caused it: they caused the trouble, they caused the tension, they caused the fights, they caused the divorce. It's all their fault. The partners in a bad marriage get hurt, too. Nobody wants to be part of a painful identity. I liken marriage to a stack of blocks. It's bound to totter from time to time, and you've got to stop and straighten out the stack.

Divorce happens when partners get to the point where there are no more options. It's like being trapped in a room without doors or windows, and a fire starts. Somehow you are in a closed area and there's no way out. You break out: you break out into a divorce. You run. That happens when you don't get help. You're so hurt, angry, and depressed that you cannot recognize options. Sometimes you do figure out all the possibilities and say, "But none of these options will work as well as divorce."

When one person decides to leave, the other person feels really abandoned. Judging from the letters I get, it doesn't make any difference whether the one left behind is a man or a woman. There's a tremendous sense of rejection. Frequently men are surprised that there's a problem in the marriage at all. What could have been a working-out comes too late a year later.

A man has a tendency to feel abandoned by his children—really lost at sea. The wife generally has the children, so she's got a focus. However, he can usually recover economically quicker than she can. But again it's the children who are devastated. They're hurt more by divorce than by death. They are so sure that they're at fault.

You have to get rid of the anger and the adrenaline of a bad relationship. When I see people torn apart by divorce, I think it's often because they have not had therapy. They are frozen in their trauma. If you're going to have the courage to break up a relationship and start anew, you've got to nourish yourself by cleansing your mind and your emotions and getting rid of your anger.

Divorce is the death of an identity. The partners have created a marriage, created an identity, and then they take the extraordinary step of killing that identity.

Children who are in a hopeless marriage are always in terrible turmoil and unhappiness. Many of them feel deeply relieved when they realize the marriage is over. They don't want it to be done with, but they need out. Where kids can benefit is when parents who may not have been honest in their marriage are honest with their kids by talking frankly to them: "I'm very worried, but we're going to make it. I really need you to help out. We're in this together, and we'll come through."

All members of the family want to know what they're dealing with. In a marriage that breaks apart, the kids have the right to know: "This is how much money we have, we can stay in this house this long," or, "We can do that next year." Children need to know all the pieces. What causes anxiety is when they don't know what's going to happen to them.

If the marriage was sound in the beginning and full of hope, therapy can help to put it back together. If the divorce decision has been made, therapy can reduce the pain load. Therapy is also a means of learning from the situation. Otherwise, you may very well make the same damn mistakes again.

Enough people have been the products of divorce that they are seriously rethinking divorce as the first option. It's certainly the last option. It was the first option for so long. I can't tell you the number of people I know well who have said, "I'm sorry I got a divorce."

Father Ed Pritchard on Forgiveness

Forgiveness is something that has to happen to you, not the other person. Unforgivingness makes you embittered. It makes you less happy, less peaceful. Forgiveness is a process of separating the person from the action. We equate both together. What God asks us to do is forgive the person. He helps us look at the person and see him as He sees him. Then the action by that person becomes less painful to us.

We can't judge a person, because we don't know all that has gone into him as a human being that caused him to act in a particular way. God says, Forgive the man, forgive the woman. If a dog is abused and then comes into a loving home, it's still going to act abused. When you reach out to touch it in a loving manner, it's going to snap at you because it's not been loved; it's been hurt. Human beings do that, too.

We can either take our hurt and feed it with resentment, anger, and self-pity, or we can move beyond our suffering and be willing to give the other person another chance or give another person a chance in this same kind of relationship.

Marie Balter on Self-examination

In order to forgive, it's necessary to look at yourself. It's important really to know yourself, not just who you are, but what you are, with all your weaknesses. Don't just see the negative; see your good qualities as well. That's very, very important. When you also understand that you too can hurt others and make mistakes, you begin to know what your imperfections are. When you see the things you do in your life and take responsibility for what you've done wrong (let the other person take responsibility for what he or she did), then you find it easier to forgive.

I wasn't an ideal child. Many of my actions were wrong. I couldn't blame my family for everything. At that time I never considered the other person: I was a kid who wallowed in self-pity. I wanted a lot of attention.

Sure you can say I was deprived. That's perhaps the reason I was the way I was. But there is still the fact that I have to take responsibility for my actions and attitudes. I can't erase who I was. Reason is one thing and excuse is quite different. I can't excuse myself. I can have a reason for why I did something, but I cannot excuse my actions.

When I came out of the hospital, the first people I had to encounter were my family. I had to start looking at all the interactions there. My concern wasn't whether I forgave my brother. I had made some mistakes too. Was he going to accept me? I wasn't the most kindly sister as a teenager; I was always self-involved. You see those traits in yourself and you begin to assess them. I saw the reasons people behaved the way they did. I looked at my mother and tried to understand her marriage. The kind of life she led with my father was far from happy. Living with my husband, Joe, I saw what I had with him, and what was lacking in my mother's life. I loved Joe and trusted him; I could enjoy him and I wasn't afraid of him. My mother was deathly afraid of my father, and passed some of that fear on to me. I had to see that, and to see that was sad. How could I hate my mother when I saw what life had dealt her? She wasn't all bad; nobody is.

Bill Russell on Greed and Selfishness

Greed, in my estimation, is what causes most of the strife in the world. If you and I get to a door at the same time, do you go through the door by yourself first, or do you hold the door for me? That's the kind of greed I'm talking about, not just money. When you get in a line, do you always have to be first, or can you say to someone, "Would you like to go ahead?" I used to think that the only way for me to be accepted, understood, and well thought of was if I was first in line, had the best clothing, was first in the family and first with my friends. "Selfishness" might be another word for it. What I see in today's world are greed and selfishness in many forms, causing disharmony and strife.

When I see you on the street today, I treat you as a human being and I recognize that you have emotions and wants and needs. I attempt to be good to you, to be kind and gentle. In so doing, I think that I will then get the same treatment from you. What I learned as a youngster was to treat you poorly, not knowing that you would treat me poorly in return. The more grief I gave, the more grief I got. I did not understand that. Today I don't believe anything that I believed when I was younger.

Probably the craziest thing I've ever seen is the T-shirt that says "Those that have the most toys when they die win." In essence, I believed that for fifty years. In fact, what happened was I lost, because what I lost was me. My greatest prize went out the door with greed and selfishness. Nobody whom anybody would want to love or to be with was available. What I ended up with was isolation. God, it was awful; isolation is a terrible place to live in. Loneliness, anger, resentment, unhappiness—that's why I drank. I really had no other recourse, no other relief.

Missy LeClaire on Twelve Rules for Living

These rules apply to people going through any illness, a divorce, the breakup of a relationship, the death of a loved one, or the loss of a job. They're about how to cope with life. The alternative to coping is not to cope, and that's not an option. People have to have developed coping skills throughout their life. However, if they haven't, they can be taught. Coping means the ability to go with the flow. My dad always says, "Don't sweat the small stuff. Take life as it comes. If you can't change it, you can't change it. If you can change it, then change it."

The way I see it, when you have an AIDS diagnosis you have a choice—to cope or not to cope. That is the question. For me, the answer was very simple. One of the hardest lessons I had to learn was that I wasn't going to die anytime soon and that I had a lot of living to do. And live I do!

The following are things that have worked for me for the past five years and that I hope will work for years to come:

1. GET OVER IT! You've got the virus. Now what? Get on with life.
2. GET A LIFE! Your life after diagnosis may be very different from the life you had before. It is up to you to make this new life full of love, successes, and rewards.
3. Find FAITH in a higher power of some sort and GRACE wherever you must. The words to the hymn "Amazing Grace" have been a great help to me. "Was grace that taught my heart to heal and grace will lead me on."

4. Take care of your EMOTIONAL SELF. Communicate! Join a twelve-step program, a support group, or get one-on-one counseling—whatever works for you. AIDS is a tough road to go alone or with the wrong kind of support (such as negative support messages).

5. PARTICIPATE in your care and treatment. Learn all you can about the disease and the treatments for various infections. Don't always count on information received from friends—always check it out with someone you know is knowledgeable. Don't be afraid to educate your doctor or other health-care professionals about new treatments, etc. Establish a team relationship with your physician.

6. KNOW YOUR BODY—but don't become obsessed about your health. Yes, you may become ill but you will likely recover with proper care, treatment, and attitude. Try not to look for things to go wrong! It's perfectly natural to have very healthy periods (days, months, years) and have AIDS too!

7. Be OPTIMISTIC but REALISTIC about everything—life, health, death, money, love, etc. Don't set yourself up for disappointment, but don't deny yourself an opportunity for fear of taking a risk.

8. Don't BELLYACHE! Besides your doctor, no one wants to hear it. Complaining is just negative reinforcement that you don't need to hear over and over.

9. PITY PARTIES are only allowed for an afternoon! Really! Before the end of the day, give yourself a swift kick, dust yourself off, put one foot in front of the other, and keep going.

10. Be THANKFUL for what you DO have—whether it be a roof over your head, a day without a fever, or rain to make the flowers grow. The world owes you nothing; try to earn what you gain.

11. Make PEACE with yourself, those you love, and even those you don't. Anger, jealousy, pettiness, resentment, fear, and hatred are extremely heavy bags to carry around all the time—let them go!

12. Be KIND to yourself and others—it will be returned threefold.

Father Ed Pritchard on Healing

Jesus said, "Go forth and lay your hands upon the sick. And those who believe these signs shall follow and they shall be healed." When Jesus made that commission, He said, "Proclaim the Gospel, the good news. Go forth and lay hands on the sick that the blind may see, the deaf may hear, and the lame may walk; raise the dead and cast out demons. This is your ministry. Go out and do it."

What did people come to Jesus for? To be healed. I don't believe healing is always a physical thing. There's a healing of the inner person who is willing to accept that the Lord wants him to come home or gives him meaning in his suffering. I have been with people who, after having had hands laid on them, died with the greatest sense of peace. There's no resentment or anger at all, even though they may still be physically suffering. There's a different attitude in them.

We don't know God, not that He's unknowable. I think we're afraid to know Him. We're afraid if we know Him something will happen that will make us act differently. We're afraid we're not going to be able to do what we want to do. If we let Him into our lives, we think He's going to rain on our parade. That is the opposite of what He does. God is our greatest cheerleader.

I get visual images when I pray over people. I see the person in adoration of God. Adoration is complete surrender to God, complete trust and wonder in the magnificence of who He is. Often when a baby sees his parents, there is an incredible openness and love that's exchanged between the infant and his mother and father. That's kind of the picture I see in the face of a person as I pray over him. It's an emotional experience of intense love. Sometimes I'm not even aware of what I'm praying, I'm so caught up with the image. The Holy Spirit is praying through Jesus to the Father in perfect prayer for whatever the need is of that person.

I've seen a woman who was completely filled with cancer cured without a trace of it. I've seen people who tested HIV positive test HIV negative. I've seen legs grow. I've seen people with cataracts who become able to see. I've seen people who were losing their hair come back the next week with a full head of hair. I've seen many amazing things; but I'm not so caught up in the results. I expect those results. It confirms to me that the Lord knows what people need most.

I see an awful lot of inner healing, too. People accept the things that they're not physically healed of. That's a miracle in itself. God doesn't waste time or energy. He's always doing something. Sometimes when I pray over a person those miracles don't happen instantaneously. It may take months. With that person's perseverance of coming back, the healing takes place.

Healing is a process of accepting God's love, accepting that He wants to do this healing for you, and having the trust and the will that He's going to do it for you. Then you see it.

Final Thoughts

In our daily lives, all of us encounter people struggling with adversity. How we relate to them is about us, not about them. Are the emotional triggers pulled inside of us hostile or hospitable? Do we meet those who are in pain with understanding and respect or do we recoil from them and hide behind a wall of fear and apathy? Do we really believe that we all face our own difficult times?

Shifting the focus from personal stories of inspiration to a broader look at America's unfinished business, some distinguished leaders and experts in their fields examine several of our country's major social issues—the very worst that can happen.

Americans can be the most caring people on earth; but prejudice, discrimination, ignorance, disregard, ridicule, and rejection are not qualities that speak well for any of us. We are good people; however, we can do better. Role models of inspiration in meeting adversity can be found on the streets of our toughest cities, in the halfway houses for runaways and addicts, group homes for battered women, refugee centers, shelters for the homeless, and veterans' hospitals. Our teachers may be found in wheelchairs, rehabilitation centers, the AIDS wards of hospitals, special schools for the handicapped, nursing homes, prisons, or on unemployment lines.

Forty-three million Americans have a disability. This figure represents about one fifth of our population. Some of the greatest inspirational teachers for educating us in conquering difficulties are those who grapple daily with their own disabilities. Unfortunately, they must also overcome society's often times negative attitude toward them as well. That attitude may be the worst that can happen.

Digest the wisdom, love, and frustration of three professionals who have dedicated their careers to advocating for persons with disabilities, and take to heart what they ask of us in return.

Paul Marchand is the Director of the Governmental Affairs Office of ARC, the Association for Retarded Citizens, in Washington, D.C.

Patrisha Wright is the Governmental Affairs Director of the Disability Rights Education and Defense Fund, Inc., in Washington, D.C.

Celane McWhorter is the Director of the Office of Government Relations for TASH, the Association for Persons with Severe Handicaps, in Alexandria, Virginia.

"Look Beyond What You See"

Paul Marchand, Patrisha Wright, Celane McWhorter

Paul

Working definitions of disability vary. Most of them deal with functional ability or functional incapacities. Those things are generally concerned with what we call major life activities, such as eating, dressing, walking, talking, thinking, mobility, and working.

Pat

Quadriplegia, paraplegia, cerebral palsy, and some forms of mental retardation are more visible. Not-so-visible disabilities include mental illness, epilepsy, cancer, AIDS, head injury, and learning disabilities.

There's also a big difference between a person who was traumatically injured and became deaf and someone who is congenitally deaf, born deaf; or between somebody who lost mobility because of an accident as opposed to somebody who never had it from birth.

The highest divorce rate is in parents who give birth to congenitally disabled children, and it's mainly the men who leave. The father imagines he's going to have a son, they will play baseball and go fishing, and the son will grow up and run track. All of a sudden, they've got a child whose arms flap up and down or don't move. Generally, the man freaks out and runs.

Paul

There are two ways of depicting disability; either as totally heroic or as suffering. There's never normal. There's never the guy or gal who leads an optimal life-style despite the disability. What you get is the guy with no arms and no legs who climbs a mountain or the blind guy who sails around the world. On the other hand, you get the homeless, the hopeless, and the guy on the street with the tin cup. You never get the mainstream of disability, which is typical of mainstream America. They go to work every day, they slug it out, they've got kid problems, they've got wife-and-husband problems—they've even got eviction problems because they can't make the rent. People with disability are much poorer than other Americans because of the disability.

Pat

I'm legally blind. I think I can do everything except drive. I'm very limited if I don't have a reader. I read print, but I don't read script; I have double vision all the time. But if you give me ten hours' worth of reading services a week, I can work, and I do get a salary. Up until the Americans with Disabilities Act, a person with a disability either had to be inspirational or pitiful. Those were the only ways that the press related to us.

Celane

I'm more familiar with the more challenging, more severe individuals who end up in institutions. Nobody wants to deal with those people. They're severely mentally retarded. They have multiple handicaps. They may have cerebral palsy. They might not speak, or they have a severe communication problem. They might look awfully funny. They might have autism. They might have serious, very unacceptable behavior disorders. Any number of these kinds of disabilities put them in the lowest one to two percent of our society.

Pat

There is a hierarchy, like a caste system, in disability. The jock para is on the highest rung. They're generally athletes who have been injured in their sports, so they're likely to be pretty muscular. Society also has at the top those of us who are the easiest to deal with because they're less of a problem for the non-disabled to cope with. It goes from the easiest to relate to to the hardest to relate to. The hardest ones in society are the people Celane's talking about. Paul's folks are one up from that.

Paul

You've no doubt heard the "vegetable" word. "The vegetables" is a term that makes us cringe. I heard it yesterday from a high-ranking federal official. It's individuals who have hardly any cognitive ability and no muscle tone to move. They are literally there. If left, they will remain there. They can't move. They can't feed themselves. They can't walk. They have massive cognitive impairment and massive physical impairment together. Some of them are easier to cope with than others.

In mental retardation—just using that as one disability—we have over seven million people in this country today. The vast majority of them are what we call "mildly mentally retarded." That means they're going to be identifiable in that category when they're in school. They're not going to be able to succeed alongside their non-retarded peers in the academic work.

Yet most of them will have families; most of them will work. They'll never be lawyers and doctors, but they'll be truck drivers, cooks, and waiters if they luck out and if they've got a family and friends to rely on. Most moderately retarded people will learn a number of skills, but will always need some kind of help. They might need social supervision to help them make decisions. They'll be able to feed themselves and dress themselves. But without help they won't know it's time to eat or time to pay a bill. They may not know how to write a check or how to make change.

There are two kinds of people society, including professionals, tends to write off: those who are called "medically fragile," and those others with severe, bizarre behaviors—in other words, those who are not only retarded but also very difficult to manage. Those two populations tend to remain in segregation and isolation—in institutions—the longest. There'll be a day, and it's darn close to being here, where the only people who'll be left in institutions are those people.

In such environments, normal social development is literally impossible. We're finding if you take the individuals and integrate them as successfully as you can in a family-type, loving, and caring home environment, they are likely to prosper more than they would if you kept them in an institution. Even those who may have been called "vegetables" at one time are able to acquire skills, especially if we reach them at the earliest possible age. If you've left somebody in a hostile, segregated environment for forty years with little or no stimulation, you're going to reap what you sow.

Pat

The public policy that we have developed in this country for years said, "If you are disabled, you should be in a separate program, segregated away, and taken care of." The answer was to throw money to create separate segregated programs. If you took any other minority in this country and tried that, you wouldn't get very far.

The first disability policy started when injured veterans came home from the war. A man gave up part of his body fighting a war, so we couldn't throw him into a segregated place. Then the parents got involved and said, "Wait a minute, my kid didn't fight in a war, but he's missing a limb, too. Why can't he be involved in society just like the veteran?" Parents' anger got filtrated into developing parent organizations.

Running concurrently was the advancement in medical technology. People started to live with traumatic injury or congenital defects. We know how to fix those now.

With advancements in education, teachers said, "This person can do more than lick ice cream or string noodles." The teachers and other professionals made it clear they could educate these children.

Celane

The attitudes of people anger me. The systems that refuse to change and the schools that, in spite of federal policy, continue to segregate kids who are different really make me mad. You still have kids in wheelchairs who have to go to separate schools because their own schools won't put in elevators. That's one of the simplest things that we can do for kids who use wheelchairs. All these Ph.D.s, the leaders of the field, won't change; they won't learn new ways. I walk in and I say, "Gee, we're doing a wonderful thing up in Syracuse. We're teaching people with autism how to communicate for the first time." In another city, they'll say, "Don't tell me that, that's hearsay."

Paul

Policy makers, for the sake of expediency, are willing to pay much more for dead-end programs, dead-end opportunities, or no opportunity rather than make the necessary public policy changes that are aimed at promoting independence and economic self-sufficiency.

Pat

It's a system that wants to hold on to old stereotypes and fears, whether it's the professional system, the congressional system, the presidential system, or the general public.

Paul

I've spent my entire professional career in disability policy. In addition to people with disabilities, I also work with their families. They are fabulous people—talk about commitment and parenthood beyond the norm. I know a great number of parents who have had to be parents for forty years non-stop. They're there every day for their children. That's parenting.

Celane

I grew up in a very intolerant society—in the deep South during apartheid, if you will. I grew up fearful of differences. When I started studying special education and working with people who were different, I began to see them as people. In terms of my own personal life, I can get into the car and drive without any problems; Pat can't. If I'm in the car and I'm cursing and angry and frustrated, I think, I should be damn glad that I'm in the car.

Paul

Labeling, inappropriate use of terminology, and making a verb a noun is one of the biggest problems we have with the press. The press always has to find its shortcuts. We cringe almost every day when we see the headlines. The way they treat "the language of disability" is horrendous. When discussing disability, never violate the "people first" principle in your use of language. Never refer to people as "the disabled." Never refer to them as "cerebral-palsied." Always use a noun that designates the person first: an individual with mental retardation, a child with cerebral palsy.

Pat

Language actually binds us to our stereotypes. When you read the paper about us, we're always "suffering"—poor, pathetic, and victims. Never call us victims. We could bore you with stories about disabled women who've gone to the doctor because they had pains in their stomach. It turned out they were several months' pregnant. The doctor never assumed they were being sexual and never treated them as if they could possibly be pregnant.

Celane

The systems just totally screw people with disabilities: the federal Medicaid system, the educational system, the Social Security system.

Pat

One out of every twelve dollars in the federal budget is spent on dependent disability programs, and we have a sixty-eight percent unemployment rate. All three of us would argue that there's not a disabled person we know who couldn't do some type of work. It's the systems Celane's talking about that are disabling us. I'm disabled by society, I'm disabled by the systems. I'm not disabled by my disability. That's the last thing that disables me.

Celane

When you see a young retarded kid or a person in a wheelchair or a homeless person, look into his eyes and look to his soul. Look beyond what you see. Take an extra minute to bother to get to know that person as a person and not as a disability. We step over the man on the street who's lying there because he's homeless. We don't even see the person. Take time at least to look at the person and say to yourself, "That's a person." If that's all you do, that's a beginning. What you've done is at least acknowledged that he's an acceptable member of our society. If you can get to that point, then you can take time to look into his eyes and try and find his soul.

Paul

Disregard the label, whatever the label might be, and attempt to disregard the disability for the moment, and see that individual is clearly a human being, a person first. Once you accept that, then you can look at his strengths and weaknesses. Simply realize that people with disabilities are people first; they all have their own skills, values, likes, and dislikes. Some of the people I know with disabilities are truly heroes in my mind, and some aren't.

Disability cuts across all lines, all socioeconomic lines, all racial and religious lines. You've got everything within forty-three million people. The same thing holds true of the parents. You have some heroic parents, and some who simply stepped away, didn't want to deal with it, and gave up. You've got others who worked like hell to make it work and couldn't.

Pat

Some of the best books I've read had some of the worst-looking covers. The same thing is true for people with disabilities. I believe that our disabilities, in some ways, do make us a little better than the average person, because I think dealing with daily discrimination teaches you a lot of ways to make yourself more adaptable in society. Where the non-disabled person can get out of kilter by a minor bump in the road, the disabled person expects potholes and will go right around them or through them. He rearranges himself and continues.

Dealing with disability on a daily basis changes your life. Being disabled, I feel I am a keener judge of character. I know who's going to look me in the eyes and talk to me. I can judge when someone's being real and when someone's patronizing me, because it happens to me every day.

Our society is an expendable society; it's very fast-moving. We don't smell the flowers on a daily basis. Folks with severe disabilities can teach us a thing or two. They also force us to slow down and appreciate what we have every day.

I listen very closely to the people I know who are mentally retarded. I listen to their opinions, because they're not covered with flowery language. They get right to the heart of things, and they tell you exactly what they think. The individual who is severely disabled—"the vegeta-ble"—as some call them, can teach us, too. There is such joy in watching someone be able to sit up for the first time, or be able to notice color or notice movement. It makes me appreciate what I miss every day in life.

A disability opens your eyes to a way of living that most people never experience. That's why a lot of people who have a disability don't believe that they "suffer" from it. They think they've been educated by their disability and are richer for it.

In the fall of 1991, the National Commission on AIDS reported to the President and the American public its latest data, findings, and recommendations. This global health epidemic, the most destructive in contemporary history, has yet to register in the American psyche as the very worst that can happen. Dr. June E. Osborn states "HIV is now part of human ecology and we must change our behavior accordingly." Dr. Osborn speaks of sexual behavior; however, AIDS may play a role in changing our entire health-care system, infuse us with new dimensions of understanding each other, and teach us how to support those who are ill and dying.

June E. Osborn, M.D., is the Chairman of the National Commission on AIDS, a fifteen-member committee appointed by Congress and the President to advise legislators and the White House on developing a national AIDS policy. Dr. Osborn is also the Dean of the School of Public Health at the University of Michigan in Ann Arbor, Michigan.

"This Virus Will Never Go Away"

———

June E. Osborn

AIDS is a terrible thing, both individually and collectively for our society at every level. The illness is a real creation of the Devil—a slow loss of vitality and energy, coupled with other manifestations that almost seem random because of the opportunism of infections and their unpredictability. For some people toward the end there is a loss of the self in the ability to think clearly. The so-called AIDS dementia happens in possibly a third of people very late in the disease. AIDS dementia can make people seem to leave their friends before they've left, so that it gets harder and harder to get a sense of feedback when you care for them. It's horrible.

Another thing makes AIDS especially awful. Losing a child or a loved one is a dreadful thing when it happens. To have to do so and also do one's grieving in secret is unthinkable. Most of the people in the AIDS epidemic are in that position. Imagine losing your child and not being able to say, over months of illness, that your child is very ill, however old—two, twenty, forty.

For our country, it's an awful epidemic because we've not responded well. We've behaved in a superficial way, which looks like indifference. Our behavior has been a combination of diffuse panicky fear out of ignorance and denial that it has anything to do with us. I think people are now increasingly aware that AIDS does have something to do with us—if not us, then our children, and if not them, our children's children. AIDS is not going to go away.

By now there've been enough polls to show that people have heard the superficial message: it's sex, it's drugs, and nothing else. But if you follow up as a pollster and ask, "Are you comfortable that AIDS cannot be transmitted by doorknobs, handshakes, hugs, and kisses?" then you discover that a much larger percentage of people are still very uneasy about it. Similarly, if you ask teenagers (not in the middle of the country, but on the coasts) who know a lot of what you want them to know whether they have responded as if it had anything to do with them, the answer is no.

The language that's been used in this epidemic has been so categorical: "gays," "addicts"—they are largely classifying kinds of labels. Very few people think of themselves with labels. It isn't kinds of people, it's kinds of behavior that we really need to be talking about. When we talk about behavior, we're terribly prudish in this country.

The most recent poll I saw, which was some months ago, stated that twenty-nine percent of the people polled knew somebody with AIDS. Probably lots more than that would know someone with AIDS if the truth was known. Given the horrible dynamics of what's coming in the next two years, our problem of capturing attention may be solved pretty soon. As of the end of January, 1992, 209,693 people have been diagnosed with AIDS; 135,434 have already died. The Centers for Disease Control projects more than one million people are HIV positive beyond the diagnosed AIDS category. The great influenza pandemic of 1918–19 killed 20 million people worldwide. In the United States, deaths numbered about 500,000. Fairly soon now, we're going to pass those figures. When the flu pandemic was done, what we were left with was the fear that flu would come back. But what we have here today with AIDS is the knowledge that this virus will never go away. We're not going to get rid of it; it's part of human ecology.

People should be aware that we are the epicenter, and so the U.S. is the worst off. Of the more than one million people who are infected in the United States, the CDC says, only twelve percent know they are infected. The ramifications of that are nowhere near as severe as the ramifications of people not knowing they're at risk if they don't learn how to protect themselves. The take-home message about the epidemic is that one can avoid this virus. We know enough to teach individuals they can do things to avoid it. They can learn that their choice of sexual partners—particularly plural, but any sexual partner—cannot be initially knowledgeable. You cannot know from meeting somebody, and even falling in love with him, what his sexual past has been. Therefore, protected sex, minimizing number of sexual partners, and committed monogamy are good ideas. A lot of people think "multiple sexual partners" means more than one at a time. People have many sexual partners through "serial monogamy," one at a time. If you are thoughtful and alert about sexual relationships, and if you can maintain a standard where there isn't any sense of personal mistrust in negotiating condom usage, safe sex practices, and not injecting drugs, you are now in a position to help, because everything else—hugs, care, compassion, and so forth—is okay.

Systematic, well-instructed condom use—from the beginning to the end, as Dr. C. Everett Koop used to say—will diminish the likelihood of transmission at least tenfold, and probably eliminate it when it's done properly. Anal intercourse does carry a higher risk unprotected. It may carry a higher risk in the context of condom use, too, because anal sex adds to the potential for condom breakage. What people have to recognize is that this virus doesn't transmit efficiently, even sexually.

Can you catch the virus of AIDS from doorknobs, from hugs? No. Can you become infected from sex? Yes. You must do everything you can to minimize the risk on the "yes" side. People don't want to look at the risks they may be taking when they go to a convention and get blotto and go AC-DC for the weekend.

We should have settings in which people can acknowledge they're a little frightened, take themselves off to a confidential or anonymous place and find out their status, learn through counseling how to avoid further risk, and then protect themselves in the future. If we were trying, that's what we'd be doing. We'd make it easy. We'd make it private. We'd make it inexpensive or free. Also we would not construct hazards to the people who turned out to be positive. They wouldn't face discrimination or lack of health care. It's a terrible thing to let ourselves get backed around so that testing sounds punishing and mandatory testing is on every legislator's agenda. It's counterproductive, not just to people with HIV, but to everybody.

The debate about health-care workers has been grotesquely misphrased. The concern is, and should be, the safety of everyone in the health-care workplace. Safety is the concern. "Universal precautions," working as if everyone carried an infectious disease risk, is something one can learn. It has been recommended since 1987. Hepatitis B is a hundredfold more infectious than HIV. Before 1987, when the universal precautions idea came about on recommendation from CDC, there were about twenty instances in which Hepatitis B–infected health-care workers had infected patients over a decade.

Since universal precautions came in, there has not been a single documented instance in four years. There are two that may be, but that's a dramatic drop, nonetheless, given that it's a hundredfold more sensitive an indicator than HIV.

There has never been a documented clear-cut HIV transmission from an infected health professional directly to a patient under his care, including Dr. David Acer, the dentist, whose circumstances are most unusual. It's never happened, and yet we are now at risk of diverting enormous resources to prevent something that's never happened. The circumstance in Dr. Acer's dentist office is most likely due to contaminated instruments and not to Dr. Acer. In other words, he could have been uninfected. You can't explain five patients spread out over time in that way. Congressman William Dannemeyer loves to say, "It's been happening all this time." That's not true. We do know.

The other direction is really quite exceptionally rare, too, even when you have a known needle *stick* from a known AIDS patient straight into a health-care professional. That's a very inefficient, rare thing. The estimate that's used is four per thousand needle sticks, and you can do things about that in the universal precautions mode by double-gloving, by analyzing the contexts of a given kind of surgery where it happens, and adding protections.

If we focus on safety, we should be focusing on Hepatitis B. People say, "Ah, but it doesn't kill." Not true. In 1987, with about four million health-care workers in the United States, there was a total of four hundred deaths of all causes that OSHA would say were work-related. Of those, over two hundred were due to Hepatitis B; nineteen were due to electrocution; and none had anything whatsoever to do with HIV.

The next couple of years are going to be terrible. With 206,000 cases of AIDS now, that number will double in the next two years—and that's AIDS, of course, not HIV infection. We have already had more people die from AIDS than died in the Korean and Vietnam wars combined, and we're just beginning.

This virus isn't going to go away. A vaccine isn't going to replace what we have to do now. It may supplement it, but it can't replace the education and the strategies of avoidance. If one is careful about sexual behavior and if people educate themselves, one can personally avoid this virus. Vaccine research is desperately important. But a vaccine may be ten years away and possibly only eighty percent effective. The optimists would say five years. I don't share their optimism. Keep in mind if we had a perfect vaccine in hand right now, it would probably take five years to do the trials. A cure, unfortunately, is intellectually very hard to imagine.

The virus is in the heterosexual community as well as the homosexual community. It's in the white community as well as the black and Hispanic communities. It's everywhere.

The basic approach to sex as we have known it and experienced it as human beings and Americans must change. The sex drive and the desire to be satisfied will always be there, no matter what. The way we have done it before has to be changed. The unprotected, one-night stand ought to be a dinosaur. People have to be thoughtful about sex; they can't be frivolous. They have to be thoughtful about it as a potentially life-threatening aspect of life as well as a life-fulfilling one. We have to grow up enough so that discussion about it can go on without having people either so terrified that they thwart their total development, or so rejecting that they take chances they shouldn't. We've got a societal maturation to achieve that's long overdue.

One reasonable approach for people who have met and think they want to establish a monogamous relationship is to make it routine to use condoms and not let it be a negotiating issue—to build the relationship until the time came when they thought they really wanted a monogamous relationship. If that's six or more months after the beginnings of this relationship, then I think getting tested and making sure that both partners are fine is probably a reasonable thing to do.

Six months after risk behavior is probably, for the person without a very high-risk pattern of behavior, very reassuring. The vast majority of people who become infected will show that they are infected within three to six months.

If a person tests positive, does that mean he will get AIDS? It's so likely that it would be irresponsible to say no to that question. Obviously, we don't know with a ten-year-old epidemic where the median incubation interval is ten years and some people have been infected and symptom-free for thirteen. That's about as far out as we can go, because the first collections of serums are 1978. There may be an occasional person who goes so long that something else takes his life.

For the people who have tested positive or who have *AIDS*, there's a lot of hope. We must stress the pace of research progress. For affluent-connected people now, it's not uncommon to live several years after the diagnosis of AIDS, because there are things that can be done and care that can be given. The chance to live a rich, final interval of life is there now, and it really wasn't at first. Life can be very meaningful and contributive, with relationships that are loving, for people with HIV infection. In that sense, there's hope.

For many, the worst that can happen consists of the very circumstances into which they were born. For them, the conditions of life are so bleak, the prospects of change so unlikely, and the rewards so unattainable that the tragedy they face is not a specific event but an entire lifetime of anguish and struggle. While some do triumph, we hate to admit that America—this land of opportunity—continues to deny so much to so many.

For many others, it is not the circumstances they were born into that doom them, but the life-styles they choose or the self-destructive actions they perform that abuse their own health. They themselves create the very worst things that can happen.

Louis W. Sullivan, M.D., is the Secretary of Health and Human Services. Dr. Sullivan oversees the federal agency responsible for the major health, welfare, food and drug safety, medical research, and income security programs serving the American people. He was also the founding dean and former director of the Medical Education Program at Morehouse College in Atlanta, Georgia.

"Not Everyone Is So Lucky"

Louis W. Sullivan

My father was shot when I was about eight years old. Fortunately, the wound itself was not life-threatening; it was one of those things where had the bullet penetrated something like a quarter of an inch off the path it took, it would have severed his jugular vein and he would have bled to death. As it turned out, it went through his neck and damaged his brachial plexus, the nerve network coming out of the spinal cord into the arm, so it affected the strength in his right arm. The damage was significant. After that, his writing was always scratchy. My brother and I were away with my mother on a shopping trip. When we came back, my father was in the hospital.

My father was an activist and had founded the Blakely, Georgia, chapter of the NAACP. At that time, blacks could not vote in state primaries and he was fighting for them to get that right. Georgia also had what was called a "county unit system" in state elections, which was a device whereby each county had a certain minimum number of votes for primary elections. The result was that three or four rural counties could actually carry more weight in the voting process than the city of Atlanta; twenty thousand people in four counties could have greater voting strength than Atlanta with three hundred thousand.

Later, the system was found to be unconstitutional by the Supreme Court. My father, among others, was fighting to challenge the county unit system. As he worked in developing the businesses of the black community and organizing the people, he was considered by many whites to be a rabble-rouser, a troublemaker upsetting the status quo.

There was another dimension in our living in Blakely. My mother was a schoolteacher, but because of my father's activities she could never get a job in Blakely or in Early County, where Blakely was the county seat. The school system, which was controlled by whites, would not hire her. She had to teach in other communities; eventually she became a superintendent of schools for the counties down in Colquitt. When we first moved to Blakely, my mother taught in Bluffton; my brother and I went with her and attended school there. When I was in the fifth grade and my brother was in the sixth, we went off to Savannah to live with relatives for a year. The following year we went to Atlanta and lived with friends and attended schools there.

My parents had a great commitment to education. My father often said, "People can take money away from you, but they can't take away an education."

My father never finished college. He was one of eleven children, born in Alachua, Florida, a rural community just north of Gainesville. He was in his freshman year at Claflin College, South Carolina, when his father died, and he had to leave and go back to help on the family farm supporting his mother. He had several jobs after he left the farm, first of all as a tailor, then as an insurance salesman during the Depression. Since nobody was buying insurance at that time, my father almost starved to death. He went into a business partnership in Albany, Georgia, in a funeral home, and when that partnership broke up, he moved to Blakely and started his own funeral home.

The day I graduated from medical school, my father told me for the first time that I was the realization of his dream. He had wanted to be a doctor, and was so pleased that I was able to achieve what he had wanted for himself.

As an undertaker, my father catered only to the black community. At that time, people died of, among other things, tuberculosis, heart attacks, cancer, farm accidents, and homicides. Within the black community on weekends, people who had menial jobs would go drinking and dancing in the local cafés for relaxation. Sooner or later, there would be a fight over some girl or an argument, and often there'd a stabbing or a shooting.

In the years of World War II, people were leaving the South. There was one train a day through Blakely, and people boarded it to leave the farm and go to Newark or Brooklyn. They were escaping poverty, going to a place where people with relatively few skills could be trained to earn a reasonable income working in the shipyards. The farm economy was declining because of mechanization and the resulting scarcity of jobs. Leaving meant not only escaping poverty, but also escaping to freedom, for the Northeast was considered a place without segregation. Around southwest Georgia, the Klan would gather and lynchings occurred from time to time. The police were never the blacks' friends. They were part of the enemy. Living there was like being in a sort of encampment.

Over the last fifty years, the South has gone beyond the segregation question. What is startling, and pleasantly so, is the fact that integration is working, not only in large cities like Atlanta, Columbus, and Macon, but also even in small towns. There are, obviously, still some areas with racial problems. While the South progressed, however, Northern cities have become in a different sense places under siege for the black community. Now we have the mass of the black community in large urban areas being virtually ghettoized, without job opportunities and with many signs of continuing racial division. While there are still things that happen in Southern cities, the real confrontations today are in the Northern cities. Things have shifted in a number of ways.

We don't hear about problems in Birmingham or Houston or Atlanta now, we hear about problems in Chicago and in New York. When people live in crowded, substandard conditions, there is a lot of frustration, a lot of anger. The violence that occurs in the black community is by and large against others in the black community. You strike out at the people who are immediately accessible.

Over the years, job opportunities in our society have changed significantly. We no longer have the situation where someone who is relatively illiterate or relatively unskilled can get a job in the auto industry, in shipbuilding, or in other industries. Now it's much more important for a person to have not only a high-school diploma but also, for jobs that are ladders of opportunity and upward mobility, a college degree. In the black community there are people who don't have those skills or education, so they are trapped. They may be married with families or single with families, and poor. It's not easy for them to go back to school. Teenage unemployment in the black community is still high; typically it has been thirty or forty percent.

I worked every summer I was in college. When I was in medical school, I was a night desk clerk at the medical school library. At one time I was busing dishes in the hospital cafeteria. I had the opportunity to enter the job market, the ability to earn money to help with my education, and also the satisfaction of doing that work. Unfortunately, there are not those job opportunities now, and that does a lot to hurt the self-esteem and self-image of young people. It warps their values and causes anger. It contributes to the kind of environment where angry people, in their antagonism, start ripping off their neighbors and committing muggings.

There are thirty million people below the poverty level in America. Poverty hurts people physically, mentally, emotionally, psychologically, and spiritually. Those who are poor are often not healthy, and that affects their lives. Poverty not only affects good health care but prevents proper diet. One of the things in a good diet is having fresh vegetables and fruits, but those happen to be more expensive than canned goods. Poverty has a strong psychological effect when people have to worry about where the rent money is coming from, whether the food is going to run out, or, if there's an emergency, where they'll get the money to take care of it. Clearly all this has a corrosive effect on one's self-image, one's sense of safety and security, and one's feeling of being in control of one's life.

In spite of all that, there are people who are poor and have developed the strength of character to be able to rise above it. Unfortunately, not everyone is so lucky. There are many who may be marginal in strength of character, or level of intelligence, or perseverance who, if born into better economic circumstances, would become very productive citizens; being born into poverty, they very well may not make it. As a nation, we have to redouble our efforts to find ways to help people work their way out of poverty. That has to be a continuing national priority.

The American family is under stress. One out of two marriages ends in divorce. When there are children, they have a much greater likelihood of then falling into poverty, becoming involved in drugs, dropping out of high school, having mental problems, and getting involved in crime. We need to do things to strengthen the family. We need to reform our health-care system to make it more accessible, as well as to get its costs under control. We have a health-care system where if you have the money, the system can do wonderful things; if you don't have the money, you're locked out. That's not right.

Educated people are usually healthier. They are less dependent on doctors or on other health professionals giving them information. What is most important is education. We have all the marvelous machinery and highly trained personnel, but if you insist on smoking, then there is nothing that technology can do to prevent you from getting lung cancer. If you get it, your chances of being alive five years later are about ten percent, even with all our wonderful X-ray therapy and surgery.

The top ten causes of death of Americans in 1991 are all conditions that are influenced by personal behavior. It might not be the primary cause, but the health behavior of the individual has a significant effect on the likelihood of infant mortality, on getting heart disease, diabetes, lung cancer, breast cancer, alcoholism, drug addiction, AIDS, and on suffering unintentional injuries—of which motor vehicle accidents lead as number one and half of those involve alcohol.

We need to get this message across to the American people, poor and affluent alike: there really is a lot that you not only can do, but must do in order to protect your own health.

Though death is a fact of life, we do not deal with dying and death very well at all. Dying people undergo more pain than they should, and too many die without dignity and love.

Ignorance in the medical profession plays a part; our own lack of knowledge about dying also plays a part. Moreover, as Dr. Robert Buckman told us earlier, perhaps our fears of "being tainted" by death cause us to remain far away from meaningful dialogue, reflection, and direction on this subject.

How we treat those in chronic pain and those who are terminally ill reveals a great deal about us. When facing death without pain or fear, the ultimate wall of life offers us the greatest opportunity for the most meaningful experience of mortal existence. In death, there is hope.

Josefina B. Magno, M.D., is a medical oncologist. She was the first Executive Director of the National Hospice Organization and is currently President of the International Hospice Institute. She also serves as the Director of Hospice Education Research and Development for the Henry Ford Health System in Detroit, Michigan.

"Love Is Really the Key"

Josefina B. Magno

"Pain" is a word that is accessible to everyone, so whenever a person is hurting, he or she very conveniently says, "I am in pain." In physical terms, pain would be what the patient or a person feels if there is something anatomically, physiologically, or pathologically wrong. We are talking about physical pain when there is an infection, an inflammation, a pressure on a nerve, a mass. Pain may be very much a part of suffering, but it is not the only element in suffering.

The human being is not just composed of a body that can have disease and thus can have physical pain. Rather, the human being is a composite of the physical, the social, the psychological, and the spiritual. Therefore, any lack of harmony or disturbance in any of these composites of a human being can cause him pain. All of these could really comprise suffering.

Social pain involves broken relationships: sometimes a quarrel with a brother, a sister, a husband, a wife, or children. This can be very painful to a person. He is not in physical pain in the sense that you can ascribe the cause to anatomical problems. Relationships with others are causing the pain.

Psychological pain is obviously the result of a person's physical, social, and spiritual pain. For the longest time, I could not put my finger on the nature of spiritual pain. But a specific incident taught me a great deal about it. I was taking care of a forty-two-year-old woman, named Florence, in Michigan. She had cancer of the lung. She had severe physical pain and could not breathe well. However, I was able to put those symptoms under control, and that was the end of the physical pain.

One day, a member of her family called and asked me please to come and see Florence. When I got to the house, the woman was screaming and moaning. I asked, "Are you in pain?" and she said, "No, Doctor." I asked, "Well, what's wrong?" and she said, "I don't know, Doctor." She just kept moaning and crying. In desperation I said, "Florence, would you want me to pray with you?" She said, "Please do." So just because there was nothing else I could do, I held her hand and prayed and asked God to take care of her and to make her feel comfortable, and the woman quieted down. Then I asked, "May I leave?" and she said yes. So I left.

Two hours later, the family called again: "Doctor, please come. Florence needs you." So I went quickly to the house, and found her crying and screaming again. By this time, I had discovered that her life was really a mess: a broken marriage here, and a man there, and all kinds of other problems. I began to feel that maybe Florence was afraid of something. So I asked her once more. "Would you want me to pray with you?" and she said, "Doctor, please do." Then I prayed for God's forgiveness of Florence and for God to assure her how much He loved her and that He was waiting for her to come home. Florence quieted down; she died thirty minutes later.

Unfortunately, in medical school they do not teach us much about pain. If you look at the medical textbooks, there are hundreds of pages on all kinds of diseases, problems, and disorders, but there are very few pages on the management of pain. In fact, we are taught in medical school never to treat pain, because pain is the important symptom that tells the physician there is something wrong. It is the duty of the physician to find out what is causing the pain. Treat the cause of the pain and the pain will go away. That is the practice of good medicine if the patient is somebody who is going to recover from the illness.

But when we are dealing with patients who are terminally ill, these patients have been diagnosed and treated. The treatments have failed, and they are in pain. Therefore, that pain serves no useful purpose, and they should not be allowed to be in pain. This is where we physicians are really obliged to relieve patients of all physical pain so that when death comes, it can come painlessly and peacefully and with dignity.

When the International Hospice Institute was organized, in 1984, the first thing it did was to create a task force to find out why physicians were not believing in or getting involved in hospice care. The answer was ignorance. Physicians feel they know how to take care of their dying patients, and therefore don't need any new ideas.

The International Hospice Institute provides training opportunities for physicians so that they can better understand what pain is, what pain control should be, and how it can be accomplished successfully. Sir William Osler, one of the greatest internists of all times, was quoting a fifteenth-century writer when he defined good medicine. "Good medicine," he said, "cures sometimes, it palliates often, but comforts always."

We physicians should never say to a patient, "I can no longer cure you, and there's nothing more I can do for you." It is our obligation as physicians to cure if we can. If we cannot cure, it's our obligation to palliate—remove the pain, remove the other symptoms—and make the patient as comfortable as possible. When we cannot palliate, we should comfort always. This is what hospice is all about. The hospice concept means the last days or weeks or month of a human being's life can be and should be the most meaningful part of that life. It's the time when goodbyes can be said, when the material things of life can be set in order, when broken relationships can be healed, when forgiveness can be extended or received, when love that has never been expressed before can finally be expressed. In order to make this possible, the patient should not be allowed to be in pain. All the symptoms must be controlled. The patient must have the physical, emotional, psychological, and social support that he and the family need at this stressful time in their lives.

Statistics from the World Health Organizations say that 75 percent of the people who are dying in the world today are still dying in great pain. This is not because we don't have the drugs; we do have the drugs. It is really lack of knowledgeability on the part of physicians. Sometimes a patient's pain needs three or four hundred milligrams of narcotics. But we physicians have been taught to stay away from narcotics because it might cause addiction.

If the patient is taking the narcotic for pain, that patient will not be addicted. Enough dosage, the correct drug, or the correct combination of drugs, and the pain will go away. It is when the patient is taking the narcotic for euphoria that he becomes addicted. The goal of pain control is to have a patient who is free from pain, fully alert and really living a normal life. That can be achieved. Patients who are on hundreds of milligrams of narcotic are fine.

Sometimes it's not the fault of the physicians; it's the fault of the regulatory agencies. For example, in New York there's a system where the agency examines all the physicians' prescriptions, and when they exceed a certain number of narcotics a month, that physician is called to find out if he's making money or dealing narcotics. This puts a sense of considerable hesitancy on the part of physicians to prescribe necessary narcotics, which is very unfair. One of the goals of the State Pain Initiatives, which were started in Wisconsin, is to work on the regulatory agencies to stop this sort of harassment.

In America, we are afraid to take care of a loved one who is sick. Feeling incompetent, we say, "Let's take the patient to the hospital where he can get the best of care," which is reasonable.

In hospice care we try to help the family learn how to do the little things that make the patient feel comfortable. We give the family members a sense of competence. We teach them how to give injections of morphine, how to turn the patient, and how to perform some nursing techniques that make them feel they know what to do. Then we alert them about the possible things that might happen.

When I was practicing at a hospice in Virginia, I would give my home telephone number to all the patients. In three years, I was called in the night only twice. The families understood what to expect, and what to do when something happened; therefore, they were not frightened. We send our loved ones to hospitals because we don't know what to do and because hospitals are places where patients often get well and recover.

Clarence Edward Crowther, who used to be an Episcopal bishop in southern California, interviewed hundreds of dying patients in the United States and England. He categorized their problems under the three big headings of pain, loneliness, and loss of control. That's in the dying patient. But one of my sons was recently hospitalized with pneumonia in a big hospital in Washington, D.C. I could see the terrible inconvenience, discomfort, and frustration that so many patients in a big city hospital go through. You order a soft-boiled egg for breakfast and, of course, they bring you a hard-boiled egg. You are in pain, you call the nurse, and it takes thirty minutes for somebody to come. You want to talk to a doctor and you wait two or three hours before the doctor comes. You feel that you are a victim; you are there and you have no control. I am a physician and I was watching my son, and I could see how painful the whole situation was in terms of loss of control and loneliness.

You cannot drug a patient out of his loneliness. You can alleviate loneliness only with a lot of love and care and attention. That's why in hospice care we use volunteers so often. The patient and family know

I may be a caring physician, but they also know that I'm doing a job. When it's a volunteer who does the wonderful things they do, patients and family know that the volunteer is not getting paid to do a job. The volunteer is there doing these things because he or she wants to do them. Therefore, I think the loving becomes much more visible and tangible. That love is really what makes the patient more peaceful.

I was at a conference in Washington, D.C., once where somebody from the Hemlock Society said from the audience, "We know that when people are lonely and miserable and suffering and in great pain, they want to kill themselves, and we should allow them to kill themselves." I was compelled to get up and say, "But that is why we have hospice. Hospice relieves that suffering, it relieves the loneliness, it relieves the being uncared for. You start by surrounding the patient with love."

At St. Christopher's Hospice in England, where hospice care was developed, a patient would come in in great pain begging the doctor to give an injection to terminate life. Three days later, after the patient had been surrounded with love and care and provided with freedom from pain and the other symptoms, that patient no longer wanted to die. You can see it with your eyes and you can touch it. Love is really the key.

People sometimes ask me, "How do those who don't believe in God die?" I look back on my experience, and I would say I have taken care of five patients who told me bluntly, "Doctor, I don't believe in God so let's not talk about God." I said, "That's fine," because when we say a patient must be in control, we must respect what he wants, so we don't talk about God. But those patients died as peacefully as the patients who believed in God. Because God is love, and love is God, nobody really dies without having an experience of God. That's my own personal observation. That's why love really for me is so important.

Some Catholics are taught to offer the pain as a sacrifice. We have to respect that. It is making the patient be in control of what he wants. As a general rule, however, unless the patient so specifies, we should not allow him to be in pain. It's so much harder for the family to manage their grieving process if they see a loved one screaming in pain. Several years after the patient has died, the family may say, "If only I could forget her screams. If only I could forget her begging the nurse for an injection to relieve the pain, and the nurse refusing because it wasn't ordered on the chart.' " Seeing your loved one die without pain, peacefully and with dignity, makes it much easier to grieve over the loss of that loved one.

In people who are dying with a sincere faith that there is an afterlife, you can really see the difference. These people look forward to life after death. They can feel the presence of God.

My husband was terminally ill with cancer. He had melanoma and, of course, that is an incurable disease. My marriage was one of those marriages made in Heaven. I brought him to Sloan-Kettering. I took care of him for six months, day and night. When he died, I was so exhausted—not because of having taken care of him, but from having prayed so hard that God might heal him. During the last two weeks of his life, he said to me, "You know, if I'm not going to get well, why don't you ask God not to make it too long and just take me. It would be easier for you and for everybody else." And I did that. I said, "Lord, if he's not going to get well, please take him, but make it as easy for him as possible, and just take care of all of us."

One day I was inside his oxygen tent, reading prayers to him, and he just looked at me, and then closed his eyes and died. I never even shed a tear because it was so peaceful. All those prayers that I said for six months worked. They prepared me to ask God to take him, which meant that he was not being wrenched away from me; I was giving him to God. Maybe that's what happens with prayer.

I really believe with all my heart that God does not allow pain to come into our lives to punish us. Pain is allowed in our lives to help us grow, because it's so much easier for us to pray and reach out to God when we are hurting than when we are happy and content. When we are hurting because we've lost somebody, or lost a job, or have no money, or we are sick, it's much easier to call on God to help. And He knows that.

When I had cancer myself, all my friends were very upset with God. "How can He do this to Jo?" I was the only parent alive for my seven children. I should have been upset, but I was very peaceful. I think I was peaceful because about two months earlier I had read a book containing a prayer that said: "Lord, I give you my life and you use it according to your purpose and your will." I thought, I guess He heard my prayer, and this is probably what He's going to do. And I just let Him. If it had not been for my cancer, I would not have gone into medical oncology. I wanted to be a great oncologist, but that was not His purpose. His purpose for me was hospice. But I first had to get into oncology to see what we were doing to the cancer patients, treating them until they were dead when we should have allowed them to be comfortable and die in peace.

I see my breast cancer as the beginning of God opening new doors for me. I felt that, and therefore I could trust Him. I was peaceful. I'm able to say every morning, "Lord, just tell me what to do in my heart and let me listen, and then I'll work as hard as I can to make it happen." I tell God, and mean it with all my heart, "You may use my life as you will." So I feel this is what He's doing, and I just do what He wants me to do.

If I am a janitor, I must be the best janitor in the world because that is the job that God gave me and this is where I find my holiness. If I am a physician, I must be the best physician that I can be because that's the job God gave me and this is where I find my holiness. This is a divine plan, which we don't understand. It's like a tapestry. You see that the underside is all chaotic, but there's a plan there. If it is God's plan for me to be on a hospital bed sick with cancer, then maybe this is where I find my holiness. That's so hard to see because we are very human.

All of us have known people with great troubles, and yet were at peace. The most important thing in our lives as human beings is to have peace in our hearts. That peace comes from God, who promised it to us. "My peace I give you." It's not the peace that the world gives, it's His peace."

Ask God to be there for you to give you peace. He promised that He will never leave us alone. We have to take His word on that. All we need to do is trust God.

God did not create a human race; He created individuals. Everyone is so unique. God created each of us for a specific purpose in His divine plan. For you to fulfill that purpose, He gave you certain gifts, talents, physical characteristics, intelligence, emotions. If you don't do what He intended for you to do in His divine plan, that portion of the divine plan will forever be empty, because nobody else can do the things that you can do. No matter how many billions of human beings there have been in this world, you have your own set of fingerprints. It's almost as if God is saying, "You are unique to me." Nobody will fulfill your mission; only you can do it.

At my church there is a book where you write your requests. If you read those petitions, there are principally three subjects; job, broken relationship, and physical health. Why are so many people so unhappy? Maybe we are looking for the wrong things. I like what St. Augustine said. "My heart is restless until it rests in You." We are not supposed to find happiness in the material things of the world. We find happiness only in God. I like what Pascal said, too: "In every human being there's a hole which is the shape of God." If we try to fill that hole with wealth, power, or fame, it never works, because the hole is in the shape of God, and only God can fill it and make us complete, truly peaceful, and happy.

God reveals Himself constantly in every event, every circumstance. Sometimes it's a terrible crisis in our lives. Sometimes it's a minor incident. Suddenly you see what it is you are supposed to do.